Looking Ahead

Developing Skills for Academic Writing

ELIZABETH BYLEEN

University of Kansas

SERIES EDITORS

PATRICIA BYRD
Georgia State University

JOY M. REID
University of Wyoming

Video notes in Instructor's Manual by
Elizabeth Mejia
Washington State University

Heinle & Heinle Publishers
I(T)P An International Thomson Publishing Company

Pacific Grove • Albany • Bonn • Boston • Cincinnati • Detroit • London
Madrid • Melbourne • Mexico City • New York • Paris
San Francisco • Tokyo • Toronto • Washington

The publication of *Looking Ahead: Developing Skills for Academic Writing* was directed by members of the Newbury House ESL/EFL at Heinle & Heinle:

Erik Gundersen, Editorial Director
Jonathan Boggs, Market Development Director
Kristin M. Thalheimer, Senior Production Services Coordinator
Nancy Mann Jordan, Senior Developmental Editor
Stanley J. Galek, Vice President and Publisher

Also participating in the publication of this program were:
Project Manager/Desktop Pagination: Thompson Steele, Inc.
Managing Developmental Editor: Amy Lawler
Manufacturing Coordinator: Mary Beth Hennebury
Associate Editor: Ken Pratt
Associate Market Development Director: Mary Sutton
Photo/video Specialist: Jonathan Stark
Media Services Coordinator: Jerry Christopher
Interior Designer: Sally Steele
Cover Designer: Ha Nguyen
Cover Artist: Katherine Stuart

ISBN 08384-7902-2
10 9 8 7 6 5 4 3 2 1

Thank You

The author and publisher would like to thank the following individuals who offered many helpful insights, ideas, and suggestions for change during the development of _Looking Ahead: Developing Skills for Academic Writing_

Victoria Badalamenti, _LaGuardia Community College, New York_
Karen Batchelor, _City College of San Francisco_
Cheryl Benz, _Miami Dade Community College_
Pam Butterfield, _Palomar College, California_
Lisa Camp, _Hunter College, New York_
Marvin Coates, _El Paso Community College, Valle Verde Campus_
Carol Culver, _San Francisco State University_
Kathleen Flynn, _Glendale Community College, California_
Barbara Foley, _Union County College, New Jersey_
Byrun Hauser, _Miami Dade Community College_
Gayle Henrotte, _Mt. San Antonio Community College, California_
Mary Hill-Shinn, _El Paso Community College_
Cynthia Howe, _Seattle Central Community College_
Sheila McKee, _University of North Texas_
Lynne Nickerson, _DeKalb College, Georgia_
Norman Prange, _Cuyahoga Community College, Ohio_
Jennifer Ross, _LaGuardia Community College, New York_
Dawn Schmid, _California State University at San Marcos_
Catherine Sessions, _Hunter College, New York_
Bob Shiel, _St. Augustine College, Illinois_
Joe Starr, _Houston Community College_
Christine Tierney, _Houston Community College_
Patricia Weyland, _Ohio State University_

$\mathscr{C}$ontents

v

Chapter 3 Explaining   62

PUTTING IT ALL TOGETHER   114

Looking Ahead: Academic Assignments   117

Chapter 5   Summarizing and Responding   120

GETTING READY   122

FOCUSING   127

PUTTING IT ALL TOGETHER   147

Looking Ahead: Academic Assignments   149

Chapter 6 Arguing   152

GETTING READY   154

• • • • • • • •

Chapter 7   Synthesizing   184

PUTTING IT ALL TOGETHER   207

$\mathcal{W}$ill your students be ready to meet the academic writing expectations of their instructors and professors when they leave your ESL program?

$\mathcal{T}$hey will if they use *Looking Ahead,*

Heinle & Heinle's new 4-level academic writing/grammar series.

SUCCESSFUL WRITING WITH *LOOKING AHEAD*!

Will your students be ready ... to perform various types of academic writing?

Looking Ahead focuses on the various types of writing that successful students must learn to employ: *investigating, explaining, evaluating, summarizing, organizing, describing, analyzing,* and others. In practicing these various forms of academic writing, students call upon a host of rhetorical modes such as *definition, classification,* and *contrast* to support their ideas and opinions. They also develop facility in using a host of academic writing formats such as *paragraphs, essays, reports,* and *memos.*

Will your students be ready ... to understand and meet challenging academic expectations?

Each chapter begins with authentic academic assignments from across the disciplines (e.g. sociology, history) for the students to analyze and discuss. These assignments show how writing tasks are used in the "real world" of academic course work.

Sample Authentic College/University Writing Assignments

In your academic courses, you will use the skills you learn in this chapter to complete assignments and test questions like the examples below.

Business Administration

In a two- to three-page paper, give advice to a new manager about how to successfully per-

Will your students be ready ... to apply their own writing skills to academic situations?

Each chapter contains several short writing activities and one longer writing assignment designed to prepare students for the writing tasks they will encounter in college classes. Throughout the chapters, students practice writing activities that are appropriate for a specific academic setting. The writing activities in each chapter end with a writing assignment that guides students step-by-step through the process.

Revise, Edit, and Proofread

1. Read your essay again. Does it say what you want it to say? Use your partner's comments to make improvements.

2. Edit your essay for the following and correct any errors that you find. After you have edited for each of these features, check (✓) the box as a reminder that you have done that task.

❑ complete sentences

❑ correct punctuation

❑ spelling and correct pronoun reference if you used any proper names

❑ verb tense choices

❑ appropriate transition words and phrases showing logical or chronological relationships

❑ reporting verbs

4. Describe an audience that would have difficulty understanding this article. Why would they have difficulty? Was it easy for you to understand? Why or why not?

Activity 3-12   Reporting Other People's Words and Ideas

1. *Quotations:* The writer included the "voices" of many other people in the examples in this article. Find all the quotations in the article. How many different people speak?

2. *Punctuation:* Add the necessary punctuation to these quotations from the article.

   a. I have more of a real life she says. I'm not relying on the computer to make me happy.

   b. It may give them a false sense of security Kandell says. The quality of the relationships they form is limited . . . it makes it more difficult for them to engage in face-to-face contact with people.

Will your students be ready . . . to exploit a variety of academic skills in writing?

Being a successful student means being a successful academic writer. In *Looking Ahead,* students learn essential academic writing skills like *brainstorming, seeking* and *using input from peers, gathering ideas from various sources, giving recognition to sources,* and *editing.*

Will your students be ready . . . to exercise key vocabulary acquisition skills?

Special focus is given to developing vocabulary acquisition skills necessary for success in a variety of academic fields. Students gain strategies for learning new vocabulary and the relevant grammar associated with these vocabulary items.

Activity 5-4   Vocabulary Matching

The following words are from Reading 1. With a partner, match the word on the left with the meaning on the right.

____ f _ 1. ambiguity   a. basic and necessary

____ 2. fundamental   b. designed to correct or cure

____ 3. unconventional   c. mathematical problem-solving

____ 4. prerequisite   d. not usual

____ 5. remedial   e. something that is necessary before something else can happen

____ 6. calculation   f. something unclear because it has more than one meaning

Will your students be ready . . . to apply the reflective skills necessary for fluency in academic writing?

Each chapter contains several *Learner's Notebook* activities that accomplish two purposes. First, *Notebook* activities give students an opportunity to gain fluency through reflective writing that will not be evaluated. Second, this type of free-writing helps students generate ideas for the academic writing tasks to come later in the unit.

LEARNER'S NOTEBOOK

Difficult Test

Describe the most difficult test you have ever taken. Why was it difficult? What kinds of questions did it include? Did the questions ask you to restate information or analyze or apply the information? If you were going to take the test again, how would you study differently?

Will your students be ready . . . to look ahead to their academic future?

Chapters end as they begin—with information about authentic academic tasks and assignments. Students can analyze these assignments to learn more about the work that will be required of them when they enter degree programs. These sample assignments motivate students by showing them that they will apply the skills they are learning with their work in *Looking Ahead.*

LOOKING AHEAD

Academic Assignment

You do not have to write the following research paper. However, analyzing this assignment will give you a clearer understanding of some types of assignments you will face in your undergraduate courses.

Read the following assignment and discuss the questions that follow.

Political Science

Research Paper: Education in the United States: What Is Wrong with the System?

For years the United States led the world in education. In recent decades, the U.S. has fallen behind other industrialized nations in educating its youth. There is general agreement that there are many problems with our educational system. However, the solutions to these problems are controversial. Educational reform theories present two different solutions:

SUCCESSFUL GRAMMAR ACQUISITION
WITH *LOOKING AHEAD*!

Will your students be ready . . . to recognize the different discourse types found in academic writing?
Authentic readings and writing assignments in *Looking Ahead* were selected based on the academic discourse types that students most often need to read and produce in academic settings. These authentic materials give students many opportunities to see and analyze how English grammar and rhetoric "work."

Grammar Preview

When you write an evaluation, you must convince your reader that your information and interpretations are accurate. In this chapter, you will look at ways to present persuasive evidence with numerical information, comparative interpretations, and quotations of the words and ideas of experts. You will also work with passive sentences, which focus on process or product, instead of the people who do the process or make the products, since passive sentences are frequently found in evaluations and other academic writing. In addition, you will look at transition words to help you show logical connections in your writing and make your writing more cohesive.

Activity 5-17   Discovering Features of Past Time Narrative

1. Past time narratives, like this one, can be used for historical accounts. This kind of writing often contains many proper nouns (John Napier, Blaise Pascal, Ada Lovelace, Charles Babbage . . .). Highlight the proper names of the people in this article and the pronouns that refer to these people. For additional information, see Section 2D on proper nouns in the GLR .

2. Past time narratives frequently use many time expressions, chronological organizers, to show when events happened. The most frequently used are dates, such as "in 1642." With a partner, circle at least four time expressions in the article "Early Computing Devices." Refer to Section 2C in the GLR for more information on chronological organizers.

Will your students be ready . . . to apply the grammar of academic writing?
Recent research has shown that specific grammar structures appear in clusters within types of discourse. By concentrating on one or two grammar clusters in each chapter, *Looking Ahead* focuses only on the grammar that is essential for the writing typical of a specific discourse type.

Will your students be ready . . . to easily access important academic grammar information?
The Grammar and Language Reference (*GLR*) section at the back of the book pulls together all of the grammar explanations and authentic examples for easy student access. An icon tells students when to refer to the *GLR*.

4B   Understanding the Grammar of Definitions

Students are expected to learn and use many new words in each of their university classes. This work will be easier if you understand the way that **definitions** are structured so that you can more easily memorize them and repeat them accurately in your own writing, especially on tests but also in other required writing assignments. Definitions of terminology are often presented in the following formats where X = the term and Y = the definition.

X is Y	Psychology is the science of behavior and mental processes.
X means Y	Addiction to a drug means that the individual is physically dependent on the use of the drug.
X refers to Y	Evaluative criteria refer to those features that the buyers use to make a choice between brands.
Y is called X. Someone calls Y X.	The number of brands that a consumer actually considers in making a purchase decision is called the *evoked* set. A consumer recognizes a need (or want) when something that he or she requires is found lacking. Some

---

SUCCESSFUL ACADEMIC READING
WITH *LOOKING AHEAD*!

Will your students be ready . . . to apply essential reading skills for successful writing preparation?
Simply stated, effective reading skills are essential for success as an academic writer. Academic writing requires that you draw on reading sources in a variety of ways—to get ideas for writing, to get background information on a topic, and to use the information you find to support your ideas. Given this, each chapter in *Looking Ahead* has a "reading theme," which allows students to become familiar with the vocabulary, ideas, and issues within that topic. In both content and style, readings reflect the types of selections that students encounter in their academic classes.

CONSUMER DECISION-MAKING

Figure 7.1 shows an outline of the major steps buyers go through in the purchase process. This process has been termed by some as the consumer's "black box." That is, it represents the invisible activity that goes on in the consumer's mind as he or she makes a buying decision. The process is a series of responses to various internal and external stimuli. Some of these stimuli are initiated by marketers, such as advertising or a call by a salesperson; some have other sources. Some marketer-dominated stimuli are successful in moving the consumer toward the marketer's product and some stimuli may actually accomplish the opposite effect.

```
         ┌─────────────────┐
         │ Need Recognized │
         └─────────────────┘
                  ↓
       ┌──────────────────────┐
       │  Information Search   │
       │    Accomplished       │
       └──────────────────────┘
                  ↓
       ┌──────────────────────┐
       │ Alternatives Compared │
       └──────────────────────┘
                  ↓
       ┌──────────────────────┐
       │   Decision Made and   │
       │     Implemented       │
       └──────────────────────┘
                  ↓
  ┌─────────────────────────────────┐
  │ Satisfaction/Dissatisfaction Realized │
  └─────────────────────────────────┘
```

Figure 7.1 The Process for Making Buying Decisions

CNN Video
with
Looking Ahead!

Will your students be ready . . . to use a variety of authentic media to prepare for their academic future?
Each chapter in the *Looking Ahead* series has a CNN video clip related to the chapter theme and designed to further stimulate authentic discussion and writing. Appealing to the learning style preferences of auditory and visual students, the videos connect the content of *Looking Ahead* to the real world. An introduction to video use in the ESL classroom by Elizabeth Mejia (see the Instructor's Manual) provides the foundation for sound teaching strategies with video.

The CNN videos are provided at no charge for teachers who adopt one or more of the *Looking Ahead* textbooks for their classes.

The World Wide Web
with
Looking Ahead!

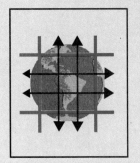

Are you ready . . . to provide all you can for your students' academic preparation?
The authors and editors of *Looking Ahead* have created an on-line system of support for teachers using the series. At **http://lookingahead.heinle.com**, teachers can find expanded versions of the Instructor's Manuals, lesson plans provided by teachers who are using the books, additional materials to supplement the books, and other support materials. In addition, the site offers opportunities to communicate with the editors and authors—to ask questions, share ideas, and make suggestions for improvements in the *Looking Ahead* series and its support materials.

Get Ready with *Looking Ahead*!

The four textbooks in the *Looking Ahead* series are designed to prepare students to be successful in their academic courses in U.S. colleges and universities. Specifically, *Looking Ahead* teaches students to read academic texts and materials, understand academic assignments, apply effective study skills, and respond appropriately to writing assignments. Each book "looks ahead" to the next in the series, and together as a group they look ahead to the writing students will do in their degree programs.

To the Teacher

Looking Ahead Book 3: Developing Skills for Academic Writing is a high-intermediate writing and grammar textbook for ESL students. The books contains seven chapters followed by the Grammar and Language Reference section. Each chapter is organized into the following sections and activities.

Goals: A list of writing, grammar, and content goals helps teachers and students understand the learning objectives for each chapter.

Sample Authentic Academic Assignments: Examples of content-area college and university assignments illustrate how students will use the chapter's writing focus (e.g., explaining, evaluating, summarizing) in undergraduate assignments.

Getting Ready: This introductory section contains an introduction and Learner's Notebook assignments.

Chapter Introductions: Students gain knowledge and practice through the introductory explanations of the writing and grammar highlighted in the chapter.

Learner's Notebook Assignments: Short writing tasks encourage students to explore and analyze writing topics, as well as reflect on their writing strategies and progress.

Focusing: This section contains authentic readings on one central theme, activities, and short writing assignments.

Authentic Readings: Readings with accompanying pre- and post-reading activities provide rich content, vocabulary, and grammatical structures for the students' writing.

Writing Assignments: Short writing assignments help students build fluency and accuracy for the final writing assignment.

Grammar Activities: Key grammatical features of academic writing, examples in context, and activities are presented. For additional explanations, students can consult the Grammar and Language Reference section at the end of the text.

Putting It All Together: Students apply their knowledge in a final writing assignment that builds on the materials presented in previous sections and chapters.

Final Writing Assignment: Each writing assignment guides students through the process of choosing a topic, considering audience and purpose, gathering and organizing information, drafting, peer response, revising, self-editing, and proofreading.

Looking Ahead Assignments: Discussing these authentic undergraduate assignments helps students strategize about how they will handle future academic writing assignments.

The Grammar and Language Reference (GLR): A quick and easy reference supplies additional explanations and authentic examples of the grammar features discussed in the chapters. The GLR can help teachers individualize grammar instruction for students who need extra work on particular structures.

*T*o the Student

Are You "Looking Ahead"?

Are you looking ahead to getting your degree? Do you want the work you do in your ESL writing class to help you succeed in future writing assignments?

Developing Skills for Academic Writing helps you look ahead and prepare for those academic writing assignments. In each chapter, you will discuss several examples of real undergraduate assignments from a variety of academic fields such as psychology, chemistry, anthropology, business management, marketing, art history, biology, and political science.

Of course, it is not enough to simply discuss sample assignments. You also need practice in writing. Academic writing assignments in many different fields of study require you to do similar writing tasks. These tasks are the focus of the chapters in this book: Instructing (telling how), Explaining, Evaluating, Summarizing, Arguing, and Synthesizing. So, for example, after you learn how to write clear explanations (Chapter 3), you can use that skill in answering test questions or in written assignments in psychology, business, biology, and other subjects. When you learn to write effective summaries (Chapter 5), you can handle any assignment in any course where you are expected to summarize a lecture, a journal article, textbook passage, or other research source. And when you learn how to synthesize information for answering test questions (Chapter 7), you will be more successful on short answer and essay tests in all your courses.

How Will This Book Help You?

This book combines writing and grammar skills to help you communicate successfully in academic writing. It contains many features that will help you look ahead to future assignments.

- step-by-step explanations of each type of writing
- authentic and interesting readings from textbooks, academic journals, newspapers, and other sources
- opportunities to practice many types of writing
- grammar activities to help you be more accurate in your writing
- a Grammar and Language Reference (GLR) section [icon] at the end of the text with explanations and examples

Best wishes for academic success!

Acknowledgments

To make an integrated series of textbooks takes incredible teamwork. Joy Reid and Patricia Byrd, Series Editors, inspired teamwork throughout this project, and gave freely of their insights, patience, and guidance. They were there every step of the way. My author colleagues, Sharon Cavusgil of Georgia State University, Linda Robinson Fellag of Community College of Philadelphia, and Christine Holten of University of California at Los Angeles and Judith Marasco of University of California at Los Angeles and Santa Monica College, added their unique perspectives and ideas. It was an exciting experience to be a part of this team.

The people at Heinle and Heinle guided this project with their many talents. Special thanks go to Nancy Siddens, Nancy Jordan, Amy Lawler, Ken Pratt, and Kristin Thalheimer for their contributions. The staff at Thompson Steele carefully guided the books through the production process. Joanne Lowry was remarkable!

I want to thank Betty Soppelsa, Director of the Applied English Center at The University of Kansas, for her support during this project. Thanks also go to AEC students who used these materials in the classroom and provided ideas for refinement.

Most importantly, I thank Earl, Adelé, Michael, Karl, and Marie for the tremendous encouragement and perspective they have always given me.

Elizabeth Byleen
University of Kansas
Lawrence, Kansas

Chapter 1

*A*cademic Writing

Success

GOALS

WRITING
◆ practice four basic sentence structures
◆ review paragraph organization and cohesion devices

GRAMMAR
◆ learn basic features of informational and interactive writing
◆ become acquainted with the Grammar and Language Reference

CONTENT
◆ read and write about success

ACADEMIC FIELDS
Psychology
Philosophy

Sample Authentic College/University Writing Assignments

Each chapter in this book begins with examples of assignments from a variety of academic fields. *You do not need to complete these assignments*. Instead, these examples will help you look ahead to the kinds of assignments you will be asked to do in your college or university courses. This textbook will help you prepare for these academic writing tasks.

Biology

Explain what a mutation is and why it is important in the process of natural selection.

World Geography

How did the first urban centers develop? What were the underlying reasons for and subsequent effects of this urbanization?

Sociology

Describe the effects that the mass media can have on a person's socialization.

GETTING READY

LEARNER'S NOTEBOOK

Warm-up Writing

You will keep a learner's notebook throughout this course. In it, you will write your ideas about topics for writing and your reactions to readings, as well as analyze your progress. This collection of writing will help you to do the major assignment for each chapter.

Topic: Write about a time when you were successful. It could be a small success or a major success.

An Introduction to Academic Writing

Writing is one of the keys to your academic success. In your courses, you may be assigned various types of writing:

short-answer test questions	essays	research and term papers
essay test questions	journals	reaction papers
summaries	evaluations	lab and project reports

At first, this variety of assignments may seem intimidating, but it is important to remember that you begin each writing task in the same way: connecting one sentence to another. In this chapter, you will practice the four types of English sentences and organize sentences into paragraphs.

Activity 1-1   Writing Survey

Think about your writing habits, your successes, and areas for improvement. Answer the following questions in complete sentences in your learner's notebook.

1. Do you like to begin writing assignments immediately, or do you wait until the last minute? For example, if you are given an assignment on Monday and it is due Friday, when will you most likely start to work on it? Why?

2. How do you gather ideas for your writing? For example, do you write down what you already know? Make drawings or diagrams? Go to the library? Search the Internet? Talk to others?

3. Where is the best place for you to write? What atmosphere do you prefer?

   (Examples: silence, music, solitude, working with others, food, bright lights)

4. Do you put your first draft on the computer or write it by hand? Why?

5. What do you use to check your work? (Examples: spell-check computer program, dictionary, a friend's help)

6. What is one important thing you learned from a past writing assignment or writing course? Give an example.

7. What are three things you would like to improve about your writing?

8. Describe a time when you were successful with a writing assignment. Why were you successful?

Activity 1-2   Discussion

In a small group, discuss your answers. Talk about your personal writing habits and strategies. Which are most effective? Are there other strategies you would like to try?

Gathering and Developing Ideas for Academic Writing

You will be expected to gather and develop ideas for your academic writing assignments from a wide variety of sources. Students depend on three main sources to gather information to develop their writing: *personal experience, interaction with others,* and *reading,* all of which we will work with in this text. Different assignments will require different kinds of information gathering.

Personal Experience

The first source of ideas for your writing is you, the writer. You can rely on all of your previous education and experience. These ideas will help you get started. Although your personal experience and background can often be strong components of your writing, you will need more to successfully complete most academic writing assignments.

Interaction with Other People

In addition to relying on what you already know, you can gain many ideas through your interaction with other people. You may:

- *interview* an expert on your topic
- *discuss* your ideas with a friend, lab partner, or a classmate

- *survey* a group of people
- *get feedback* from other students about your ideas
- *participate* in a class discussion, discussion section, or study group
- *talk* to your professor about the assignments

Each of these techniques will help you think about and develop your topic more completely.

Reading

Students also depend heavily on reading to learn and develop ideas for writing tasks, so effective reading skills are important to your academic success. This reading may include:

textbooks	journal and magazine articles
books	lab manuals
sources on the Internet	

In this text, readings within each chapter will help you develop ideas for writing. You will also gather material from other sources to help with ideas for your assignments.

For your writing assignments, you will not usually use all of the information you gather. Instead, you will select and put together the information that best supports your ideas. This process is called *synthesis*. Throughout this textbook, you will synthesize information from your personal experience, reading, and interaction with others and see how others use a variety of sources to support their ideas in their writing.

Grammar Preview

Learning more about the grammar of *academic writing* will help you improve your writing. In this chapter, you will see how grammar is used in various types of writing. In addition to working with the four basic sentence types, you will see some features of *informational writing*, which is writing about generalizations, theories, definitions, and other academic topics. You will also work with some features of *interactive writing*, learning about how the grammar of conversation is sometimes used in writing.

Go to pages 211–262 in the back of this textbook and spend some time becoming acquainted with the Grammar and Language Reference (GLR) section 🔘 . See how the GLR is organized and the kind of information it contains. Notice that Section 8 includes grammar terminology and examples to help you learn and review grammar terms. Throughout this textbook, you can refer to the GLR for further explanations and examples of the grammar in each chapter.

FOCUSING

READING 1 DEFINITIONS OF SUCCESS
(DICTIONARY ENTRIES, PARAGRAPH, AND QUOTATIONS)

Activity 1-3   Pre-reading Questions

People define success in many different ways. In Reading 1, you will read dictionary definitions, a paragraph definition, and quotations about success.

1. As a class, make a list on the chalkboard of 10 to 20 successful people. Why do you consider each of them a success?

2. What is your personal definition of success?

DICTIONARY DEFINITIONS

suc·cess /sək'sɛs/ *n.* **-es 1** [C] accomplishment of a task, the reaching of a goal: *The meeting was a success: we agreed on everything.* **2** [C;U] a good event, an achievement: *She had success in medical school and became a fine doctor.* **3** [U] wealth, good luck in life: *The man has had a lot of financial success and has no money worries.*

suc·cess·ful /sək'sɛsfəl/ *adj.* with success: *No one likes the new movie; it's not successful. A successful result brings happiness.*

Source: *The Newbury House Dictionary of American English* (Boston: Heinle & Heinle Publishers, 1996).

PARAGRAPH: WHAT IS SUCCESS?

People often use the words *success* and *successful,* and we have a general picture in our minds about what these words mean. However, there is no single accurate definition because individuals, families, and cultures have their own ideas about success. Some may value success with relationships, academics, careers, or money. Others may feel successful when they serve other people, or when they achieve wisdom or understanding. While some may think of success as being defined by awards, prizes, and advancements, others see it defined by the individual. *Success* means different things to different people.

QUOTATIONS

The ability to concentrate and to use your time well is everything if you want to succeed in business—or almost anywhere else, for that matter.

Lee Iacocca

There is only one success—to be able to spend your life in your own way.

Christopher Morley

I do not care for socially recognizable success. I only value that success which I can feel within me, which satisfies me, and which basically stems from self-knowledge.

Anwar El-Sadat

The whole secret of a successful life is to find out what it is one's destiny to do, and then do it.

Henry Ford

I must admit that I personally measure success in terms of the contributions an individual makes to her or his fellow human beings.

Margaret Mead

I have learned that success is to be measured not so much by the position that one has reached in life as by the obstacles which he has overcome while trying to succeed.

Booker T. Washington

Activity 1-4   Post-reading Questions

1. Has your own definition of success changed after reading these definitions? Are there other people you want to add to your list of successful people?

2. Dictionary definition

   a. What type of information is given in this entry?

   b. Use each of these forms of *success* in a sentence:

   success (noun)   succeed (verb)

   successful (adjective)   successfully (adverb)

3. Paragraph

   a. How does this definition of *success* differ from those in the dictionary entry?

   b. What is the main idea of the paragraph? Which sentence expresses this main idea?

    c. Look again at your list of successful people on the chalkboard. What does your list show about your own beliefs about successful people?

4. Quotations

    a. Read the quotations again and discuss the meaning of each one.

    b. Which definitions are closest to your own definition of success?

Activity 1-5 Recognizing Four Basic Sentence Types

1. Understanding the basic sentence structures of English will help you connect your ideas in a variety of ways. Go to Section 1 in the GLR GLR to review the four basic sentence types: *simple, compound, complex,* and *compound-complex.*

2. Write the correct sentence type before each of these sentences from Reading 1.

    a. _____simple_____ Success means different things to different people.

    b. _compound_ People often use the words *success* and *successful,* and we have a general picture in our minds about what these words mean.

    c. _complex_ However, there is no single accurate definition because individuals, families, and cultures have their own ideas about success.

    d. _simple_ Some may value success with relationships, academics, careers, or money.

    e. _complex_ Others may feel successful when they serve other people, or when they achieve wisdom or understanding.

    f. _complex_ While some may think of success as being defined by awards, prizes, and advancements, others see it defined by the individual.

    g. _complex_ I must admit that I personally measure success in terms of the contributions an individual makes to her or his fellow human beings.

    h. _simple_ I do not care for socially recognizable success.

    i. _compound_ The meeting was a success; we agreed on everything.

3. Describe the basic characteristics of each of the four basic sentence types.

LEARNER'S NOTEBOOK

Successful Sentences

In your learner's notebook, write four of your own sentences about success (or another topic you choose). Use these four basic sentence types: *simple, compound, complex*, and *compound-complex*.

READING 2   THE SUCCESS OF OPTIMISTS

A *paragraph* is a group of sentences that work together to express one main idea. The main idea is often in the first sentence of the paragraph or near the beginning. The sentence containing the main idea is the *topic sentence.*

The other sentences in the paragraph *support* the topic sentence. The support may be by definitions, examples, details, facts, or other explanations. A concluding sentence, which is especially helpful in long paragraphs, helps end the paragraph.

A paragraph can stand alone. When it does, it is often given a title. A paragraph can also be connected to other paragraphs in a longer piece of writing, such as an essay, report, or research paper. The first line of the paragraph is *indented* to help show the reader where each new paragraph begins.

THE SUCCESS OF OPTIMISTS

Optimistic thinking helps fuel success. Of course, to succeed, people need to do more than just think optimistically. Hard work and persistence are key ingredients to success, but add optimism and you have an even higher chance of success. For example, imagine 5 two company employees, both intelligent and hard-working, collaborating on a long-term project. They make substantial progress working together until they encounter a difficult problem. The pessimistic person becomes increasingly discouraged, and he finally sees 10 no alternative but to quit the project. In contrast, the optimistic person is temporarily discouraged but knows that the problem can be solved. The optimist begins looking at the problem from several different angles, and she consults several other people until a 15 solution is reached. *Even though the two employees were both hard-working and intelligent, optimistic thinking led the project forward to success.*

Title

Topic Sentence
• giving the main idea of the paragraph

Supporting Sentences
• giving evidence and examples to further explain and support the main idea

Concluding Sentence
• restating or summing up the main idea

Activity 1-6 Post-reading Questions

1. Explain the difference between an optimist and a pessimist.

2. Do you agree with the paragraph?

3. Is it sometimes beneficial to be a pessimist?

4. What's the main idea of this paragraph? Where is it expressed?

5. In the supporting sentences, the author gave an example. What phrase introduced this example?

6. What are other types of support that can be used in the supporting sentences?

7. What does the concluding sentence do?

Activity 1-7 Writing Topic Sentences and Controlling Ideas

A good topic sentence guides both the reader and the writer. It is usually the first or the second sentence of a paragraph. The topic sentence contains the subject of the paragraph and a controlling idea (what you want to say about the subject).

Possible topic sentences are given below. For each one, underline the topic of the sentence and circle the controlling idea. (The topic and the controlling idea can both be more than one word.)

EXAMPLE

        topic   controlling idea
Optimistic thinking (helps fuel success.)

1. Mastering a musical instrument can take more than a decade of practice.

2. Job status is not the only indicator of success.

3. Optimism sometimes leads to failure.

4. Effective time management is the key to keeping up with college classes.

5. Putting your first draft on the computer can save you considerable time when revising.

Now, write five of your own topic sentences, underline the topic, and circle the controlling idea.

6. _____

7. _____

8. _____

9. _____

10. _____

Activity 1-8   Writing Assignment

1. In a small group, choose five of the ten topic sentences in Activity 1-7. Then discuss possible supporting ideas to include in each paragraph. Remember that these ideas must all relate to the topic sentences and help to develop them further.

2. Choose the topic sentence you are most interested in. Make a list of possible supporting ideas. How will you gather and develop more ideas? How can you use personal experience, interaction with others, and reading?

3. Write a paragraph. Include a title, topic sentence, supporting sentences, and a concluding sentence.

4. Read the following section on cohesion devices and then edit your paragraph in Activity 1-9.

Cohesion Devices

All of the sentences in a paragraph work together to express one main idea. Therefore, the sentences and ideas in a paragraph should be logically arranged and flow smoothly one after the other. To show that sentences in a paragraph are all working together, a writer uses *cohesion devices*. Cohesion means "to stick together."

Three common cohesion devices are:

1. *Repetition of key words and phrases.* In the paragraph that follows, forms of the word *success* have been repeated several times to add cohesion. Each use of success is circled. Because this paragraph defines success, the word success appears very frequently.

2. *Use of pronouns to link sentences.* Pronouns (*she/her, he/him/his, they/them, it*) refer to a noun. In this way, they help link two or more sentences together. In the paragraph below, each pronoun has been underlined.

3. *Transition words and phrases.* It is important for a writer to be able to use a variety of words and phrases to present ideas. Transition words and phrases help connect your ideas. Words and phrases like *first, however, consequently, therefore, as a result,* and *in conclusion* help readers "travel" from one sentence/idea to another. These

words show the relationship between sentences or ideas. You will find brackets [ ] around the transition word in this paragraph.

WHAT IS SUCCESS?

People often use the words (success) and (successful), and we have a general picture in our minds about what these words mean. [However,] there is no single accurate definition because individuals, families, and cultures have their own ideas about (success). Some may value (success) in relationships, academics, careers, or money. Others may feel (successful) when they serve other people, or when they achieve wisdom or understanding. While some may think of (success) as being defined by awards, prizes, and advancements, others see it defined by the individual. (Success) means different things to different people.

Activity 1-9   Identifying Cohesion Devices

1. Go to Reading 2 and identify the cohesion devices in the paragraph "The Success of Optimists."

    a. Circle forms of the key words *success* and *optimism*.

    b. Underline the pronouns. What noun does each pronoun refer to?

    c. Put brackets around transition words and phrases.

2. Check your markings in a small group.

3. Why are these cohesion devices important?

4. Look at the paragraph you wrote in Activity 1-8 above. What kind of cohesion devices could you add to improve your paragraph?

5. Use the checklist below to be sure your paragraph is complete. Make any necessary changes.

    Self-Editing Paragraph Checklist

    ❑ complete sentences

    ❑ topic sentence and controlling idea

    ❑ supporting sentences

    ❑ concluding sentence

    ❑ cohesion devices

Activity 1-10   Using Transition Words and Phrases

1. In Section 3D of the GLR ⬤, you will see charts containing transition words and phrases. Read through the charts, putting a small mark by any words and phrases you currently use in your writing. If you have only two or three "favorite" transition words and phrases that you use repeatedly, work to become confident using others.

2. From the chart, choose five transition words and phrases that are new to you. These may be ones you have seen in your reading, but have never used in your writing. Practice using each new word in a sentence in your learner's notebook.

3. Share your sentences with a partner or with the class on the chalkboard.

4. Use these new transition words and phrases in your next writing assignments.

READING 3   VICARIOUS REINFORCEMENT (PSYCHOLOGY TEXTBOOK)

People are not usually successful at everything they try to do. What makes people want to try to do certain things? How do our feelings about ourselves influence our success?

Activity 1-11   Pre-reading Questions

1. Match each word with its definition. Use information from your previous experience or skim the reading to locate the words and then guess their meaning or, if necessary, consult a dictionary.

      _d_ 1. vicarious   a. continuing to do something despite difficulty

      _b_ 2. imitate   b. to do the same thing as someone else

      _c_ 3. reinforcement   c. something that encourages repetition of a behavior

      _e_ 4. doubt   d. substituting someone else's experience for your own

      _a_ 5. persistence   e. to consider unlikely

      _f_ 6. venture   f. a chance or risk

2. The following reading is from an introductory psychology textbook. First read the excerpt quickly for the main ideas. Then read it again more slowly. Notice how the author used many examples to explain two main terms: *vicarious reinforcement* and *self-efficacy*.

VICARIOUS REINFORCEMENT

Six months ago your best friend quit a job with Consolidated Generic Products in order to open a restaurant. Now you are considering whether you should quit your own job with Consolidated Generic and open your own restaurant in a different part of town. How do you decide whether or not to take this step?

Perhaps the first thing you do is to find out how successful your friend has been. You do not automatically imitate the behavior of someone else, even someone you admire. Rather, you imitate behavior that has proved reinforcing for that person. In other words, you learn by vicarious reinforcement—that is, by substituting someone else's experience for your own.

When a new business venture succeeds, other companies try to figure out the reasons for that success and try to follow the same course. When a venture fails, other companies try to learn the reasons for that failure and try to avoid making the same mistakes. When a football team wins consistently, other teams copy its style of play. And when a television program wins high ratings, other producers are sure to present look-alikes the following year.

Something to Think About

Might vicarious learning lead to a certain monotony of behavior? Might it contribute to the lack of variety in the television programs and movies that are offered to the public? How can we learn vicariously without becoming like everyone else?

The Role of Self-Efficacy in Social Learning

You watch an Olympic diver win a gold medal for a superb display of physical control. Presumably you would like to earn an Olympic medal too; so because of this vicarious reinforcement you should go out and try to make some spectacular dives into a pool. Do you? Probably not. Why not? Why does that vicarious reinforcement fail to motivate you to engage in imitative behavior?

If you are like most people, the reason is that you doubt you are capable of duplicating the diver's performance. People imitate someone else's behavior only if they have a sense of **self-efficacy**—the perception that they themselves could perform the task successfully.

We achieve or fail to achieve a sense of self-efficacy in two ways. One way is by observing ourselves. If I have tried and failed to develop even simple athletic skills, I will have no sense of self-efficacy when I think of trying to duplicate the behavior of an Olympic medalist. A student who has studied hard and has done well on several exams will have a strong sense of self-efficacy when faced with the next exam.

We also learn self-efficacy from role models. If your older cousin has studied hard and has gained admission to medical school, you may believe that you can do the same. Psychologists sometimes help students overcome test anxiety by having them watch students similar to themselves displaying good test-taking skills (Dykeman, 1989).

People's persistence or lack of persistence in coping with a difficult task is strongly influenced by their sense of self-efficacy. For example, kidney patients undergoing dialysis treatment are advised to curtail their fluid intake sharply. Patients who are confident they can follow the instructions generally restrict their intake and respond well to the treatment. Those who confess that they "can't tolerate frustration" generally yield to temptation, go on drinking fluids, and soon die (Rosenbaum & Smira, 1986).

Similarly, people who believe they can quit smoking have a reasonable chance of succeeding. People who doubt their ability to quit may try hard at first, but sooner or later they have one cigarette, decide they are a hopeless case, and give up (Curry, Marlatt, & Gordon, 1987).

Source: J. Kalat, *Introduction to Psychology* (Wadsworth Publishing Company, 1993).

Activity 1-12   Post-reading Questions

1. Look at the words in Activity 1-11 again. Use each word in a sentence related to Reading 3.

2. What is vicarious reinforcement? Give an example of a behavior someone would want to imitate.

3. Give an example of how vicarious reinforcement has influenced you to try something new.

4. Explain self-efficacy. What are two ways a person can gain a sense of self-efficacy?

5. What is a role model? Give examples of positive and negative role models.

LEARNER'S NOTEBOOK

Role Model

Write about a role model who has influenced you in a positive way. Describe this person and how he or she influenced your life.

Activity 1-13   Practicing Four Basic Sentence Types

Practice writing these four types of sentences. For the first sentence in each group, complete the blanks based on your understanding of Reading 3. For the second one, create your own sentence.

1. **Simple**

   a. People often imitate _____.

   b. _____.

2. **Compound**

   a. People with high self-efficacy _____ and

   _____.

   b. _____

   _____.

3. **Complex**

   a. We will only imitate the reinforcing behavior of others if/when _____

   _____.

   b. _____

   _____.

4. **Compound-Complex**

   a. When _____ was successful at _____,

      I _____ and I _____.

   b. _____

   _____.

Activity 1-14   Analyzing Topics

For every academic writing assignment, the first step is to analyze the topic so that you can respond appropriately. In the following activity, you will examine the kind of information you should include in your response to a variety of topics based on the readings in this chapter.

As a class, define each of these types of information.

definition	personal experience
opinion	comparison
example	explanation
cause/effect	

Look at the eight possible paragraph topics below. What kind of information is each topic asking you to give? For some topics, you may need to choose more than one.

1. Are there different cultural expectations of success for males and females?

2. Explain the difficulty a person might have if he or she were the first person in their family to succeed in getting a higher education.

3. Describe a situation when a person would be likely to have a strong sense of self-efficacy.

4. Compare your definition of success with that of someone else—your family, parents, culture, grandparents, friends.

5. Discuss how vicarious learning could lead to imitation (and monotony) in one of the following: the movie industry, restaurants, retail stores, new product development, or musical groups.

6. Write about a successful person. What contributed most to their success—intelligence, hard work, luck, talent, or fate?

7. What is the most important quality of a successful researcher?

8. What are two primary effects that a lack of a positive role model could have on a young adult's development?

Activity 1-15   Pre-writing

In a small group, write an appropriate topic sentence with a controlling idea for each of the topics above. Have a few class members write theirs on the chalkboard. Discuss which ones are best and why.

LEARNER'S NOTEBOOK

Paragraph(s)

Choose one of the topics in Activity 1-14. Take a few notes about key ideas. Write one or two paragraphs on this topic in your learner's notebook.

When you are finished, use the self-editing paragraph checklist below. Make necessary changes to your paragraph(s) so each contains all five elements.

Self-Editing Paragraph Checklist

☐ complete sentences

☐ topic sentence and controlling idea

☐ supporting sentences

☐ concluding sentence

☐ cohesion devices

Features of Informational Writing

Reading 3 is an example of informational writing, which is used to write about generalizations, theories, definitions, and other academic topics. By learning two features of informational writing described below—complex noun phrases and present tense, you will be able to use this type of writing for written tests and academic assignments.

1. *Complex noun phrases:* The most common feature of informational writing is the complex noun phrase. A complex noun phrase contains a central or core noun. Other words and phrases come before or after this core noun to form a noun phrase. Reading 3, which is from an introductory psychology text, contains several complex noun phrases. They helped create sentences that included a lot of information.

    One type of noun phrase is formed by putting two nouns together. Some examples from Reading 3 are *business venture, football team,* and *television program.*

    Another type of noun phrase is formed by adding a prepositional phrase after a core noun. Two examples from Reading 3 are *sense of self-efficacy* and *the behavior of someone else.*

2. *Present tense:* Another common characteristic of informational writing is that it is generally written in the present tense. Remember that when you use the present tense, you must use the rules for subject-verb agreement.

> **GLR** See Section 3B in the GLR to learn more about noun phrases and 3G to learn more about subject-verb agreement.

Activity 1-16   Using Features of Informational Writing

1. Match these words (one noun from the left-hand column with the core noun from the right-hand column) to make a *noun + noun* noun phrase.

role	anxiety
test	treatments
kidney	patients
dialysis	model
fluid	intake

2. Match the nouns on the left with the appropriate prepositional phrase on the right.

admission	of an Olympic diver
the lack	to medical school
reasonable chance	of succeeding
the behavior	of variety

3. Write five sentences about the content of Reading 3. Use five of the above noun phrases, either *noun + noun* or *noun + prepositional phrase.*

4. Quickly skim Reading 3 and circle the present tense verbs.

Features of Interactive Writing

Reading 3 is also a good example of *interactive writing*, a style frequently used in introductory college textbooks. In interactive writing, the author tries to involve the reader by using grammatical structures that are more commonly found in conversation than in writing. These features include asking questions and using the pronouns *you* and *I*.

> **GLR**   See Section 7 for more information about interactive writing.

Activity 1-17   Learning Features of Interactive Writing

1. Underline the questions in the following paragraph from Reading 3.

You watch an Olympic diver win a gold medal for a superb display of physical control. Presumably you would like to earn an Olympic medal too; so because of this vicarious reinforcement you should go out and try to make some spectacular dives into a pool. Do you? Probably not. Why not? Why does that vicarious reinforcement fail to motivate you to engage in imitative behavior?

2. Circle the uses of the pronoun *you.*

3. Who is the *you* the author is referring to? Who is the author asking the questions to? Why? Where does the author answer his own question?

Activity 1-18   Acknowledging Other Writers' Ideas

1. Underline the three places in Reading 3 where the author shows he is using other people's ideas.

2. What reference information is given? Where is it given?

3. Spend a few minutes becoming acquainted with Section 5 in the GLR ⬤. Learn what kinds of information it contains. You will refer to this often as you use the ideas and words of other people to support your own writing.

READING 4   ANATOMY OF A CHAMPION (MAGAZINE ARTICLE)

Activity 1-19   Pre-reading Questions

1. What is an *athlete*?

2. Name several successful athletes and the sport they excel(led) in. What has contributed to their success?

ANATOMY OF A CHAMPION

Successful athletes can show us how to be champions in life

What makes a champion? What has been learned from studying gold medalists?

Self-analysis. The successful athlete knows his or her strengths and weaknesses. This critical appraisal should be honest but never negative. A negative self-analysis decreases your motivation and doesn't offer solutions.   5

Self-competition. When an event ends, a champion doesn't ask himself, "Did I win?"; he asks, "How did I do?" You can only control your performance. It doesn't make sense to compare yourself to others. Winning or losing becomes secondary and at times irrelevant.

Focus. The athlete must always be in "the present," concentrating on the task at hand, not on the outcomes. If you regret the past or worry about the future, it inhibits your perfor- 10
mance.

Confidence. Successful athletes control anxiety by setting tough but reasonable goals. By facing a challenge where the outcome is within your ability, you achieve a state of "flow," which leads to increased confidence.

Toughness. This is a mental trait that involves accepting risk and trying to win rather than 15
trying not to lose. A "tough" athlete accepts commitment, sees change as opportunity and believes in control of his or her destiny.

Having a game plan. Even for elite athletes, talent is not enough. They need a game plan. Your own game plan for living can be simple or complex, depending on your level of ability and experience.   20

These are the lessons we can learn from Olympians. Let the Games begin.

Source: George Sheehan, "Anatomy of a Champion," *Runner's World* (Rodale Press, May 1993).

Activity 1-20   Class Discussion

Think about the six traits described in Reading 4.

self-analysis	self-competition
focus	confidence
toughness	having a game plan

With a partner, discuss how each of these applies to you as writers. Share your examples with another set of partners or with your class.

Activity 1-21   Paragraph Writing Assignment

In Activity 1-20, you applied the six traits to writing. Now, you will apply two of the traits to some other activity or skill. Here are some possible ideas:

- being an employee, student, teacher, or parent
- being an artist, second language learner, musician, or researcher

Write two connected paragraphs. Each paragraph will be about one of the traits and how it applies to the activity or skill. For example:

Paragraph 1: Having a game plan + being a second language learner
Paragraph 2: Self-confidence + being a second language learner

When you are finished writing, use this self-editing paragraph checklist to check your work. Revise your paragraphs and rewrite them.

❑ complete sentences

❑ correct sentence punctuation

❑ topic sentence and controlling idea

❑ supporting sentences

❑ concluding sentence

❑ cohesion devices

❑ paragraph hooks (see next page)

Paragraph Hooks

We have practiced using transition words and phrases, repetition of key words, and pronoun reference to connect the sentences in a paragraph. These cohesion devices help each sentence of your paragraph flow smoothly to the following sentence.

You can use these same cohesion devices when you begin a new paragraph to help you hook (connect) your new paragraph to the previous paragraph. In fact, notice how this paragraph is hooked to the first paragraph by repeating key words ("cohesion devices" and "paragraph"). Circle these words and phrases in the topic sentence of this paragraph and in the first paragraph. This repetition makes it easy for the reader to go from the ideas in the first paragraph to the ideas in this paragraph.

Throughout this text, notice how authors move smoothly from sentence to sentence, and also from paragraph to paragraph. Check your two paragraphs in Activity 1-21 to see that you smoothly connected your sentences and also your two paragraphs.

PUTTING IT ALL TOGETHER

FINAL WRITING ASSIGNMENT

For your final writing assignment, write two or three connected paragraphs related to success.

Plan

1. *Choose your topic.* Select one of the following ideas.

    a. Choose one of the eight topic ideas in Activity 1-14.

    b. Look at the paragraphs you have already written in this chapter. Are there ideas you want to expand or connect? If so, check your ideas with your teacher.

    c. Select one of the following topics:

        • a challenge and how a person successfully met that challenge

        • a person who successfully contributed to a field of study

2. *Gather and organize your ideas.* Collect ideas to support the topic of your connected paragraphs by doing two or more of the following:

   a. Read your entries in your learner's notebook. Circle ideas that you might use in your new paragraphs.

   b. Reread the readings in this chapter. List ideas that might fit in your paragraphs.

   c. Think about your personal experiences about the topic and make notes about those experiences.

   d. Interact with others. Talk with others about your topic; take notes and list possible supporting ideas.

   Then organize your ideas. Write possible topic sentences and a list of supporting ideas for your paragraphs

3. *Topic workshop.* With a partner, share your selected topic, proposed topic sentences, and list of supporting ideas. Help each other improve your topic sentences. Do all the supporting ideas help explain and clarify the idea in the topic sentence? Discuss additional possible supporting details to include in the paragraphs.

Write Your First Draft

Based on your discussion with your partner, arrange your ideas in two or three connected paragraphs. Don't worry about saying everything perfectly. You will have a chance to revise and edit your paragraphs before you put them in final form.

Peer Response

1. Courtesy-edit. Before you exchange your paper with your partner, read your own paper carefully to make sure your meaning is clear. You want your partner to be able to read your ideas easily, so check for anything that would make it difficult for your partner to understand your paper. If some sentences are confusing, rewrite them. Correct any problems with spelling, punctuation, and grammar that might confuse your reader. This is a courtesy to your reader.

2. Exchange the first draft of your connected paragraphs with your partner.

   a. Read your partner's draft. Write answers to the following questions to give to your partner. Discuss the answers together. What makes these paragraphs interesting? What would make them more interesting?

b. Does each paragraph have a topic sentence with a controlling idea?

c. Is there enough support in the paragraphs? What could be added?

d. What is something you learned from your partner's paragraphs that you didn't know before?

e. Was anything difficult to understand? Explain.

f. Which paragraph did you like best? Why?

Revise, Edit, and Proofread

1. Read your paragraphs again. Do they say what you want them to say? How will you use your partner's comments to help you improve your paragraphs? Make any changes needed to make your paper clearer and more interesting.

2. Edit your individual sentences for the following, and correct any errors that you find. After you have edited for each of these features, check (✓) the box to remind yourself that you have completed that task.

   ☐ complete sentences

   ☐ correct sentence punctuation

   ☐ verb tense choices

   ☐ subject-verb agreement

   ☐ cohesion devices: repetition of key words and phrases, pronouns, transition words and phrases

3. Make any necessary changes and rewrite your paragraphs.

4. Proofread your paragraphs by checking the spelling, grammar, and punctuation. Use the GLR ⬤ and a dictionary or computer spell-check program to help you. (If you use a computer program, be sure that what it suggests makes sense in the context of your paragraphs.)

• •

**L
O
O
K
I
N
G
A
H
E
A
D**

Academic Assignment

At the end of each chapter in this text are authentic college/university assignments like the one below. *You do not have to complete these assignments.* However, analyzing these assignments will give you a clearer understanding of the types of assignments you will face in your undergraduate courses.

Read the following information from an art course syllabus and then discuss the questions about the course requirements.

Post-Modernism

We will explore the phenomena of Modernism and Post-Modernism in contemporary culture, focusing (for the most part) on Post-Modernism. We will examine a selection of artists and review readings together. We will have a series of student-run panel discussions. You will have readings assigned for these panels and I have also assigned some outside artists to several of these panels. Each of us will keep a course journal and we will share our writing from these journals. In conjunction with this course, visiting scholars and artists will speak to various aspects of the Post-Modern experience.

Course Requirements and Evaluation: This class is rather unusual in that I will conduct the class like a graduate seminar.

1. Discussion is an important part of the course and I value your input. After all, we are all part of the Post-Modern era. Each of us has our own pool of knowledge and experience more than we may be aware of. We will try to access that experience in this class. (25% of your course grade)
2. We will keep a course journal throughout the semester. Your journal will include 14 weekly reviews, three responses to visiting lecturers, two responses to museum visits, four responses to readings, and other assignments done in class. (25% of your course grade)
3. You will also write a research paper on a particular artist, work of art, or topic (not the same topic as your panel). (25% of your course grade)
4. You will participate in one "issues" panel and write an accompanying summary paper evaluating yourself and the other members of the panel. (25% of your course grade)

There will be no exams in this course.

DISCUSSION

1. What are the writing assignments for this course?

2. How would you use personal experience, interaction with others, and reading to gather information for these writing assignments?

3. This syllabus only gives general information about these assignments. What questions would you want to ask the instructor about the course journal and the research paper?

4. How much of your course grade is affected by these writing assignments?

5. What other skills are necessary to be successful in this course?

6. In this course, there are no exams. Would that fact influence whether or not you took this course? Why or why not?

Chapter 2

*I*nstructing

Academic Skills

G O A L S

WRITING
◆ write clear, organized instructions
◆ write a memo

GRAMMAR
◆ practice giving instructions using imperatives, modals, and conditional sentences
◆ explore the differences between spoken and written English

CONTENT
◆ read about academic skills
◆ explore the instructional resources on your campus

ACADEMIC FIELDS
Multi-disciplinary

Sample Authentic College/University Writing Assignments

In your academic courses, you will use the skills you learn in this chapter to complete assignments and test questions like the examples below.

Business Administration

In a two- to three-page paper, give advice to a new manager about how to successfully perform the four functions of management—planning, organizing, leading, and controlling.

Geology

Explain how fossils are formed.

Human Physiology

After the brain organizes incoming messages, it sends responses to the body. Describe this process.

 CNN video support is available for this chapter.

Turner Le@rning

GETTING READY

LEARNER'S NOTEBOOK

Warm-up Activity

In your learner's notebook, make a list of skills a college or university student needs to be successful. When you finish, write a short paragraph about the two most important skills on your list. Why are they important? How can students improve these skills?

When you are finished writing, collect everyone's ideas on the chalkboard. Are there other skills you can add to the list?

An Introduction to Instructing

Instructional writing is used to explain how to do something or how something is done. In any bookstore in the United States, you will see hundreds of "how-to" books. These books instruct you in how to make a million dollars, develop a positive attitude, fall in love, dress for success, build your own house, study for important tests, cook nutritious meals, or repair your own car.

As a student, you are also surrounded by *instructions*, both written and oral. Receiving instructions is a way to learn new material and skills, so, naturally, it is a vital part of your education. These instructions may be directions, advice, rules, or steps of a process, and they come from a variety of sources.

Activity 2-1   Receiving Instructions

Write at least one kind of instruction you might receive from each of the following sources.

Source	Instruction/How to
lab manual	how to do a lab experiment, how to use a microscope, how to be safe working in a lab
campus map	
course syllabus	

textbook   _____

test   _____

registration materials   _____

on-line library catalog   _____

classmate   _____

reference librarian   _____

teacher   _____

computer lab personnel   _____

Writing Clear Instructions

In addition to receiving instructions, you will be expected to give and write instructions as part of your academic work. There are several important steps to remember.

1. **Analyze your audience.**

   Your audience is who you are writing the instructions for. Depending on your audience and their prior knowledge or experience, you may need to explain some information very carefully or you may only need to mention other points briefly.

   • How much do they already know?

   • What new terminology will they need to be defined or explained?

2. **Know your purpose.**

   Your primary purpose is to write clearly so that others can easily understand the instructions. Your purpose may also be:

   • to have people follow/perform the steps of your instructions

   • to persuade people that they can or should follow your instructions

   • to demonstrate (on a test, for example) that you are able to explain how something is done or how something occurs

3. **Include all the necessary information.**

   Before you begin to write, list all the necessary information. Check again when you are finished to be sure the information is complete. If something is missing, the reader may not be able to understand the instructions.

4. Organize your instructions.

Time: Instructions for a step-by-step process should be given in chronological (time) order. You begin with the very first step and continue through the steps to the end. When you put the steps in chronological order, you may see that several can be grouped together in a paragraph if they are all about one main idea, such as *preparation, first steps,* or *final steps.*

In writing, chronological steps are sometimes numbered (e.g., 1, 2, 3, 4, 5); words can also be used, like *first, second, then, next, after that, finally.*

Importance: Some instructions can be organized according to importance. You can begin with the most important information and end with the least important, or you can start with the least and end with the most important.

Situation: Instructions can also be organized according to location or activity. For example, instructions telling the reader how to be safe could be organized by location: *safety at home* and *safety on vacation.* Study skills could be organized by activity: *reading textbooks, attending class,* and *preparing for tests.*

5. Guide the reader through difficult parts of the instructions.

Anticipate unfamiliar vocabulary and other ideas or steps the reader may find difficult, and be sure to give detailed explanations. In some cases, you can use illustrations or diagrams to help the reader.

Activity 2-2   Finding Examples of Instructions on Campus

1. Find an example of instructions for students on your campus. There are several possibilities, such as how to enroll, register, add/drop courses, use the library, evacuate a building in an emergency, change a major, manage time, drink alcohol responsibly, manage stress, or use the laundry facilities in a dormitory.

2. Either bring the printed instructions to class or write them down to share with your class.

3. Share your examples in class. Analyze each example, asking:

    a. Who is the audience?

    b. What is the purpose?

    c. Are the instructions complete?

    d. How are the instructions organized?

    e. How does the author help the reader with difficult parts of the instructions? How is this done with words and/or pictures and diagrams?

LEARNER'S NOTEBOOK

Effective Instructions

What did you learn from your class discussion about writing effective instructions? Give examples to support your ideas.

Grammar Preview

When you write instructions, you must write clearly and persuasively so your readers will accept your instructions as valuable and accurately presented. In this chapter, you will use commands, warnings, comments, and various types of advice to write convincing instructions. You will also use modal auxiliary verbs to set the correct tone for your advice and conditional sentences to show causes and results (what happens if someone follows your advice, for example). In addition, this chapter will help you to understand differences between spoken English and formal written academic English. This will help you think about which features of spoken English can be used in your writing and which cannot be used in formal academic writing.

FOCUSING

A variety of skills can help you become a more effective student. Your campus undoubtedly has many resources to help you successfully meet your academic goals. In this chapter, you will explore some of those campus resources. You will also read several articles that explain how to stay alert in classes, prevent computer disasters, predict test questions, gather information about course requirements, and evaluate materials from your campus library and the Internet.

READING 1   THE IN-CLASS OXYGENATOR (ACADEMIC SKILLS TEXTBOOK)

Activity 2-3   Pre-reading Questions

1. Have you ever fallen asleep in a class? Explain when and why this happened.

2. What advice could help students stay awake and alert in their classes?

THE IN-CLASS OXYGENATOR

When you become sleepy in class, the problem might be lack of oxygen. You can run through the following process in 30 seconds.

1. Straighten your spine. Put both feet on the floor, uncross your arms and legs, sit up straight, and hold your head up straight.

2. Take a deep breath and while you're holding it, tense the muscles in your body. Start with the muscles in your feet, then the legs, thighs, stomach, chest, shoulders, neck, jaw, forehead, arms and hands. Hold these muscles tense for the count of five and then relax and exhale. 5

3. Breathe deeply three times. Inhale slowly and deeply, breathing into your belly as well as your chest. Pause momentarily at the top of the breath and then exhale completely. When you have exhaled as much as you can, force out more air by contracting the muscles of your stomach. Do this breathing three times. 10

4. Repeat step #2. You've now activated all of your muscles and filled your body with oxygen. You are ready to return your attention to the task at hand.

Practice this exercise now by completing it twice. Then make a mental note so that the next time you're sleepy in class or while you're studying, you can use this exercise. With a little practice, you can make it subtle. Your instructor and classmates won't even notice you're doing it. 15

Source: Dave Ellis, *Becoming a Master Student,* 7th Ed. (Boston: Houghton Mifflin Company, 1994).

Activity 2-4   Post-reading Questions

1. In a small group, practice this process. Go through it step by step.

2. Who is the audience for this piece of writing? What is the purpose?

3. Is the reading organized by time, importance, or situation?

4. In Reading 1, find one example of each of the four basic sentence types you practiced in Chapter 1: *simple, compound, complex,* and *compound-complex.*

READING 2   PREVENTING DISASTER (ACADEMIC SKILLS TEXTBOOK)

Students in almost all disciplines find computers vital for doing assignments and accessing the ever-growing amount of information available in the library and on the Internet. The reading in this section offers instruction in the most basic computer skills.

Activity 2-5   Pre-reading Questions

1. What expectations do your teachers have for word-processed work or basic computer skills?

2. On your campus, what resources are available to help students expand their computer skills?

PREVENTING DISASTER

Whether you're using your own computer or another computer, take precautions to avoid the most serious catastrophes.

1. Don't do anything silly to a computer. Don't spill things on it. Don't drop it. Don't hit it. However, yelling and screaming are okay and often fairly common and acceptable behaviors.   5

2. Learn how to start, stop, and restart the computer you are using. Two common problems are (1) a computer gets "hung up" so that no matter what you do, absolutely nothing changes on the screen, and (2) you get "lost" in an application program and suddenly don't know what you're doing and can't figure out how to move back to doing something that was making sense. In both cases the last (and very desperate) option is to turn the com-   10 puter off and then restart it. Usually you will lose whatever work you had done since the last time you saved or filed your work. But at least you will be back in operation.

3. Learn how to make "backups." Be sure you understand the different ways to make backup copies and know where you can save and store copies of your computer work (your computer *files*). Learn what *diskettes, hard disks, internal memory,* and *network server*   15 *shared storage* are and whether each is available to you. Learn how to use them. Always think about how serious a problem it would be for you to recreate (from notes and memory) your current work. If it's no big deal, then don't worry about it. However, for your most important projects, you should probably:

a. *Save* the document at least every five or ten minutes while you work on it. Give the   20 file or document a name that you can easily recognize and remember. Use numbers to help identify the version number of the document. (Is it your first draft or your fourth rewrite?)

b. *Make a backup copy.* Desktop computers such as an IBM-compatible (sometimes called a Windows computer) or a Macintosh allow you to copy documents (*files*) from the computer to a diskette (and vice versa). Be sure you save your work on the document fre-   25 quently and also at the end of each work session. If what you're working on is extremely important, keep the diskette in a different room or building than the computer.

c. *Print a "hard" (paper) copy* of your draft version at the end of every work session. If you think you wouldn't be able to produce a copy of your work to date on short order, then print a copy of the most up-to-date version at the end of each work session and keep   30 it in a safe place.

Source: J. N. Gardner and A. J. Jewler, *Your College Experience—Strategies for Success,* 2nd Ed.
(Wadsworth Publishing Company, 1995).

Activity 2-6   Post-reading Questions

1. Who is the audience for this piece of writing? What was the author's purpose?

2. Find at least three words or phrases that were defined. Why do you think the author defined these particular words?

3. What purpose does typeface—**bold** and *italics*—serve in this reading?

4. Look at the organization of Reading 2.

   a. How are the numbered sections (1, 2, 3) organized? Why is "1. Don't do anything silly to a computer" given first?

   b. How is Section 3 organized?

5. Form a small group. First, learn about your group members.

   a. How much computer experience do they have?

   b. How familiar are they with computer terminology? Then, keeping in mind the level of computer experience of your group members, explain how to start, stop, and restart the computer you use and how to back up your work.

Two Common Sentence Types in Instructions

Positive and negative commands with implied *you* as subject

Imperatives command someone to do or not to do something. The imperative uses the root form of the verb. The subject of the sentence, which is *you,* is implied but not stated in the command.

EXAMPLES

Positive command: Learn how to use them.
Negative command: Don't drop it.

Sentences with stated *you* as subject

Instructions also include sentences with *you* as the stated subject. These subjects are not commands; instead, they explain how to follow the instructions by giving further description or comment.

EXAMPLE

Usually you will lose whatever work you had done since the last time you saved or filed your work.

Activity 2-7   Using Two Common Sentence Types

1. Find two examples of positive or negative commands with implied *you* as a subject in Reading 2.

2. Find two examples of sentences with stated *you* as the subject in Reading 2.

Activity 2-8   Analyzing Reading 1

Return to Reading 1 and analyze the sentences used. Do you find these two sentence patterns there? Is one more common than the other?

Activity 2-9   Conditional Sentences

Conditional sentences are complex sentences that are often used to show that if something happens, then something else happens. Examples of conditional sentences are given in Section 6D of the GLR 🔵.

1. In "3. Learn how to make 'backups'," you will find three conditional sentences. Highlight or underline them. Scan for the word *if.*

2. What is the purpose of these conditional sentences?

3. How would Reading 2 be different (besides being shorter) if these conditional sentences were omitted?

Write four conditional sentences related to computer use:

1. If you do not know anything about computers, _____

_____

_____.

2. If _____

_____

_____.

3. _____

_____ if _____

_____.

4. If _____

_____

_____.

Guidelines for Writing a Memorandum (Memo)

A memorandum (memo) is a written message often used to give or ask for information. Memos are frequently used by people in the same work environment. Unlike a business letter, which is generally put in an envelope and mailed to someone at a distance, a memo is usually distributed within an organization, such as a business or school, to help people communicate with each other.

A memo has two main parts:

1. the heading, which has four lines of information

2. the message

Memo

DATE:	When the memo was written.
TO:	The receiver of the message.
FROM:	The person who wrote the memo.
SUBJECT:	This line should be short but informative. For example, "Upcoming Meeting" could announce a meeting.

The message discusses the subject clearly and directly. You can begin with a general sentence about the purpose of your memo and then give supporting details.

Most memos are written in block style, which means that the paragraphs are not indented. Paragraphs are single-spaced with a double space between paragraphs.

Activity 2-10   Writing a Memo

Using the correct format for a memo, write a memo to other students in your ESL program. Choose one of the topics below.

1. Avoiding Computer Disaster: Have you ever had a computer disaster? What advice can you give others to avoid a computer disaster you have had? What should students do if it happens to them?

2. Learning about Computers: What advice can you give students who know little or nothing about computers? Explain how they can learn. What resources are available to them on your campus or in your community?

READING 3   HOW TO PREDICT TEST QUESTIONS
(ACADEMIC SKILLS TEXTBOOK)

When a test approaches, students are often concerned about the format of the test and what material will be covered. The following article explains how you can guess what will be on a test.

HOW TO PREDICT TEST QUESTIONS

Predicting test questions can do more than get you a better grade on a test. It can keep you focused on the purpose of the course and help you design your learning strategy. It can be fun too.   5

First, get organized. Have a separate section in your notebook labeled "Test Questions." Add several questions to this section after every lecture and assignment.

You also can create your own code or   10 graphic signal—maybe a "T!" in a circle— to flag possible test questions in your notes.

The format of a test can help you predict questions. Ask your instructor to   15 describe the test—how long it will be and what kind of questions to expect (essay, multiple choice). Do this early in the term so you can be alert for possible test questions from the very beginning.   20

During lectures you can watch for test questions by observing not only what the instructor says but also how he says it. Instructors give clues. For example:

Instructors might repeat important points 25 several times, write them on the board, or return to them in subsequent classes.

They might use certain gestures when making crucial points. They might pause, look at notes, or read passages word for   30 word.

Also pay attention to questions the instructor poses to students, and note questions other students ask.

When material from reading assign-   35 ments also is covered extensively in class, it is likely to be on the test.

Put yourself in your instructor's head. What kind of questions would you ask? Make practice test questions.   40

Save all quizzes, papers, lab sheets, and graded material of any kind. Quiz questions have a way of appearing, in slightly altered form, on final exams. If copies of previous exams are available, use 45 those to predict questions.

For science courses and other courses involving problem solving, practice working problems using different variables.

You can also brainstorm test questions 50 with other students. This is a great activity for study groups.

Finally, be on the lookout for these words: *This material will be on the test.*

Source: Dave Ellis, *Becoming a Master Student,* 7th Ed. (Houghton Mifflin Company, 1994).

Activity 2-11   Post-reading Questions

1. Who is the audience for this piece of writing? What is the author's purpose?

2. In your opinion, is this advice helpful? If so, what are the two or three most helpful pieces of advice? Explain.

3. Look at the organization of this article, which contains 14 short paragraphs and is organized according to the situations below. Write the number of the correct paragraphs that relate to these general topics.

Paragraph	Situation
1	introduction
_____	note-taking
_____	listening to the lecturer
_____	studying outside of class
14	conclusion

Activity 2-12   Using Modal Auxiliaries in Instructions

The author uses only three modal auxiliaries in Reading 3—*can, might,* and *will.* If you understand how he uses these modals, you can try this approach in your own writing when you are giving instructions. The first step is to find the modals; the second is to analyze the strategy used by the author; the third is to try these techniques in your own writing.

1. Circle all of the uses of *can* in Reading 3. Underline all of the uses of *might.* Put a box around the uses of *will.*

2. Match the meanings of these modals (as they are used in the reading) with the best definition.

    a. can   _____ possible actions for readers to take themselves

    b. might   _____ statements of certainty made by teachers

    c. will   _____ possible but not predictable actions by teachers

3. Why is *can* used so frequently by this writer? How can you use this technique in your own writing?

GLR   Refer to Section 6C for more information on modal auxiliaries.

Activity 2-13   Writing Assignment

Write a humorous paragraph about how to fail a test. Organize your paragraph by time, importance, or situation. Use examples and experiences to support your ideas. You can use your imagination to create this paragraph! Try to include at least one of each of the following:

- conditional sentence
- implied *you* sentence (imperative)
- stated *you* sentence
- modal sentence

Peer Review: Share your paragraph in a small group. Answer these questions about each shared paragraph.

1. Is the paragraph humorous? Why?

2. What is the topic sentence and controlling idea?

3. What is the most interesting detail?

READING 4   COURSE REQUIREMENTS (INTERVIEW)

An important academic skill is being able to discover new information. You will often do this by asking questions of other students, your teachers, academic advisers, or librarians. While many of these questions will be spontaneous, sometimes you will want or need to prepare questions for an interview.

The interview may be informal, such as talking to a friend who is taking a course you will take next semester. For a more formal interview, you could prepare a list of written questions, and at the interview, you would probably think of other questions to ask. You might take brief notes or audiotape the interview. The key to both informal and formal interviewing is asking good questions and showing genuine interest in the other person's opinions. Answers that only require a "yes" or "no" will not give you many new ideas for your writing. However, questions that encourage the speaker to give more information often will.

The following reading is part of a transcript of an informal interview. In this interview, one person is trying to get information about a course called Western Civilization, commonly called "Western Civ."

Read silently first. Then read it with a partner, each taking one of the parts. Occasionally you will find interruptions, repeated words, and hesitations by the two speakers.

TRANSCRIPT OF AN INFORMAL INTERVIEW

E: Tell me about Western Civ. How much time do you spend on Western Civ? Because that's probably . . .

S: As little as possible (laughter)

E: Now, why are you taking Western Civ?

S: It's required for all undergraduates and you can't take Western Civ until you are either   5
a junior or a senior.

E: Oh really? Oh, for some reason I thought that was a freshman. . . . you had to be a freshman.

S: No, I wish it was. No, you have to be a junior or a senior in order to take it. I don't know why. I guess their reasoning is that you'll be able to write better papers, um, but   10
the first semester of Western Civ you write a lot of little papers and then one big paper. This semester, um, we have one, um, BIG paper, anywhere from 15 to 20 pages and then two exams and that's it.

E: And what format are these exams?

S: Uhhhhh. . . . Everything from true-false, short answer, quotation identifications to long   15
essays. I mean it runs the gamut. And they **do** take two to three hours to take.

E: So how do you study for those?

S: Pray (laughter). Ummm, ummm, well, I don't spend much time reviewing the readings, because it would take too long. I mean, you read 20 books in a semester, so I go back over my notes and particularly notes taken in the discussion sessions . . . umm.   20
Sometimes I'll, I'll go to the library and and pull out the reserve materials. Basically it's just the overhead material but sometimes it's easier if the lecturer's notes are right there rather than my notes.

E: So, what? The lecturer . . . the lecturer puts the overhead transparencies on reserve?

S: And, and their notes.   25

E: So you can compare your notes to theirs?

S: Right. In case you miss anything you can go back and—

E: Hey, that's good.

S: Um, to a degree, but I find that their notes are generally more sparse than my notes anyway.   30

E: Oh.

S: So, I mean if you don't go to class, yeah, it helps, because you can always go and get the notes.

E: Yeah. Did you do well in that course? Or are you doing well in that course?

S: Oh, I got a B last semester.   35

E: Oh, that's good.

S: And I have to admit I didn't put the effort into it I could have, um.

E: So, what advice would you give to students just starting to take Western Civ?

S: Don't get behind in the readings. Because you'll never catch up. I mean you read literally 20 books a semester and there's no way you can skim that, and Cliff Notes don't   40
help and you just can't get behind. If you do get behind, though (chuckle), it's possible to pull through, I mean I did, I got a B, but . . . (laughter)

Activity 2-14 Characteristics of Spoken Language

With a partner, try to find these common characteristics of spoken language in the interview. Write down the line number of an example of each.

1. interruption _____

2. repetition of words _____

3. fragment _____

4. laughter _____

5. conversational "fillers" (uhhh, um, etc.) _____

6. question asking _____

7. using *you* and *I* _____

8. contractions _____

Activity 2-15 Differences Between Spoken and Written Language

1. Read this summary of the information given in the interview. Compare this written language with the spoken language of the interview.

WESTERN CIVILIZATION COURSE WORK

When students are juniors or seniors at the University of Kansas, they are required to take two semesters of Western Civilization. In the first semester, students write several short papers and one long paper. In the second semester, they take two exams and write a 15–20 page research paper. Students also read about 20 books for the course each semester and so it is important to keep up with the reading assignments. When it is time for a test, it is impossible to review all the books, so students should take good notes throughout the semester. If they want to double-check their notes, they can see the lecturer's notes on reserve at the library.

2. With your partner, fill in the blanks below with differences between spoken and written English. It may be helpful to each take a part and read through the interview again, stopping when you discover a difference to add. You can also use the characteristics of spoken English from Activity 2-14. A few items have already been written in the chart to help you begin.

SPOKEN LANGUAGE : INTERVIEW	WRITTEN LANGUAGE: PARAGRAPH
everyday informal vocabulary	more formal vocabulary
more questions and answers	
body language	
	complete sentences

Activity 2-16   Interview Assignment

Interview a student who is taking or has taken a class you will probably take in the future. Another possibility is to interview the teacher of the course.

Plan your questions. Before the interview, write down at least five questions you will ask. The questions can be about:

- textbooks
- assignments
- tests
- advice or suggestions for students taking the course

Interview. If possible, record the interview on audiotape.

Write. Write a paragraph about the course and advice for new students.

Revise. Read your paragraph at least two times. Is your information correct and complete? Are your sentences clear? Does your paragraph flow smoothly?

Rewrite. Rewrite your paragraph, making necessary improvements.

Share. Share your paragraph with other students in your class who are interested in the course you wrote about.

READING 5   EVALUATING SOURCES (ACADEMIC SKILLS TEXTBOOK)

College and university students need to learn about the information resources available to them in the library and on the Internet. The amount of information available can be overwhelming; however, your educational success depends on learning how to access this information. Finding the information is just the first step. You must also evaluate the information to see if it is appropriate to your needs.

1. **Instructional Resources for Using Your Campus Library**

Each library system is different and is constantly changing and being updated. Go to your campus library to discover the instructional resources available to people learning to use the library.

These may include maps, guides to the library, on-line help, tours, workshops, reference librarians, and step-by-step instructions posted near computers, photocopiers, and other equipment.

Bring these written instructional resources, or information about them to class to share with your classmates.

LEARNER'S NOTEBOOK

Library Skills

Write a paragraph describing what you already know about finding information in your campus library. For example, write about whether you are able to:

use on-line catalogs   recall a book
use subject encyclopedias   use interlibrary loan
find journal articles   photocopy
find books   use the reserve desk

Then write about your plan to use instructional resources to learn more about your library system. Write at least two goals and tell how you plan to accomplish them. You will need these skills to complete many of the final writing assignments in this text.

2. **Instructional Resources for Using the Internet**

The Internet is a worldwide telecommunications network of interconnected computers that stores a rapidly growing amount of information. You can access a wide array of information from around the world quickly and easily using the World Wide Web (WWW).

Discover the instructional resources available to people learning how to use the WWW. These may include self-help books and handouts, on-line help, workshops, computer lab personnel, friends, and classmates.

Bring these instructional resources, or information about them, to class to share with your classmates.

LEARNER'S NOTEBOOK

Internet Skills

What do you already know about the WWW? What are the instructional resources available to you to learn more? What are your goals for learning more or which sites would you like to explore? How will you accomplish these goals?

EVALUATING SOURCES

Successfully gathering information involves more than just locating enough sources. It also involves evaluating articles, books, and other materials once you have found them. Particularly in the "Information Age," as the volume of available information increases daily, you should not settle for the first available sources. These sources may not be as relevant as others; they may be dated or inaccurate. To evaluate a source you might ask these   5
questions:

1. Is the source relevant to your information needs? You can begin by looking at the title of the book or article, its length, the type of source you need, and the type that is available or that you have at hand.

2. Is the information in the source accurate? If your topic is controversial, if you are   10
relying on just a few sources, or if you are using a questionable fact, you might want to find some reviews or additional commentary to check how accurate the information is. Compare other sources to see what they say.

3. Does the author or the source show bias? Consider why material was written or for whom it was written. When might you need to seek a different opinion?   15

4. Is the author credible or reliable? What are the author's credentials? If you have trouble answering this question, ask a reference librarian.

5. Is the information timely? That is, is it the most up-to-date information you could locate? You might consider these questions when using statistics or when you are in a fast-paced field constantly undergoing change (for example, computer science, medicine, eco-   20
nomics).

Source: J. N. Gardner and A. J. Jewler, *Your College Experience—Strategies for Success*, 2nd Ed.
(Wadsworth Publishing Company, 1995).

Activity 2-18   Post-reading Questions

1. If you are using a computer database to begin your search, you will be able to evaluate many articles quickly on-line. In other words, you may know from simply looking at the title of an article whether or not it will be appropriate for your assignment. What other things can you evaluate about the article before you actually read the article?

2. When may older material be useful?

3. If you are using material on the WWW, what special evaluation problems might you have?

4. Choose the source that would probably give you the most credible information. Explain.

   a. Topic: effects of smoking

      _____ Surgeon General of the United States

      _____ public relations firm for a cigarette company

   b. Topic: qualifications of a politician

      _____ the politician's opponent

      _____ the politician's public record

   c. Topic: effects of a natural disaster

      _____ disaster relief volunteer

      _____ tourist

   d. Topic: effectiveness of a new drug

      _____ research by the pharmaceutical company that makes the drug

      _____ research by an independent laboratory

   e. Topic: possibility of cloning human beings

      _____ 1998 scientific journal

      _____ 1980 scientific journal

Activity 2-19   Using Modals When Writing Instructions

In Reading 5, "Evaluating Sources," the authors are handling a topic much like the topic in Reading 3, "How to Predict Test Questions," so you can expect that the authors in Reading 5 will use modal auxiliaries to give advice. You can learn ways to present advice politely but effectively by studying how these writers present their ideas.

1. Find sentences 3 and 4 in the introductory paragraph of Reading 5. Sentence 3 gives some advice about something *not* to do; sentence 4 explains the reasons for the advice.

    • What modal is used for the advice?
    • What modal is used for the reasons?

    Based on your knowledge of modal auxiliaries, explain why you think the writer made these choices.

2. Plan a set of sentences that gives advice about something not to do and explain the reasons for that advice. What can you give other people advice about? Health? Money? Getting good grades? Talk over your ideas with other students in your class.

3. Write three sets of sentences following this pattern. Edit these sentences for modals and for complete sentence structure. Share your advice with the other students in your class.

Activity 2-20   Indirectness in Giving Advice

The writers of Reading 5, "Evaluating Sources," use a very polite tone. They have good advice to give about evaluating sources of information, but they do not demand that their readers take the advice. They use the modal *might* four times. Find all of those uses.

Try using another modal. For example, what is the effect on the article if you change *might* to *should*? What happens to the tone if you change *might* to *must*? If you are not sure about how the meaning and tone and meaning changes, you might ask a native speaker of English to react to the changes.

> **GLR**   Refer to Section 6C for more information on modal auxiliaries.

Activity 2-21   Using Conditional Sentences in Written Advice

1. To learn how these writers use conditional sentences, first find and highlight two conditional sentences in Reading 5. Scan for the word *if*.

2. To practice using conditionals in your own writing, complete these sentences related to doing research:

a. If your source gives outdated statistics, _____

_____

_____.

b. If you don't copy the URL address from your WWW source correctly, _____

_____

_____.

c. If you can't find the materials you need the night before your paper is due,

_____

_____.

d. If you find 80,000 entries on your library's database for journal articles related to

your topic, _____

_____.

e. _____

if you don't have time to proofread your paper before you turn it in.

3. Now try writing three conditional sentences of your own related to the research process.

LEARNER'S NOTEBOOK

Research Skills

Explain how the characteristics of curiosity and patience help someone doing research. What difficulties would a person with little curiosity or patience have?

Essay Organization

The final writing assignment at the end of most chapters in this textbook will be an essay. An essay is a set of between four and eight (and sometimes many more) related paragraphs that support one main idea. Some of the skills you will learn and practice as you write essays are:

- gathering and organizing your ideas
- writing for a specific audience and for a specific purpose
- presenting a clear main idea (thesis) for your writing
- supporting your ideas with evidence
- organizing and presenting your ideas logically

Although your academic assignments will vary in format, such as reports, research papers, and reactions, you can apply these five skills to those formats. For example, your lab report and your ten-page research paper will demand that you use these same skills. What you learn by writing essays in this course can be transferred to other academic writing assignments you will write.

An essay has three main parts.

Introduction
Body
Conclusion

Each part will vary in size, depending on your assignment and the complexity of your topic. For example, for a long research paper or a topic for which the reader needs a lot of background information, the introduction may be several paragraphs. That assignment would also demand many body paragraphs. Some conclusions may also need to be several paragraphs long, depending on the topic.

For most college essays, your introduction and conclusion will each be one paragraph. The body of your essay will probably be two to six paragraphs long, depending on the assignment.

Introduction

The introduction is the first paragraph. The introduction should catch the reader's attention so that the reader wants to continue reading.

An introduction can be represented by a triangle. The sentences in the introduction become more and more specific, leading the reader to the main idea, or thesis statement, of the essay. The thesis statement is usually the last sentence(s) of the introduction.

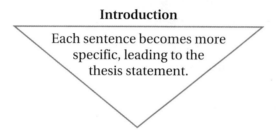

Introduction

Each sentence becomes more specific, leading to the thesis statement.

The Thesis Statement

The thesis statement tells the main idea of your essay and is the most specific and important sentence of the introduction. The rest of your essay will support the idea you present in your thesis statement. It is a promise to the reader and helps guide the writer.

The thesis statement gives both the topic of the essay and the controlling idea (what you want to say about the topic).

A thesis statement is an idea that can be developed in the paragraphs of your essay. The thesis statement is not simply a statement of fact, such as "I graduated from high school on May 25, 1997," because you can not develop this fact.

EXAMPLE: INTRODUCTION WITH THESIS STATEMENT

The first test in a course is always difficult. Students are not quite sure what kind of test the professor will give. Even so, some students feel fairly confident when they take that first test. However, many others realize that they need to find ways to be more successful on the next test. Students can accomplish this by learning more effective study strategies, developing a system for mastering vocabulary, and getting help from a study group.

Activity 2-22   Analyzing Thesis Statements

1. Underline the thesis statement in the example above and tell what you think the essay will be about.

2. Read the following thesis statements for short essays. For each one, discuss:
   - what you expect the main idea of the essay will be
   - what questions you think will be answered in the essay
   - possible sources of information that would help you gather ideas for the essay

   a. By following three guidelines for selecting your courses, you will be able to obtain your degree more quickly.

   b. A reference librarian can provide valuable help in locating resources for a research paper.

   c. Our library's on-line catalog helps students find information much more efficiently than the old card catalog system.

   d. Students should consider several sources for financing their education: scholarships, loans, and job earnings.

   e. Time management skills are essential for keeping up with course reading assignments and test preparation.

   f. You can save time and energy by following these three steps to register for a course by telephone.

Activity 2-23   Writing Thesis Statements

It is important to narrow your topic carefully so that you can adequately develop it in your essay. If your thesis statement is too broad or general, you will not be able to give enough specific support to cover your ideas thoroughly or to make your writing interesting.

For the first thesis statement in Activity 2-22, a broad, general topic for an essay would be *academic success*. We can narrow this topic to *selection of courses*. When a controlling idea is added to this narrowed topic, we have a workable thesis statement for an essay.

Narrow each of the following topics below and write a thesis statement.

EXAMPLE

Topic: academic success

Narrowed Topic: selecting courses

Thesis Statement: By following three guidelines for selecting your courses, you will be able to obtain your degree more quickly.

Topic: healthy lifestyle
Narrowed Topic: _____
Thesis Statement: _____
                  _____
                  _____ .

Topic: educational travel
Narrowed Topic: _____
Thesis Statement: _____
                  _____
                  _____ .

Topic: careers in your major field of study
Narrowed Topic: _____
Thesis Statement: _____
                  _____
                  _____ .

Topic: diversity on campus
Narrowed Topic: _____
Thesis Statement: _____
                  _____
                  _____ .

Topic: a college education
Narrowed Topic: _____
Thesis Statement: _____
                  _____
                  _____ .

Body

The body paragraphs in an essay support and develop the idea in your thesis statement. Therefore, the body paragraphs will be the longest part of your essay. Some of the
ways you will gather the ideas for your body paragraphs are through personal experience, reading, and interaction with others. You will gather and synthesize facts, details,
examples, quotations, ideas, and explanations.

Begin each of your body paragraphs with a topic sentence. Each of these topic sentences should support the thesis statement of your essay.

Activity 2-24   Planning Body Paragraphs

Choose three of the thesis statements in Activity 2-22 or 2-23, and, with a partner, discuss ideas for three or four body paragraphs for each one. After you have your ideas, write a topic sentence for each body paragraph. Discuss as a class.

Conclusion

The conclusion is the last paragraph in the essay. It can restate your main idea or main supporting ideas. It completes the ideas you have written in your essay.

Activity 2-25   Analyzing an Essay

Read the following essay and answer the questions that follow.

DOING BETTER ON THE NEXT TEST

The first test in a course is always difficult. Students are not quite sure what kind of test the professor will give. Even so, many students feel fairly confident when they take that first test. However, many others realize that they need to find ways to be more successful on the next one. Students can accomplish this by learning more effective study strategies, developing a system for mastering vocabulary, and getting help from a study group.

An important first step is to talk to successful students about how they study. Even in large classes, it is often easy to tell who the best students are. You will learn that the best students do not all study the same way, but they have developed strategies that work well for them. However, what these students have in common is that they do a lot of studying along the way and then review, instead of cram, before the test. For example, one strategy is to prepare for each class by reviewing class notes and doing the assigned reading; another strategy is to read class notes and write down any questions after each class. This way, before the test, students can review instead of trying to learn things for the first time. Other students have different strategies that work for them. By talking to several students, you will learn about a variety of successful approaches.

Another strategy is to develop a system for learning new vocabulary. To learn the basic terms of your field of study, you need to have a specific place to keep all these new words, whether it is a special place in a notebook, a list on the wall by your study area, or a stack of index cards. Add to your list after you read the text-book or after a lecture. Then spend time going over these words frequently. Research shows that you will make more progress learning these words in several short study sessions instead of one long session. Even ten minutes a day is enough to start mastering these words.

In addition to studying on their own, some students benefit from forming an informal study group. The success of your group will depend on its members, so try to choose a partner or a few partners who share your attitudes about study. These people will not do your studying for you, but together you can compare class notes, review key terminology and concepts, and often have interesting discussions about the course material. Having a study group also helps students set aside a certain time to study the course material.

Because a student's life is complicated, juggling work, friends, family, exercising, and having fun, it is sometimes hard to keep up with a course. However, when you do, you will feel more confident about tests and in class discussions. Many students find that the more time they put into a class, the more they enjoy it and the more they learn.

1. Below, fill in the outline of the essay

   Thesis Statement: _____

   _____ .

   Topic Sentence 1: _____

   _____ .

   Topic Sentence 2: _____

   _____ .

   Topic Sentence 3: _____

   _____ .

2. Notice how each of the topic sentences relates to the thesis statement. What key words and ideas are repeated?

3. Find one example in the essay of each of these grammatical structures we studied in this chapter.

   a. modal sentence

   b. imperative (command) with implied *you* as the subject of the sentence

   c. sentence with stated *you* as the subject

   d. transition word or phrase

PUTTING IT ALL TOGETHER

FINAL WRITING ASSIGNMENT

For your final writing assignment, you will give clear instructions in an essay of at least four paragraphs.

Plan

1. *Choose your topic.* For one of the following ideas, explain how to:

    a. find and evaluate journal articles in your library

    b. find and evaluate sources on the WWW

    c. be a successful language learner/student/writer

    d. buy a car or computer, or make another major purchase

    e. select a major

    f. choose a college or university

    g. be safe on your campus

    h. gather financial resources to support yourself while in school

    i. manage time as a student

    j. use a piece of equipment related to your major

2. *Consider your audience and purpose.* Your audience is the students in your class. In a small group discussion, discover what they already know about your topic by asking questions. Determine your purpose. Why are you writing for this audience?

3. *Gather and organize your ideas.*

    a. Start by listing all the necessary information. Do additional reading or interact with others, if appropriate, to gather more information.

    b. Divide this information into logical groupings.

    c. Make a list of words that need to be defined and explained.

    d. Circle steps that may cause the reader difficulty. Plan how you will give a clear explanation.

    e. Write a thesis statement for your essay.

4. *Topic workshop.* Share these preliminary notes with a partner.

   a. Does the thesis statement give the main idea of the essay?

   b. Is the information logically organized into paragraphs? Are the categories clear?

   c. Is any information omitted? Ask your partner questions about any missing information.

   d. Are there other words that will need to be defined or explained?

   e. Do you agree with your partner about the information that may cause the reader difficulty?

Write Your First Draft

Put your ideas down on paper. Later you will be able to revise and edit this first draft.

Peer Response

1. Courtesy-edit. Before you give your essay to your partner, read it carefully to make sure the writing is clear. You want your partner to be able to read your ideas easily, so check for anything that would be difficult for him or her to understand. If some sentences are confusing, rewrite them. Correct any problems with spelling, punctuation, or grammar that might confuse your reader.

2. Exchange your essay draft with a partner. At the end of your partner's draft, write the author a short note. Explain which parts of the instructions were easy to understand. Tell the author if any parts were unclear. Conclude by giving one positive suggestion that would make the instructions clearer.

Revise, Edit, and Proofread

1. Read your essay again. Is it logically organized? Do your instructions say what you want them to say? How will you use your partner's comments to help improve your essay? Make necessary changes to topic sentences and supporting sentences.

2. Edit your essay for the following and correct any errors that you find. After you have edited for each of these features, check (✓) the box as a reminder that you have done that task.

   ❏ complete sentences

   ❏ correct sentence punctuation

   ❏ vocabulary appropriate for written communication

   ❏ appropriate transition words and phrases to show logical and chronological relationships

❑ modal auxiliaries used as necessary to control the tone of commands and to be polite

❑ if conditional sentences are used, check both parts of the sentence for correct verbs

3. Make necessary changes and rewrite your essay.

4. Proofread your essay by reading it aloud and listening for errors. Make necessary corrections.

Revision and Proofreading

Writers often wish their first drafts were better than they are. All writers, inexperienced and experienced, first language and second language, can improve their writing through revision. Sometimes this revisioning is quite dramatic. Often first drafts can be more clearly organized or their content improved by adding or deleting information.

If it is difficult to see what needs to be changed to make the writing clearer, try having a friend, classmate, or teacher read your writing and help you see where it is clear and where it is unclear.

When you revise, you read what you've written and think through your ideas carefully. You consider the comments of your classmate or teacher and decide what you should add, delete, or rearrange. You may need to go back and gather more information and do more writing. In addition, you must look carefully at the grammatical structures you have used and make any necessary corrections. Depending on your assignment, you may need to revise your paper more than once.

After you revise your paper, it is important to proofread it carefully for grammatical or punctuation errors. Some students find it helpful to read their papers aloud to hear where corrections need to be made.

Discussion Questions

1. What are the steps in revising a paper?

2. What is a writing task that you might revise more than five times? Why?

3. What is proofreading?

4. Students often say they don't have time to proofread. How much time does it really take? How does proofreading help create a better impression for the reader?

Revise and Proofread with a Computer

Many students now word-process their assignments, which can save considerable time when revising and proofreading. The following tips will help you use the computer effectively for revising and proofreading.

1. Learn how to save, cut, copy, and paste your writing. When you revise, this will help you delete and rearrange parts of your writing to make the content and organization clearer.

2. Don't throw anything away. Instead of deleting sentences and paragraphs, *cut* and *paste* them at the end of your document. You may decide to use them later.

3. Proofread your writing both on-screen and off-screen. Remember that when your paper comes out of the printer, the form can look very beautiful, but you must be sure that your ideas, organization, and sentence structure are clear.

4. Use a spell-check program, making sure that what it suggests makes sense. Proofread again for spelling after you use the spell-check program.

5. Be sure to follow your professor's recommendations for font size (12 is very readable) and margins (one inch all around is standard).

● ●

L O O K I N G   A H E A D

Academic Assignment

You do not have to complete the authentic assignments at the end of each chapter in this textbook. However, analyzing them will give you a clearer understanding of the types of assignments you will face in your undergraduate courses.

The following assignment is from a course, "Introduction to University Life." There are two parts, the first on using the library, and the second on interviewing a professor or staff member. Read the assignment and discuss the questions that follow.

Introduction to University Life

Library Assignment: This assignment is designed to both (1) get you over any initial phobia you might have about using a million-volume university library and (2) show you how to use the on-line catalog (it's really quite wonderful once you are comfortable with it). The university library is the knowledge "heart" of any university, and therefore a resource with which you *must* become comfortable. It really is *not* so intimidating if you just spend some time in it. The reference librarians are all friendly and helpful folks. It's their job to help get you pointed in the right direction, direct you to possibly useful sources of information, and help you out when the computer terminal won't do anything right!

I will distribute this assignment in class on the first day and go over it with you as a group. You have six days to do it. This is because, with 71 sections of this course, the desire to get it completed early in the semester (so you can benefit from it right away), and the finite number of on-line terminals, the university simply can't have more than a few sections working on it at any one time. Be glad we are in the first group. The library staff will be fresh and enthusiastic about working with you.

Turn the completed assignment in to the reference desk (not to me) by closing time on Sunday, Sept. 20.

Interview of Professor or Student Affairs Professional Staff Member: The purpose of this assignment is to get you more familiar with the professional life of a university professor or student affairs professional person. The idea is that the more you understand about how the "other side" operates, the more likely you are to be more understanding of their situation and to utilize them when appropriate. It will also give you some possible career insights to file away in the back of your mind.

You may do your interview individually or in pairs or triples (no more than three students per group, please). You should make an appointment with your subject well in advance of the actual meeting date. If there is someone you'd like to interview but are just too reluctant to ask yourself (like the president, for example), I'll be glad to set up the appointment (if I can). Believe me, faculty and staff are used to this activity so you should not encounter any resistance. This is also a chance to explore an academic field of interest. Let's say you've long harbored an interest in the weather . . . why not go interview a meteorologist over in Atmospheric Science?

Your interview format must include answers to the following:

1. Person's name, title, departmental affiliation, and date of interview.
2. The person's academic background/training.
3. Why he or she chose (or ended up in) the field/discipline he or she is currently in.
4. If a faculty member, what is his or her favorite class to teach and why?
5. If a faculty member, what research is she or he doing at present or has done in the recent past?
6. What are the range of job possibilities open to someone with an undergraduate degree in his or her discipline?

Feel free to pursue with him or her any other issues of interest to you. (Ask the meteorologist what the weather is likely to be next weekend!)

DISCUSSION

1. According to this professor, why is each of these assignments important?

2. How long will they take to complete?

3. If you were given this assignment, who would you want to interview? Would you want to do it alone or in pairs or triples?

4. What are other questions you would want to ask the professor about these assignments?

*E*xplaining

Addictive Behavior

GOALS

WRITING
◆ write detailed explanations of
  words and concepts

GRAMMAR
◆ practice the grammar of informational writing to define, show
  cause and effect, report other
  people's words and ideas, and use
  modals to change the strength of
  explanations

CONTENT
◆ read about three kinds of addictive
  behavior

ACADEMIC FIELD
Psychology

Sample Authentic College/University Writing Assignments

In your academic courses, you will use the skills you learn in this chapter to complete assignments and test questions like these examples below:

Biology

Explain what a mutation is and why it is important in the process of natural selection.

Economics

Explain the structure of the Federal Reserve Bank system and its role in controlling the U.S. economy.

Speech Communication

Explain the three barriers to effective listening. How can you, as a speaker, help reduce or eliminate each of these barriers?

 CNN video support is available for this chapter. Turner Le@rning

GETTING READY

Warm-up Activity

Think about explanations you have heard or read. What makes a good explanation? What can make an explanation confusing?

Introduction to Explaining

Audience and Purpose

Being able to write an effective explanation of an object, behavior, historical event, concept, or process is a valuable academic skill. For example, you may be asked to explain what an anthropologist does, how comets are formed, or the results of a chemistry experiment. If you can write a good explanation, it shows that you understand something well and can present that information to others in a clear and interesting way. Therefore, teachers often ask students to write an explanation to test their knowledge of a subject.

Before you start your explanation, it is important to think about your *audience*.

- How much do they already know?
- What aspects are they most interested in?
- What can you do to help them understand the subject most effectively?

Some audiences will have considerable background knowledge, but others will know almost nothing about the subject. Remember that you need to make your explanation fit their needs. You must also know the *purpose* of your explanation. In many cases, it will be to inform and teach your audience about the subject. However, when a teacher asks you to write an explanation for an exam, the purpose is to test *your* knowledge and understanding of a subject. In this case, even though your audience—your teacher—has considerable background knowledge, your explanation must be complete and detailed enough to show that *you* also understand the subject well.

Activity 3-1   Explanations for Different Audiences and Purposes

1. Work in a small group. Explain one of these computer terms—*cut and paste* or *virus*—to three people:

   a. a 12-year-old student who has been using computers in school since kindergarten and has a basic understanding of computers

b. an older retired friend or relative who has seen computers and heard other people talk about them, but who has never worked with one

c. your computer science teacher on a written test

2. How will the purpose of your explanations be different, depending on your audience? What would the reaction probably be if you gave an explanation designed for one of these people to the other two?

Three Key Questions in Explaining: *What? Why? How?*

Once you have analyzed your audience and the purpose of your writing, you can think about the parts of a good explanation. Three important questions that are frequently answered in explanations are *what, why*, and *how*. Often, all of these will be needed to make a full and clear explanation. In some explanations, however, you will focus on *what, why*, or *how*.

Explaining *What*

First, the reader needs to know *what* you are explaining. *What* is often answered with a basic definition and background information. This is the starting point or foundation for your explanation, as you will see in this definition of psychology.

	word	general category	specific category
basic definition	*Psychology* is the	*science of behavior and mental processes.*	

background information The goals of psychology are to understand, measure, describe, and control behavior. To do this, psychologists
details study genetic and environmental influences, the workings of the nervous system, perception, learning, motivation, and the nature of the personality and social interactions. As
comparison with any science, its work is based on experiments and careful observation and collection of data.

This short explanation begins with a basic definition of *psychology*. We learn that it is a science, and more specifically, "the science of behavior and mental processes." To complete the explanation, additional information is given in the form of examples and comparisons.

An Introduction to the Grammar of Definitions

Informational writing frequently contains many definitions. In your academic courses, you will be expected to learn many definitions, which will give you the vocabulary you need to speak and write as a knowledgeable person in that field.

It is important to learn the basic structure for definitions. By understanding this structure, you will be better able to learn (and memorize) definitions that will help you successfully explain words and concepts on tests and in assignments. Below is a common pattern used for a wide variety of academic definitions.

Three basic parts of a definition

        1   2   3
the word being defined + simple present tense verb(often *be)* + complex noun phrase
    1   2   3
A drug is any chemical substance that changes mood, perception, or awareness.

A sentence or two of additional information is often given immediately before or after the sentence containing the definition. This helps make the definition clearer.

Activity 3-2   Definition Structures

1. Underline and label parts 1, 2, 3 of the following definitions. These definitions come from a variety of academic majors. Distinguish definition sentences from sentences that contain additional information. The first sentence is an example.

                     1   2   3
   a. Excessive exercisers are people who work out or run two to three hours a day and won't back off despite pain and injury. Exercise extremists can also be identified by a lack of attention to family or work.

   b. A satellite nation is one that is dominated by a more powerful nation.

   c. Employees do not work for free. Employee compensation may include wages or salary, insurance or other benefits, and intangible rewards.

    d. Atoms are the building blocks of all matter. They consist of three types of sub-atomic particles: protons and neutrons, which are tightly bound in the atom's nucleus, and electrons, which surround the nucleus.

    e. Planned obsolescence is the policy of producing goods that will soon wear out so consumers will buy new goods to replace them.

    f. A volcano is a type of mountain that forms as a result of tectonic activity. Unlike other mountains, volcanoes contain pipelines that release matter from the earth's interior.

    g. Sigmund Freud developed the psychodynamic view of personality, which posits that personality is made up of the id (primitive drives), the superego (moral conscience), and the ego (which seeks a balance between the two). Behavior is the result of interaction among the three.

    h. Chemistry is the study of matter and the transformations it undergoes.

2. Look again at definitions in *a–h* above. In a small group, write the name of the field of study that would include this definition in the margin next to it. For example, *1a* could be from psychology.

3. Write a definition of each of these terms.

    a. A definition _____.

    b. Addiction _____.

    c. Explanations _____.

4. Now choose four words related to your field of study or interest and define each one in a sentence.

Activity 3-3   Analyzing Major Field Definitions

Look at textbooks for courses you are taking or ones you will take in the future. Bring three definitions from these texts to your next class to share in a small group.

- Are the definitions constructed like the example?
- What other definition structures did you find? List all the structures found by members of your class.

GLR   See Section 4 in the GLR for common definition structures.

Activity 3-4   Strategies for Learning Definitions

In a small group or as a class, list several effective strategies for learning and remembering definitions. What works best for you? Why?

LEARNER'S NOTEBOOK

Learning New Vocabulary

Explain the strategy or strategies that help you learn new vocabulary. How do you remember these words? If possible, give a specific example from a course you are taking or have taken.

Extended Definitions

The audience for and purpose of your definition will help determine its length. For example, the word *tree* could be defined simply in a sentence or two for most audiences. However, a much longer and more scientific definition is used in the field of botany. In your writing, short definitions are often appropriate for words that help the reader understand the main idea. Sometimes, though, a definition can be the main idea of a paragraph or essay. This is an *extended definition* and may include comparisons with something similar or even opposite example(s), or other necessary background information, depending on your audience.

LEARNER'S NOTEBOOK

Writing an Extended Definition

Write a paragraph to define one of the words below. Begin with a topic sentence and provide support and detail in the paragraph. Use examples and/or comparison to support your explanation.

family	engineering	dependence	intelligence
music	respect	culture shock	abnormal behavior

Explaining *Why*

In addition to giving a definition, many explanations answer the question *why* by showing the reasons for something. The writer explains why something is the way it is—its *causes*. The results—*effects*—can also be explained. The relationship between cause and effect can also be explained; for example, a paragraph or essay can explain how the cause leads to the effect.

In explaining a serious automobile accident, the driver could give several possible causes:

- road and weather conditions
- condition of the car (poor brakes, broken headlights)
- condition of the driver (tired, distracted, drunk)
- how the driver was driving (recklessly, too slowly/fast)

The accident could be the result of a combination of several of these causes.

What could the effects of the accident be? Possible effects are:

- damage to the car
- injury to the driver and passengers
- increased insurance rates
- repair bills
- time spent without a car to drive
- a conviction for drunk driving
- death

The accident could result in several of these effects.

Some explanations may focus more on the causes and others may focus on the effects.

Activity 3-5   Determining Causes and Effects

1. With a partner or a small group of classmates, choose four topics from the list below that interest your group.

   - success in school
   - constant fatigue
   - a sports team with an undefeated season
   - good nutrition
   - illiteracy
   - drug addiction
   - rising consumer debt
   - winning a college scholarship

2. Draw two columns on a piece of paper.

3. In one column, list possible causes, and in the other, list possible effects for each of your four topics.

4. When you are finished, discuss your causes and effects with the class.

Activity 3-6   Writing Sentences Showing Cause and Effect

For each of the four topics you chose in Activity 3-5, write one complete sentence showing a cause and one showing an effect. Here are some common structures.

EXAMPLES

Constant fatigue often *results in* poor job performance.
One cause of constant fatigue is lack of adequate nutrition.

Noun	causes results in results from leads to has an effect on	+ noun.
The (One)	cause of noun is effect of noun is	+ noun.

Explaining *How*

Sometimes an explanation includes *how* something is done or *how* something should be done. In Chapter 2 we focused on organizing this kind of explanation by time, importance, or situation.

Adding Support and Detail

Support and detail will help make your explanation clear and interesting. The type of support and detail you use will depend on the topic of your explanation and your audience, but there are many possibilities:

- Examples
- Facts and statistics
- Reference to experts or research
- Interviews with authorities
- Illustrations (pictures, charts, graphs, etc.)

Activity 3-7   Planning to Use Support and Detail

You are planning a paper that explains the main causes and effects of stress on first-year students at your school. Without actually writing the paper, in a small group, discuss information you could include to give a clear and detailed explanation. Use what you have learned in this section on explaining *what, why,* and *how* to plan helpful support and detail.

- Start by listing possible causes and effects of stress on these students.
- What examples could you use in your explanation?
- What facts or statistics would make the explanation more complete?
- Who would be important people to talk to that you might quote or cite in your paper?
- What would be important research to cite?
- Describe an illustration/chart/graph to support your explanation. What type of information would it include?
- What explanation might you give of how to relieve stress?

Grammar Preview

In the following section, "Focusing," you will work with explanations of factual information. Such explanations often involve definitions and statements of generalizations that are given with present tense verbs.

To provide support for an explanation, we often want to include the words or ideas of experts, so we will look at how to cite and quote. We will also learn how to use modal auxiliary verbs like *can, could, may,* and *might* to show that sometimes there is more than one possible explanation or interpretation.

FOCUSING

Many books and articles explain the problems faced by people who are chemically dependent or addicted to nicotine, alcohol, or drugs. However, in this chapter, you will also read explanations about problems people face who are psychologically dependent on three very common activities or behaviors: computer use, shopping, and aerobic exercise. While many people make these activities a normal part of their lives, some people develop an exaggerated need for them.

The following readings explain the psychology of human behavior. They use vocabulary and content that you would find in a college psychology course. The first reading is from a psychology textbook. However, you can also find a wide variety of interesting articles related to psychology in newspapers, magazines, and academic journals because many people are interested in learning more about themselves and others through psychology.

In these readings, you will see how the authors answered the questions of *what, why,* and *how* to give full and complete explanations.

READING 1   ADDICTION (PSYCHOLOGY TEXTBOOK)

A drug can have a medical or a legal definition. But for our purposes, a *drug* is any chemical substance that changes mood, perception, or awareness. Drugs can be used to treat illness and relieve pain. Or they can be abused, or used in a way that is harmful to the individual or the society.

Addiction to a drug means that the individual is physically dependent on the use of the   5
drug. If a person is addicted to a drug, the continued use of that drug requires larger and larger doses to have the same effects. In addition, when the person stops using the drug, withdrawal symptoms occur. These can range from mild discomfort to trembling and nausea, and possibly death.

An individual is said to be *psychologically dependent* on a drug when the nonuse of it   10
causes the person to have severe feelings of distress. Psychological dependency becomes a problem when the person uses the drug to escape from the daily problems of living. (Individuals can also become psychologically dependent on such things as movies, TV, gambling, reading books, and hobbies.) A psychological dependency involves making something into such a habit or source of comfort that it interferes with daily living.   15

Source: T. L. Engle and Louis Snellgrove, *Psychology—Its Principles and Applications*, 7th Ed.
(New York: Harcourt Brace Jovanovich, Inc., 1979).

Activity 3-8   Post-reading Questions

1. What three words are defined in this passage? What makes these words easy to identify in the text? Which words are explained in extended definitions?

2. Which of these three definitions gives both a general and specific category? (See page 65 for an example of a general and specific category.)

3. What other kinds of information are given in one of the extended definitions?

4. What is the difference between addiction and psychological dependency?

5. What are the effects of addiction?

6. What are the effects of psychological dependency?

READING 2   NEW MALADY HITS COMPUTER USERS: "WEBAHOLISM" (NEWSPAPER ARTICLE)

Activity 3-9   Pre-reading Vocabulary

1. In a small group, share the information you know about computers to define these terms.

- keyboard
- virtual
- Internet
- electronic mail (e-mail)

- World Wide Web site
- on-line
- "chat" rooms
- terminal

2. You will notice that these words are used but not defined in the following article. What does this tell you about the audience for this article?

Activity 3-10   Pre-reading Questions

1. If you work on a computer, how much time do you spend using it in a day/week?

2. Have computers had a positive, neutral, or negative effect on your life? Why?

3. What are the possible effects of spending too much time on the computer?

NEW MALADY HITS COMPUTER USERS: "WEBAHOLISM"

Hard core on-line users are living artificial lives that some say can be dangerous to their health and emotional stability.

By Susan Fernandez
Knight-Ridder News Service

College Park, MD.—Lisa Bowes had a wonderful life as a student at Humboldt State University in California.

Every day she chatted with her pal Johan from Sweden. She'd discuss 5 movies and her favorite hobby, quilting, with girlfriends from California. And, for about a year, she flirted with her special friend Jason from Pennsylvania.

There was only one problem. Bowes 10 had hardly a friend on campus.

Instead she spent long hours alone each day typing at a keyboard to ghostly "on-line" buddies. "I'd spend hours and hours . . . and hours on the computer," she 15 recalls.

Bowes has since recovered from her on-line addiction. To get better, she had to give her computer away. But the curious virtual life she lived is not unique. 20

Across America, growing numbers of students-and some of their elders—are finding it difficult to walk away from their computer keyboards.

For some, computer compulsion is simply a fresh form of the kinds of obsessive behavior that college students seem prone to. Spending all of one's free time in a computer lab is like going out drinking every night of the week, or eating enough dorm food to gain the "freshman 15" pounds of fat.

But for others, especially the introverted who have a hard time finding a place in the college scene, the computer can practically fill a life—with large consequences, both good and bad.

The good is that the computer helps withdrawn young people reach out, make friends and learn to interact. The bad, experts say, is that hard core on-line users are living artificial lives likely to be dangerous to their health and emotional stability.

Computer addiction has grown so serious that officials at one school—the University of Maryland at College Park—are forming a "Caught in the Net" support group to help wean students from their computer habits.

Other schools are banning students who spend too much time on-line from computer labs or limiting the amount of time they can log on.

Another addiction

At Maryland, where all students have free access to the Internet and 32,000 of 35,000 students have electronic-mail accounts, staff psychologist Dr. Linda Tiptan says the support group was being formed because more and more students had been coming to her in the last year with computer-addiction problems.

For most, addiction stems from a bigger problem, such as low self-esteem, she says. "It's comparable to gambling or shopping addictions. It's something that makes you feel good about yourself."

Bowes recalls that she was much more comfortable talking to people through a computer screen. So instead of hanging out at parties, she made friends playing computer fantasy games and talking in on-line "chat" rooms for up to eight hours at a time.

Now 26 and a graduate student at Maryland, Bowes says she likes her off-line life better. She's set on getting her master's in library science and spends her free time engaged in such activities as going out with her roommates or watching television with friends.

"I have more of a real life," she says. "I'm not relying on the computer to make me happy."

But while Bowes has signed off, thousands are signing on—and staying on.

School daze

A recent study from Nielsen Media Research based on more than 4,200 telephone interviews of randomly selected households in the U.S. and Canada, found that 11 percent of the population 16 years and older, or 24 million people, use the Internet; of those users, 12 percent gain access to the computer from school.

One-third of Internet users log-on at least once a day and spend an average of 5 hours and 28 minutes on-line per week. That comes out to 35 minutes a week per person of the total population—as much time as the population as a whole spends watching rented videotapes, according to the study.

Some college students spend as much as half of every day on-line. This may be in part because access to the Internet, e-mail and other computer activities is free and easily available at most schools.

Some of these compulsive computer users are reaching out for help at an Internet World Wide Web site called

"Webaholics." Last month, about 75 people told their personal computer compulsion stories to "Webaholics."

"I am attending Penn State so I can have free access to the Internet. Penn State's tuition is less than what my Internet bill would be otherwise," wrote "Nancy" from Penn State University.

"I'm a freshman at University of Cincinnati. I haven't met anyone here at this school of 30,000 or so people, but that just doesn't bother me as long as I have this terminal in front of me," said "Aaron."

And "Reb Kline" wrote from an undisclosed school: "I'm at the computer 15 to 18 hours a day. Soon I will probably be taking showers with this dumb machine. Actually, it's not the machine that has a problem, it's me . . ."

Unhealthy trick

Getting people to say they're hooked on computers is not easy, notes Dr. Jonathan Kandell, another psychologist at Maryland's counseling center. So far only three people have signed up for the university's "Net" support group. The counseling center wants to get five people before it schedules a meeting.

"Many just see spending hours at a time on-line as an enjoyable part of their life, as something to do," Kandell says.

Chris Najewixz, a computer science major at Maryland who spends between five and seven hours each weekday on the computer, says he doesn't consider himself an addict.

"Most people think that computer geeks are dumb intellectuals with no self-esteem and no interests in life," he says. "Well that isn't true for me. I have tons of interests, that's what spawned my interest in computers."

Kandell worries that students who spend most of their time with a computer and who make a lot of on-line friends trick themselves into believing they have a healthy life.

"It may give them a false sense of security," Kandell says. "The quality of the relationships they form is limited . . . it makes it more difficult for them to engage in face-to-face contact with people."

Source: Knight-Ridder/Tribune Information Services, Lawrence (Kansas) *Journal World,* Nov. 28, 1995, 3A.

Activity 3-11   Post-reading Questions

1. What is "Webaholism"?

2. What are the main ideas of the article? Write them in two or three sentences (a short summary). Compare your summary to your classmates' in a small group. Do you agree about the main ideas of the reading?

3. Now focus on the details and support for those main ideas. The author used many techniques to explain Webaholism. Find examples in the article of each of these techniques to complete the chart. Remember that you will use many of these techniques when you write your major essay in this chapter.

Techniques	Examples and line numbers from the article
Comparison	Spending all of one's free time in a computer lab *is like* _____ Lines _____.
Examples	people: universities: Lines _____.
Causes	Lines _____.
Effects	Lines _____.
Experts quoted or cited	Lines _____.
Facts and Statistics (skim the reading again for numbers	Lines _____.

4. Describe an audience that would have difficulty understanding this article. Why would they have difficulty? Was it easy for you to understand? Why or why not?

Activity 3-12   Reporting Other People's Words and Ideas

1. *Quotations:* The writer included the "voices" of many other people in the examples in this article. Find all the quotations in the article. How many different people speak?

2. *Punctuation:* Add the necessary punctuation to these quotations from the article.

   a. I have more of a real life she says. I'm not relying on the computer to make me happy.

   b. It may give them a false sense of security Kandell says. The quality of the relationships they form is limited . . . it makes it more difficult for them to engage in face-to-face contact with people.

3. *Reporting verbs:* In both of the examples above, the author used the verb *say* to report the words of the speaker. With a partner, list at least six other verbs that could be used to report what a speaker says.

_____   _____   _____

_____   _____   _____

Now, check your list with the reporting verbs in Section 5B of the GLR .

4. *Writing direct quotations:* Interview a partner (or your teacher) about his or her computer use. Write two direct quotations reporting what this person said.

LEARNER'S NOTEBOOK

Developing Ideas

Choose one or more of the following topics.

1. In Reading 2, the author said that it is easy for college students to develop some form of obsessive behavior. Do you think this generalization is true? Are certain types of students more likely to develop these obsessive behaviors? Explain.
2. The article stated that some schools are limiting students' time on-line in their computer labs. Is this a reasonable policy? Explain why or why not. Write a one-page memo to the computer lab director explaining your opinion. Use correct memo format.
3. Do you think "virtual" friends can be "real"? Explain the advantages and disadvantages of virtual friends.
4. Describe your own positive or negative experiences with computers.

READING 3   YO-YO SHOPPING (NEWSLETTER ARTICLE)

In this reading, the author explains another addictive behavior, compulsive shopping. As you read, you will learn about compulsive shoppers and their financial status, reasons for shopping, and the effects it has on their lives.

Activity 3-13   Pre-reading Questions

1. Some people know exactly what they want to buy and go to a store to quickly purchase it. Other people like to shop more slowly without a clear idea of what they will buy. Explain how you like to shop.

2. Do you know anyone who shops too much? What are possible causes of this behavior? What are its effects?

YO-YO SHOPPING

At the mall, flea market, or weekend yard sales, people shop for the fun of it, especially at holiday time. This is a harmless pastime for those who like it, but a few (perhaps as many as six percent) like it so much that they become addicts—compulsive shoppers who shop the way an alcoholic drinks or a compulsive gambler bets. Our culture is geared to consumption; indeed, from early childhood we are exposed to ads urging us to buy. A whole new world of shopping is upon us, too: electronic shopping, via television or computer. Millions already belong to cable TV shopping clubs and/or cruise the information superhighway in search of worldly goods. Banks are gearing up to supply online cash, cyber-money, and electronic "purses," so that at the touch of a button shoppers can buy, buy, buy. Of course, it's the shopping that's "virtual." The debt will be real.

When shopping becomes an addiction, it can destroy lives, and like other forms of addiction it has been the subject of scientific study. Obsessive spending—"fiscoholism," or the need to spend money to create a mood change—may not do serious harm to those with unlimited funds, time, and closets. But at some point it can result in personal, financial, and legal problems. These, ironically, may produce depression in the shopper and lead to more binges. As reported in the *Journal of Consumer Policy* in 1990, researchers found that compulsive shopping correlates with low self-esteem as well as anxiety. Addicted shoppers may feel elated as they purchase but depressed afterward. They often have no use for the goods they carry home and may not even open the packages. Credit cards rather than cash are almost always used for shopping binges.

Another study in the *Journal of Clinical Psychiatry* this year described the typical compulsive buyer as a 36-year-old woman who had been obsessive about shopping since her late teens. (Other studies have emphasized, however, that men are not immune.) Clothing, shoes, jewelry, and makeup are the top four items purchased during splurges. All these have to do with appearance, and indeed compulsive buyers seem more concerned than most with how they look and how others react to them. They are more likely to succumb to their compulsion when feeling bad about themselves.

Mercifully, that shop-till-you-drop urge does appear to decline as a person grows older. But if a member of your family is forever spending, in the face of mounting debt and crammed closets, you might propose storing credit cards in a safe deposit box or canceling them. Keeping a diary of purchases may also be useful. As with other forms of compulsive behavior, sessions with a qualified psychotherapist may be useful.

One support group that can help is Debtors Anonymous, modeled after Alcoholics Anonymous. Check your phone book for a local chapter, or write to it at P. O. Box 400, Grand Central Station, New York, NY 10163 for an information kit. The National Foundation for Consumer Credit (800-388-2227) can also help you find financial counseling.

Source: University of California at Berkeley Wellness Letter, Volume 11, Issue 3, December 1994.

| Activity 3-14   Post-reading Questions |

1. a. What effects does our consumer culture have on how people shop and what they buy?

    b. List all the places you have seen advertisements in the last week.

2. The author used many techniques to give an explanation of shopping addiction. Complete the chart with examples from the article.

Techniques	Examples and line numbers from the article
Definitions	addicts obsessive spending Lines _____.
Example of a typical compulsive shopper	 Lines _____.
Causes	 Lines _____.
Effects	 Lines _____.
Research cited	 Lines _____.
Practical suggestion to help solve the problem	 Lines _____.

Controlling the Strength of Generalizations in Explanations

When you give an explanation, you write some statements of fact. Generally, these use the *present tense*. For example, look at this factual statement from the shopping article.

EXAMPLE

Our culture *is* geared toward consumption; indeed, from early childhood we *are* exposed to ads urging us to buy.

In an explanation, you may also write interpretations or draw conclusions from these statements of facts. To do this, you will often use modals, especially the modals, *may, might, can,* and *could.* These words will help you control the strength of generalizations, as you'll see in Activity 3-15.

Activity 3-15   Using Modals to Control the Strength of Generalizations

1. Look again at the reading about shopping addiction. In the second paragraph, circle the six times the modals *can* and *may* are used.

2. Now compare the meaning of the pairs of sentences below. The first sentence in each pair is a statement of fact and uses the present tense. How does the meaning of the sentence change when you add a modal?

    • When shopping becomes an addiction, it destroys lives.
    • When shopping becomes an addiction, it *can* destroy lives.

    • At some point, it results in personal, financial, and legal problems.
    • At some point, it *may* result in personal, financial, and legal problems.

    • Addicted shoppers feel elated as they purchase but depressed afterward.
    • Addicted shoppers *may* feel elated as they purchase but depressed afterward.

3. Why was it necessary to use *can* and *may* in paragraph 2 of the article?

> **GLR**   Refer to Section 6B, Controlling the Strength of Generalizations.

READING 4   ARE YOUR PATIENTS EXERCISING TOO MUCH?
(JOURNAL ARTICLE)

Activity 3-16   Pre-reading Questions

1. Look at the title of the article. What does this tell you about the audience?

2. What kinds of physical exercise do you do? How often do you exercise? What are the benefits to your physical and mental health?

3. Why do you think some people exercise too much?

ARE YOUR PATIENTS EXERCISING TOO MUCH?

Research suggests that some people may harm themselves physically and mentally by exercising too much.

Many people exercise far too little, but many others exercise far too much. Often obsessed with increasing their strength, stamina, and cardiovascular fitness, these zealous exercisers work out to the point of jeopardizing their physical and mental health. The question is: How much is too much?

The American College of Sports Medicine recommends aerobic exercise for up to 60 minutes at least three times a week to maintain fitness.* Less clearly defined, however, is the other end of the exercise spectrum—the point where exercise becomes a detriment.

Which Patients Overdo It?

According to James G. Garrick, MD, director of the Center for Sports Medicine at Saint Francis Memorial Hospital in San Francisco, excessive exercisers are people who work out or run 2 to 3 hours a day and won't back off despite pain and injury.

Exercise extremists can also be identified by a lack of attention to family or work, says Rosemary Agostini, MD, clinical instructor in orthopedics at the University of Washington School of Medicine in Seattle and a family practice and sports medicine consultant at the Virginia Mason Sports Medicine Center in Seattle. They may consider exercise to be more important than anything else in life, she adds.

When injured and forced to stop exercising, exercise extremists often become depressed. Agostini says some of her patients have reported sleeplessness, restlessness, and loss of appetite—symptoms similar to those seen with drug withdrawal. These people may be addicted to the endorphins released by exercise—the so-called "runner's high," she says.

Some athletes exercise to extremes because they mistakenly believe it is good for them or that it is the proper way to exercise. Many of these people are converts to exercise. "We see this a lot in cardiac rehabilitation," says John D. Cantwell, MD, director of preventive medicine at Georgia Baptist Hospital in Atlanta, and an editorial board member of *THE PHYSICIAN AND SPORTSMEDICINE*. Some patients—thinking that if a little exercise is good, then a lot is better—may exercise for an hour a day when they were advised to work out for 30 minutes every other day, Cantwell adds.

The Physical and Mental Costs

Injuries occur in excessive exercisers because of the sheer magnitude of their activity, says Garrick, who is an editorial board member of *THE PHYSICIAN AND SPORTSMEDICINE*. Minor problems with equipment, such as worn-out running shoes or a new tennis racket, won't bother the average recreational athlete, but they can cause big problems in athletes who overdo it. In other words, says Garrick, "When you are doing too much there is less margin for error." Likewise with minor injuries, which can more easily develop into serious conditions in patients who don't know when to stop. "These people can be hard to take care of because they amplify their injuries through their zeal," he says.

Excessive exercise increases the risk of orthopedic problems, says Michael L. Pollock, Ph.D., professor of medicine at the University of Florida in Gainesville. 80 "There is a direct relation between injury rates and how much you do," he says.

Overdoing exercise may also play havoc with a person's psychological well-being and affect his or her social life, says 85 Agostini. "When you see someone who is exercising to the extremes despite injuries, that person may need psychological treatment," she says. Such psychosocial problems are not rare, adds Agostini. "I see a 90 patient like this maybe once a week."

*The American College of Sports Medicine: "The recommended quantity and quality of exercise for developing and maintaining cardiorespiratory and muscular fitness in healthy adults." *Med Sci Sports Exerc* 1990;22(2):265–274.

Source: Valerie DeBenedette, *The Physician And Sportsmedicine,* Vol. 18, no. 8 (August 1990).

Activity 3-17   Post-reading Questions

1. Compare the effects of a reasonable amount of exercise with excessive exercise.

2. Describe a person who exercises too much. What effects does it have on his/her life?

3. What techniques did the author use to write about people who exercise too much? Refer to the charts you made for the second and third reading to help you list these techniques.

Activity 3-18   Role-play

Imagine that you are an addicted *on-line computer user, shopper,* or *exerciser.* Think about your life and how this behavior affects your health, job or school work, financial situation, self-confidence, relationships with others, and day-to-day life. Jot down notes about these various effects.

In a small "support group," tell your partners about this problem and how it is affecting your life. Your partners will ask questions for more explanation and offer friendly advice.

Showing the Credibility of Your Expert Sources

In academic writing, you can strengthen your explanation by using the words and ideas of experts. To show your readers that these are people whose ideas they should respect and trust, give the experts' qualifications or credentials. You can include this information in a *non-restrictive relative clause* immediately after the person's name. Often this relative clause structure is reduced to a phrase that is called an *appositive*.

EXAMPLE OF NON-RESTRICTIVE RELATIVE CLAUSE (UNDERLINED)

Some people gradually withdraw from friends and family as the computer consumes more and more of their time, notes Dr. Susan Gregg, <u>who is a staff psychologist at Memorial Hospital</u>.

EXAMPLE OF APPOSITIVE (UNDERLINED)

Some people gradually withdraw from friends and family as the computer consumes more and more of their time, notes Dr. Susan Gregg, <u>a staff psychologist at Memorial Hospital</u>.

> **GLR** Refer to Section 5F for more information on non-restrictive relative clauses and appositives.

Activity 3-19 Showing Credibility with Non-Restrictive Relative Clauses and Appositives

1. In *a, b,* and *c* below, add the information about the credentials of each expert to the first sentence. You can use either a complete non-restrictive relative clause or an appositive. Try giving the credentials in both formats to be sure that you understand how this grammar works.

   a. According to James Garrick, M.D., excessive exercisers won't back off despite pain and injury.

      James Garrick is the director of the Center for Sports Medicine at Saint Francis Hospital in San Francisco.

   b. Getting people to say they're hooked on computers is not easy, notes Dr. Jonathan Kandell.

      Kandell is a staff psychologist at Maryland's counseling center.

   c. Michael L. Pollock, Ph.D., says excessive exercise increases the risk of orthopedic problems.

      Dr. Pollock is a professor of medicine at the University of Florida in Gainesville.

2. What kind of information is included in the credentials?

3. Why is this information important for the reader to know?

Citing and Quoting

In much of your academic writing, you will not only use your own ideas, but also the ideas of others. It is very important to use other people's ideas and words correctly in your own writing. If you use someone else's exact words or ideas without giving them credit, you are plagiarizing. Plagiarism is viewed very seriously at schools in the United States; the consequences can be failure in a course or even expulsion from school. Some other cultures have a very different view about crediting someone else's exact words or ideas.

Activity 3-20   Discussion

1. What is your school's policy on plagiarism? Where can you find this information?

2. If you are familiar with another culture, how does that culture view using someone else's exact words or ideas in academic papers?

3. Are you familiar with the MLA or APA citation systems? What resources can you use to learn more?

Rules on Citing and Quoting

Citing and quoting are the tools to incorporate other people's ideas properly in your writing. Different academic disciplines use slightly different formats, but the same key information is included. This section illustrates a common academic format.

-   You *cite a source* in your writing when you use someone else's *ideas.*
-   You *quote a source* when you use someone else's *ideas and exact words.* You must use quotation marks *and* cite the source.

In-text Citations

1. When you use someone else's ideas, put the last name (Last) of the author and the year of publication in the text. Put either just the year or the last name and the year in parentheses, depending on the sentence structure.

    EXAMPLES

    According to Last (1998), one cause of homelessness is . . .

    An article in *Time* magazine (Last, 1998) indicated that . . .

2. When you use someone else's ideas *and* someone else's words, use quotation marks around the words. *After* the final quotation mark, cite the source and include the page number. Or, depending on the sentence structure, put the last name (Last) of

the author and the year of publication in the text (as above in 1), and include the page number immediately after the last quotation mark. The final period in the text comes after the citation.

EXAMPLES

Last (1988) said, " . . . " (p. __).

The report stated that " . . . " (Last, 1998, p. ___).

End-of-text References

At the end of your paper, cite the complete references for each of the sources you used in your paper. You must reference each source that you used. However, you may *not* include sources that you did not cite in your paper.

EXAMPLES

References

Source

Book	Author. (Year). *Title of book.* Place of publication: Publisher.
	Wood, J. (1994). *Gendered lives—communication, gender and culture.* Belmont, CA: Wadsworth.
Journal Article	Author. (Year). Title of article. *Title of Journal,* volume (issue): page numbers.
	Gregg, S. (1996). Experimental approaches to group living. *Journal of Social Psychology,* 32(3): 184–189.
WWW Sites	Last, First. "Title of work." *Title of Complete Work.* <protocol and address> (date of message or visit)
	Long, Phillip. "Medications." *Internet Mental Health.* <http://www.mentalhealth.com> (10 Oct. 1997)

GLR   Refer to Sections 5G and 5H on referencing systems and plagiarism.

Activity 3-21   Analyzing Various Formats for In-text and End-of-text Citations

Different disciplines use slightly different formats for in-text and end-of-text references. It is important to learn what the expectations are for your academic department. Find and look at a journal in your major field of study. Discover how in-text and end-of-text references are given. Share this information with your class.

PUTTING IT ALL TOGETHER

FINAL WRITING ASSIGNMENT

Your essay will give an *explanation.* Remember that you can use a variety of techniques to write a clear and interesting explanation: defining, comparing to something similar or different, giving examples, showing the causes and/or effects, quoting or citing an expert or research, and using facts or statistics.

Plan

1. *Choose your topic.* Explain one of the following ideas.

   a. A topic, idea, event, trend, system, or group related to your field of study or your interests. Explain what it is and give examples that explain *how* or *why.*

   b. A common activity or behavior that people spend too much time doing that has negative effects on their lives. (It may be something in this culture or another culture you are familiar with.) Some possibilities are playing computer or video games, watching TV, gambling, working, talking, or cleaning. Use examples, quotations, causes and/or effects to interest your reader.

   c. This chapter contains readings about people whose lives are not balanced. One activity takes up most of their time and energy. Explain *what* a balanced life is, *why* it is important, and *how* it can be achieved. Note: In this particular explanation, it is possible to tell *what, why,* and *how.* However, depending on the topic, you may focus more on one of these question words than another in your explanation. You need to use the techniques that will make the clearest explanation for your reader.

2. *Consider your audience and purpose.* Your audience is your classmates. Choose one classmate to represent your audience. Interview this classmate to discover what he or she knows and doesn't know about the topic. What is he or she interested in? Your purpose is to *inform.*

3. *Gather and organize your ideas.*

   a. Write or take notes about your topic. Start with the question words *what, why,* and *how.* What support and detail can you use to make it a good explanation?

   b. Find and read one library or Internet source to support the ideas in your paper. Use the information in this source to add to your notes. Make a copy of this source to attach to your essay.

   c. Organize your information. What is your thesis statement?

What basic information does your audience need to understand your explanation?

What is the main idea for each body paragraph?

4. *Topic workshop.* Share your notes with a partner and tell about the information in your library or Internet source. Discuss your essay plans together.

Do you both have a workable thesis statement?

Are your ideas organized logically into body paragraphs?

Does your source help support your ideas?

What could you do to improve your plans before you start writing?

Do you need to find an additional source of information?

Write Your First Draft

Based on your discussion of your essay plan, try to write a well-organized first draft. Later you will be able to revise your essay to improve your explanation.

Peer Response

1. Courtesy-edit. Before you exchange your paper with your partner, read it carefully to make sure your writing is clear. This will help your partner be able to read your ideas easily, so check for anything that might make it difficult to understand your paper. If some sentences are confusing, rewrite them. Correct any problems with spelling, punctuation, and grammar.

2. Exchange your essay draft with your partner.

    a. List three or more techniques your partner used to help make his or her explanation clear.

    b. At the end of your partner's draft, write him or her a short note. Explain what the most interesting part of the essay was. Ask one question about a part that could be clearer. Conclude with one positive suggestion to make the explanation clearer or more interesting.

    c. Share your notes with your partner. Did you use any techniques in your essay that your partner did not list? Share this information with your partner.

Revise, Edit, and Proofread

1. Read your essay again. Is it a clear explanation? Are there additional techniques you can use to make it clearer? How will you use your partner's comments to help you make improvements? Make any changes needed to improve the meaning and organization of your writing.

2. Edit your individual sentences for the following and correct any errors that you find. After you have edited for each of these features, check (✓) the box to remind yourself that you have done that task.

☐ complete sentences

☐ correct sentence punctuation

☐ verb tense choices

☐ subject-verb agreement

☐ appropriate transition words and phrases

☐ modals and other grammar to avoid over-generalization

☐ if you included any definitions, check the definition sentence carefully

☐ if you used another person's words or ideas, check that you quoted or cited correctly. Should you add information about the person's credentials to show why a reader should believe his or her opinions and information?

3. Make necessary changes and rewrite your essay.

4. Proofread your essay, checking the spelling, grammar, and punctuation. Use the GLR ⬤ and a dictionary or computer spell-check program to help you. (If you use a computer program, be sure that what it suggests makes sense in the context of your essay.)

Academic Assignments

The following are test questions from academic courses. You would be expected to write at least a paragraph under time pressure to answer each of the questions. You do not have to write the answers to these questions, but with a partner or a small group of classmates,

- underline the key words in each writing task
- discuss possible organization for the answer to each
- discuss techniques for giving a good explanation

Chemistry

What happens when magnesium chloride is heated? Does a physical, chemical, or no change occur? Explain how you arrived at your answer.

Engineering

Give three reasons why the "infrastructure crisis" is so apparent in the U.S. highway system.

Business Management

Explain the characteristics of a successful manager, giving specific examples of interpersonal skills, technical knowledge, and conceptual skills.

Biology

You are the only doctor in a small, rural town. People of all ages begin coming into your clinic with the following symptoms:

headache	fever of 102 degrees Fahrenheit
aches in joints	swelling in the abdomen

These people are not familiar with the germ theory of disease, and they are very frightened. Write an explanation of the disease process for these people.

Chapter 4

Evaluating

Food and Lifestyles

GOALS

WRITING
◆ make an evaluation based on accepted criteria
◆ use a variety of types of evidence to support your evaluation

GRAMMAR
◆ practice using numerical evidence, comparisons, quotations, transition words, and passive sentences in making an evaluation

CONTENT
◆ read about the food choices of the !Kung, United States college students, and the Japanese

ACADEMIC FIELDS
Anthropology
Nutrition

Sample Authentic College/University Writing Assignments

In your academic courses, you will use the skills you learn in this chapter to complete test questions and assignments like these:

Political Science

Evaluate the effectiveness of negative TV advertisements for presidential candidates. Give specific examples from the most recent presidential campaigns.

Performing Arts

You are required to attend three instrumental musical concerts and write an evaluation of each one. Each evaluation should include:

- a copy of the program
- a brief description of the concert
- an evaluation of the overall performance

 CNN video support is available for this chapter.

GETTING READY

LEARNER'S NOTEBOOK

Warm-up Writing

No two people eat exactly the same food. What influences what you decide to eat? Describe the factors that most strongly influence your food choices. Some factors to consider are:

family background   cultural heritage   nutrition information
personal preferences   availability and cost of food cooking facilities
health concerns   time to prepare food   religious beliefs

In your notebook, explain how these factors influence what you eat.

An Introduction to Evaluating

An evaluation demands that you look at something critically and assess its strong and weak points, its positive and negative aspects. People evaluate a variety of things. Personnel directors evaluate job applicants to decide whom to hire, doctors evaluate a patient's symptoms to make a diagnosis, and business managers evaluate productivity, products, and profits. Sports teams evaluate their performance at previous competitions to prepare for the next one. Librarians evaluate the best materials to buy with a limited budget, and retailers evaluate which products to sell. Writers of college guides evaluate schools around the country, and art and music critics evaluate performances and works of art.

In your academic work, you will be asked to evaluate ideas, interpretations, decisions, and changes. You may also be asked to evaluate an object or thing, such as a computer program, an architectural plan, a piece of art or literature, a performance, or the results of an experiment. Sometimes you will be asked to evaluate your own performance, such as in speeches, presentations, projects, experiments, and your written assignments. Critical thinking is essential in all of these evaluation assignments.

To begin an evaluation, you must have a good understanding of the subject that you are evaluating. This involves direct experience and/or research. For example, if you are asked to evaluate a musical performance (see "Sample Authentic College/University Writing Assignments" on page 91), you could rely on your direct experience—your attendance and attention at the performance.

For the evaluation of the musical performance, if you merely said "I liked it," you would only be giving a reaction or an opinion. An evaluation requires more time, thought, and effort. First, you analyze several important *criteria* that are standards people generally agree are important to consider when evaluating. For a musical performance, these criteria might include:

Criteria List: the order in which the pieces are played
choice of selections
musicians' skill and interpretation
concert hall acoustics

Then you judge each of these criteria based on your direct experience at the concert. This would help you arrive at an overall judgment or evaluation of the performance. Your evaluation might be positive, negative, or mixed (some positive and some negative aspects).

Steps in an Evaluation

1. Gather information

The first step of an evaluation is to gather information through personal experience, reading, or interaction with others. This information helps you to gain a clear understanding of what you are evaluating.

This information may be comparisons, numerical information, research findings (facts, statistics), quotations from reliable sources, examples, or descriptions. You can synthesize this information/evidence to support your evaluation.

2. Select criteria

As mentioned above, criteria are standards that people generally agree are important and reasonable to consider when evaluating something. It is often helpful to have a criteria list to ensure that your evaluation is thorough and complete. For some evaluations, your instructor may give you specific criteria to use. For others, you will create your own criteria list. As you gather information, you may add other criteria to your list.

3. Evaluate each criterion

Use the information you have gathered to evaluate each criterion. You may rate some criteria positively, others negatively, and some as mixed or neutral.

4. Make an overall judgment

Based on your evaluation of each criterion, make an overall judgment. For example, all things considered, is it exciting, logical, worthwhile, significant, cost effective, accurate, educational, positive, or negative?

Use Multiple Sources

In evaluating a musical performance, you could gather information solely by direct experience, but for many evaluations, you will need to gather information from a variety of sources.

Imagine that you have just graduated. You have two job offers and are trying to make a decision about which job to take. You would gather information through personal experience by touring and interviewing with each company. You would also read about each place of employment—either information the company has given you or that you have gathered in a library or on the Internet. Finally, you would collect more information by interacting with your interviewers and other employees. Your research would help you establish and support your criteria, which might be like this:

Criteria List: salary and benefits

work environment

potential job satisfaction

appropriateness of job to your field of study

opportunity for advancement

Once you had selected your criteria, you would use the information you had gathered to analyze each item. For example, you would ask which job offers the better salary and benefits. You would consider the work environment, and proceed through the rest of your criteria. Even if you found negative aspects about some of your criteria, if most of them were positive, your overall judgment would be a positive one. Your evaluation may show that neither job is "perfect," but that one has more positive features than the other.

| Activity 4-1   Making a Criteria List |

Work together in small groups. Make a criteria list of at least three items for each of the following tasks. Then discuss the kinds of information you would gather.

1. You are on a committee that will decide what kind of computers to buy for your school's computer lab. What criteria would your committee want to investigate before the purchase?

2. What criteria do students use to evaluate teachers?

3. What criteria would you use to evaluate the food served in your college or university student center?

4. What criteria would you use to evaluate the results of a scientific experiment?

5. In a political campaign, there are three main candidates for an office. What criteria would you use to determine the best candidate?

LEARNER'S NOTEBOOK

Evaluating Group Work

Evaluate the success of your small group work. What did you learn? What did you contribute? How could the learning experience have been better?

Activity 4-2   Evaluating Sources

The information you gather and use to support your evaluation must be reliable and accurate. Therefore, it is important to evaluate your written research sources—books, journals, magazines, and the Internet—to select the best sources.

In Chapter 2, you read about criteria to use to evaluate sources. Reread that short article and make a criteria list from it. Then answer the questions that follow.

Criteria List: _____ *relevance of the source* _____

_____

_____

_____

_____

1. Why is it important to use several criteria to evaluate each source? What would happen if you only used one criterion to evaluate?

2. How does the quality of your evidence affect your evaluation?

Grammar Preview

When you write an evaluation, you must convince your reader that your information and interpretations are accurate. In this chapter, you will look at ways to present persuasive evidence with numerical information, comparative interpretations, and quotations of the words and ideas of experts. You will also work with passive sentences, which focus on process or product, instead of the people who do the process or make the products, since passive sentences are frequently found in evaluations and other academic writing. In addition, you will look at transition words to help you show logical connections in your writing and make your writing more cohesive.

FOCUSING

Activity 4-3   Vocabulary Related to Food and Nutrition

Throughout this chapter, you will read and use important terminology related to nutrition, eating, food, and nutrition-related health problems. In a small group, work together to see which words you already know. You can explain many of them by giving examples. As you go through this chapter, add other new vocabulary to this list.

Nutrition	Food and Eating	Health
calorie	cuisine	longevity
carbohydrate	consumption	infant mortality
fat	crash diet	cancer
protein	dietary habit	heart attack
sodium	subsist	cholesterol level
vitamin		
mineral		

READING 1   THE !KUNG OF THE KALAHARI REGION (ANTHROPOLOGY TEXTBOOK)

Hunting-and-gathering societies hunt animals and gather plant foods they find in nature. Very few of these remain; most societies rely on agriculture to meet many of their food needs. In this selection from an anthropology text, you will read about a group of hunter-gatherers, the !Kung, who live in the Kalahari Desert in southern Africa.

Note: The exclamation mark at the beginning of !Kung indicates that the initial sound of this word is a click.

Activity 4-4   Pre-reading Questions

1. What does an anthropologist study?

2. What are at least two criteria an anthropologist might use to evaluate the food a group of people eats?

Activity 4-5   Pre-reading Vocabulary Exercise

Match the words on the left with their definitions.

_g_	1. food-procuring	a. poor nutrition due to insufficient or poorly balanced diet
_C_	2. cultivated foods	b. having more than enough
_D_	3. edible	c. crops
_B_	4. abundance	d. fit to be eaten
_E_	5. affluence	e. wealth
_F_	6. on the brink of starvation	f. very close to suffering or dying from lack of food
_A_	7. malnutrition	g. obtaining or acquiring food

THE !KUNG OF THE KALAHARI REGION

One of the best-studied hunting-and-gathering societies, the !Kung inhabit the northwestern part of the Kalahari Desert, one of the least hospitable environments in the world. Inhabiting an area that is too dry 5 to support either agriculture or the keeping of livestock, the !Kung are totally dependent upon hunting and gathering for their food. Food-procuring activities are fairly rigidly divided between men and women. 10 Women collect roots, nuts, fruits, and other edible vegetables, while men hunt medium- and large-size animals. Although men and women spend roughly equivalent amounts of time on their food-procuring activities, 15 women provide between two and three times as much food by weight as men.

Even though the term *affluence* or *abundance* tends to be relative, Lee (1968) presents convincing evidence to suggest 20 that the !Kung are not teetering on the brink of starvation. In fact, there are reasons to believe that the !Kung food-gathering techniques are both productive and reliable. For example, the !Kung's most important sin-25 gle food item is the mongongo nut, which accounts for about half of the !Kung diet. Nutritionally, the mongongo, which is found in abundance all year long, contains five times the calories and ten times the 30 protein per cooked unit than cereal crops. Thus, quite apart from hunting, the !Kung have a highly nutritional food supply that is more reliable than cultivated foods. It is little wonder that the !Kung do not have a 35 strong urge to take up agriculture when there are so many mongongo nuts around.

Another measure of the relative affluence of the !Kung is their selectivity in what food they take from the environment. 40 If they were indeed on the brink of starvation, they should be expected to exploit every conceivable source of food. But in actual fact, only about one-third of the edible plant foods are eaten, and only 17 of the 45 223 local species of animals known to the !Kung are hunted regularly (Lee: 1968:35).

Moreover, if the !Kung were in a life-or-death struggle with the natural environment, their survival rate and life expectan- 50 cy would be low. Infant mortality would be high, malnutrition would be rampant, and the elderly and infirm would be abandoned. This is hardly the demographic picture for

the !Kung. Based on fieldwork conducted 55 in the 1960s, Lee (1968:36) found that approximately ten percent of his sample population was sixty years of age or older, a percentage that was not substantially different from industrialized societies.   60

And finally, the !Kungs' relative abundance of resources can be judged from the amount of time they devote to procuring food. While it is true that food getting is the most important activity among the !Kung, 65 it is no less true for cultivators and pastoralists. Although the amount of work varies from one hunting-and-gathering society to another, it appears that the !Kung, despite what might appear to be 70 their harsh environment, are hardly overworked. Lee (1968:37) estimates that the average !Kung adult spends between twelve and nineteen hours per week in the pursuit of food. Usually women can gather 75 enough food in one day to feed their families for three days, leaving a good deal of time for such leisure activities as resting, visiting, entertaining visitors, and embroidering. Even though men tend to work 80 more hours per week than women, they still have considerable leisure time for visiting, entertaining, and dancing.

Source: Gary Ferraro, *Cultural Anthropology* (Wadsworth Publishing Company, 1992).

Activity 4-6   Post-reading Questions

1. Describe the !Kung diet.

2. What is the overall evaluation of this diet? Starting in the second paragraph, circle words in the reading that support this evaluation.

3. The author apparently had no direct personal experience with the !Kung. What main source of information did he rely on?

4. The following chart shows a criteria list used to evaluate the !Kung diet. Complete the chart by noting whether the criteria were evaluated positively (+) or negatively (−) and citing the evidence used to support the criteria.

Criteria List	Evidence
__+__ food-gathering techniques	These techniques are productive and reliable. (Lee, 1968)
_____ nutritional status of mongongo nut	
_____ selectivity	
_____ health and longevity of population	
_____ amount of time spent to procure food	

Activity 4-7   Using Evidence to Support an Evaluation

A variety of types of evidence used to support evaluations are listed below. Check the types of evidence used in Reading 1. For each, give one example from the reading.

Evidence	Example
_____ research findings (facts, statistics)	
_____ personal experience	
_____ quotations from reliable sources	
_____ examples, description	

Activity 4-8   Using Numbers to Show Factual Evidence in Evaluations

The basis for many evaluations is numerical information. These numbers may tell you about cost, weight, quantity, volume, dimensions, distance, life span, frequency of occurrence, etc.

The following phrases all contain numbers, either in word form or numerical notation, and are used as support in Reading 1.

1. Skim *a–h* below and circle the numbers used. The first is an example.

2. Complete the right-hand column, based on the reading, with what explanation the phrase gives.

    Numerical Evidence   *This evidence explains . . .*

    a. between (two) and (three) times as much food   how much food women gather
        by weight as men   _____

    b. accounts for about half of the !Kung diet   _____

    c. contains five times the calories and ten   _____
        times the protein per cooked unit than cereal
        crops

    d. only about one-third of the edible plants   _____

    e. only 17 of the 223 local species of animals   _____

    f. approximately ten percent of his sample   _____
        population

    g. spends between 12 and 19 hours per week   _____

    h. gather enough food in one day to feed their   _____
        families for three days

3. Sometimes numerical information is used for comparisons. For example, letter *a* above compares how much food women gather and how much men gather. Which other phrase in this exercise shows comparison?

Activity 4-9   Using Transitional Words and Phrases to Create Cohesion

Academic writing is often organized "logically." That is, the author puts the writing together in ways that show the logical relationships among the subsets of information. To help the reader follow the logic of your writing, you need to include appropriate transition words to guide the reader to understand your ideas.

1. In Reading 1, find at least five transition words and phrases that were used to help the reader travel from one idea or sentence to another. As a class, list these words and phrases on the chalkboard.

2. Transition words are used to make connections between two sentences.

    a. What does starting the sentence with *in fact* add to the previous sentence?

    b. Which expressions introduce examples?

    c. Which expression(s) indicate additional information will be given?

    d. Which expression(s) show chronological order?

> **GLR**   Refer to Section 3D for more information on logical organizers.

READING 2   COLLEGE CUISINE MAKES MOTHER CRINGE (JOURNAL ARTICLE)

In this article, the author describes what college students eat and evaluates whether their diet is healthy.

Activity 4-10   Pre-reading Questions

1. What clue does the title of the article give you about the author's evaluation?

2. Do you think most college students have a healthy diet? What pressures are college students under that may affect their eating habits?

3. Have your eating habits changed since you began college? Why? Are they better or worse than they were before?

4. What criteria do you use to select your food?

5. Different countries and cultures have their own ideas about what constitutes a nutritional diet.

    a. Are you familiar with the guidelines established by the U.S. Department of Agriculture in the Food Guide Pyramid? What are the recommendations for citizens of the United States?

U.S.D.A. Food Guide Pyramid

    b. If you are familiar with the general nutritional guidelines for another country or culture, share how they are similar or different.

Activity 4-11   Vocabulary Matching

1. Match the words in the left column with their definitions on the right.

   _____ 1. versatile   a. not eat breakfast, lunch, or dinner

   _____ 2. staple   b. having control

   _____ 3. nonperishables   d. having many different uses

   _____ 4. restraint   e. foods that don't spoil easily or require refrigeration

   _____ 5. crash diet   f. an important, often eaten food

   _____ 6. skip meals   g. a plan to lose weight very quickly

2. To read this article actively:

   - circle words you do not know
   - underline the topic sentence in each of the eight body paragraphs
   - write comments in the margins when you agree or disagree with the ideas in the article

COLLEGE CUISINE MAKES MOTHER CRINGE

WHEN PARENTS SEND THEIR CHILDREN off to college, they might entertain the notion that their little darlings, having been brought up with the four basic food groups,* will continue to practice impeccable dietary habits. Little do they know that their children will skip meals, guzzle soda by the case, and subsist on a diet that would make mother cringe.

What do college students buy with their food money? Since they often cannot choke down the turkey tetrazzini or tofu stroganoff served in the campus dining hall, they will turn to whatever happens to be cheap and available. Pasta in all shapes and sizes is a popular meal. It's easy, cheap, filling, and versatile. When it is buried in different sauces, a student can almost fool herself into believing that she hasn't eaten it for five days straight.

Quick and easy meals are most attractive to students, so the microwave plays a major role in students' lives. Half of all students say they use a microwave every day, reports Roper CollegeTrack, an annual survey of student behavior and attitudes.

Cereal is another staple in the undergraduate kitchen. Two-thirds of undergraduates surveyed by Roper CollegeTrack say they bought a box of cereal in the last month. There are some college students who stock three different kinds of cereals, one for each meal. The day begins with a huge bowl of Lucky Charms and ends with a candle-light dinner of Froot Loops. There is also the famous "bagel diet." Three bagels a day might not be very nutritious, but bagels can be consumed while running for a bus. They also fit very nicely in the front pocket of a backpack.

On every college campus, there is at least a handful of restaurants and snack bars that cater to the dietary habits of students. Pizza and subs are featured prominently, but they often share the spotlight 45 with chicken wings, fried mozzarella sticks, onion rings, french fries, and any other grease-intensive snacks the cook can think of.

Far and away the most popular food is 50 pizza, according to the 1990 MTV Roper CollegeTrack report. More than half of all students say pizza is their favorite food. Second place falls to hamburgers, which gather only 7 percent of students' votes. 55

In dorm rooms, where students are usually limited to a cube-sized refrigerator to store foods, nonperishables are often the products of favor. Many students have milk crates shoved under their beds that are 60 filled with Oreos and Chips Ahoy! cookies, Cool Ranch Doritos and potato chips, Twinkies, and other tempting food from the candy and snacks aisle at the supermarket.

Exam time destroys all remaining 65 shreds of dietary restraint. In an attempt to "pull all-nighters," huge quantities of coffee and soda are consumed. The sodas of choice are either Mountain Dew, which contains the greatest amount of caffeine 70 and sugar of any mainstream soft drink, or Jolt, the eye-opening soda that proudly

claims to have twice the caffeine and all the sugar of regular Coke or Pepsi. Jolt starts appearing in campus stores right around 75 exam time, and it is often used to wash down a Vivarin or NoDoz caffeine pill.

Because of this hedonistic bingeing, some students go on crash diets after exams. Forty percent of all students say 80 they tried to lose weight by dieting in the last year; 60 percent of women and 25 percent of men dieted. These diets usually are not endorsed by any medical authority, but can be quite creative. There is the Slim- 85 Fast and beer diet, the broccoli diet, the chocolate chip cookie diet, and anything else that sounds like it would go under the heading "lose weight fast" in the *National Enquirer.* 90

College is a time for breaking away from the ideals that mom and dad professed. It is a time for new experiences, a time to expand one's horizons. More and more, it is also a time to discover the ther- 95 apeutic qualities of Pepto-Bismol.

Susannah Baker, Class of 1993, Rutgers College

*Until recently, the U.S.D.A. nutritional guidelines included four basic food groups. The current guidelines are shown on page 101.

Source: Susannah Baker, "College Cuisine Makes Mother Cringe," *American Demographics,* September 1991.

Activity 4-12 Post-reading Questions

1. Do you have some of the same eating habits described in Reading 2? Do you know other students who do? Explain.

2. Look at the title, first paragraph, and last paragraph. State the author's overall judgment of college cuisine in one sentence.

3. What are the possible effects of this kind of eating?

4. Imagine that you are designing a marketing campaign for a new food product. What features would be important for this new product to have to sell well in the college market?

Activity 4-13   Using Evidence to Support an Evaluation

What types of evidence did the author of Reading 2 use? Check the appropriate types and give an example of each type of evidence used.

Evidence   **Example**

_____ research findings (facts, statistics)   _____

_____ personal experience   _____

_____ quotations from reliable sources   _____

_____ examples, description   _____

Activity 4-14   Writing Assignment

1. Write two paragraphs that compare the college cuisine with the !Kung diet. Choose two of the following criteria to use in your comparison.

   Nutritional value

   Variety

   Cost (in terms of time and money)

   Potential nutrition-related health problems

2. Here are two suggestions of common ways you might organize your comparison paragraphs logically:

	Plan 1	**Plan 2**
Paragraph 1	Criterion 1	College cuisine
	College students	Criterion 1
	!Kung	Criterion 2
Paragraph 2	Criterion 2	!Kung
	College students	Criterion 1
	!Kung	Criterion 2

3. Peer Review. Share your paragraphs with a partner.

   a. Did you choose the same organizational plan, criteria, or evidence? Discuss your choices.

b. What is the most interesting comparison in your partner's paragraphs? Are there any other comparisons that could be made to make the paragraphs even more interesting?

c. Give one suggestion to your partner to improve the paragraphs.

d. Ask each other, other classmates, or your teacher, any questions you have about ways to improve the meaning, organization, or grammatical structure of your paragraphs.

4. Revise and rewrite your paragraphs. Proofread.

LEARNER'S NOTEBOOK

Remembering Details

Write your reaction to Reading 2. What details do you remember about the article? Why? How can you make your writing "memorable"?

Activity 4-15   Using Passive Sentences in Informational Writing

Sentence Structure: Informational writing often focuses on processes and products rather than on the people who follow the processes or make the products. Because of this focus, informational writing includes frequent use of passive sentences. For example, in the reading on college cuisine, the writer talked about bagels rather than about the students who eat the bagels: *Three bagels a day may not be very nutritious, but bagels can be consumed while you run for a bus.*

1. Fill in the passive verb forms of the following sentences using the verbs below.

> • consume   • divide   • feature   • find   • judge

a. On every college campus, there are at least a handful of restaurants and snack bars that cater to the dietary habits of students. Pizza and subs _____ prominently, but they often share the spotlight with chicken wings, fried mozzarella sticks, onion rings, french fries, and any other grease-intensive snacks the cook can think of.

b. Exam time destroys all remaining shreds of dietary restraint. In an attempt to "pull all-nighters," huge quantities of coffee and soda _____ .

c. Food-procuring activities _____ fairly rigidly _____ between men and women.

   d. Nutritionally, the mongongo, which _____ in abundance all year long, contains five times the calories and ten times the protein per cooked unit than cereal crops.

   e. And finally, the !Kung's relative abundance of resources can _____ from the amount of time they devote to procuring food.

2. Now circle the subject of each passive sentence in number 1 of this exercise.

3. Finally, determine the unmentioned "actor" in sentences 1–5. Note that a strong identifying clue for passive voice is the ability to add "by *x*" after the verb.

   a. by _restaurants and snack bars_

   b. by _____

   c. by _____

   d. by _____

   e. by _____

4. Why were these sentences written in the passive voice? What was the author emphasizing? How would the intent/meaning of the sentences change if they were written in the active voice?

> **GLR**   Refer to Section 3E for more information on passive sentences.

READING 3   EATING WELL (NEWSPAPER ARTICLE)

In the column "Eating Well," which appeared in the *New York Times*, author Marian Burros evaluates the effect that the American diet is having on the Japanese diet. While Readings 1 and 2 evaluate foods eaten, this article is different in that it evaluates the *changes* that eating certain foods has produced.

Activity 4-16   Pre-reading Questions

1. As the world is becoming more international, people are being influenced by foods from other cultures. What different ethnic restaurants are there in your city?

2. What foods do you especially like that originated in other cultures?

3. Why are more and more people eating fast food?

4. Is there a connection between what people eat and illness? What foods do you think people should avoid? Which foods are the most healthful? Why?

5. To read this article actively:

    • underline the main ideas
    • circle words you do not know
    • write the kinds of evidence used in the margins

EATING WELL

Tokyo [1] As soon as the early-morning bullet train from Tokyo to Kyoto pulled out of the station, Japanese children pulled out their breakfasts: deep-fried chicken nuggets, pork cutlet sandwiches, hot dogs and soft drinks.

[2] There may be some poetic justice here.

[3] If, as some believe, the Japanese are undermining the American economy by their trade practices, Americans may be quietly undermining the health of the Japanese public – with its eager cooperation – by selling it billions of dollars' worth of hamburgers and french fries, ice cream and Danish pastries. There are at least a thousand McDonald's in Japan today.

[4] The Japanese seem to have an ever-growing appetite for Western-style food high in fat and calories and low in fiber and complex carbohydrates. "Diet is related to the change in economic growth,"

Dr. Shuhei Kobayashi, the director of the National Institute of Health and Nutrition, said earlier this month in Tokyo. "The richer people are, the more food they eat." Especially food that is high in fat.

[5] The Japanese fascination with Western food is not based on taste alone. Western food is easier to prepare than the traditional labor-intensive Japanese meals, with their emphasis on rice and vegetables. And fast food is much cheaper than even the simplest bowl of soup in a noodle restaurant.

[6] On a recent trip to Japan, it was obvious that the trendiest Japanese adolescents, in their neatened-up version of grunge, eat fast food often, and on some of them, it is already showing, as they grow horizontally as well as vertically.

[7] "I eat hamburgers and french fries and a Coke two or three times a week,

and cakes and pastries, but not every day," said Saori Yamaguchi, standing in front of a McDonald's.

[8] Hayashi Masazumi, with the top of his hair dyed red, several earrings and a John F. Kennedy medallion around his neck, said he ate cheeseburgers, fries, milk and ice cream every day. "It tastes good and it's cheap," he added.

[9] A report by the Japanese Government released last month shows the impact of Western food. It warns that if the Japanese continue to increase their consumption of fat, which rose from 8.7 percent of calories in 1955 to 25.5 percent in 1992, they risk a much higher rate of chronic diseases.

[10] Between 1960 and 1991, consumption of grains in the Japanese diet dropped from about 14 ounces to less than 10 ounces a day per person. Rice, the staple of the Japanese diet, dropped from

a little over 10 ounces a day to less than 7 ounces, while milk and dairy-product consumption rose from about 2 ounces a day to about 8 ounces. Low-fat dairy products are unheard of.

[11] Meat consumption per person, according to the report, rose from less than an ounce a day to more than 3 ounces, and consumption of fats and oils tripled, from less than half an ounce to an ounce and a half.

[12] But the consumption of sodium, which once amounted to 20 grams a day, has dropped strikingly, to a little less than 13 grams a day.

[13] These dietary changes have resulted in a mixed bag for the Japanese. The height and weight of younger Japanese have increased strikingly, reflected in the need to buy larger school desks. The decrease in salt consumption has strikingly reduced the number of deaths from stroke and from stomach cancer. And the incidence of infectious diseases like pneumonia and tuberculosis, caused by malnutrition, has dropped.

[14] While the Japanese continue to have the longest life expectancy of any nationality, there has been a significant increase in the mortality rate from colon, lung, rectal and liver cancer among men, while breast cancer among women is also on the rise.

[15] Dr. Takashi Sugimura, president emeritus of the National Cancer Center in Tokyo, said that the striking rise in the cancer rate among men may be due to their eating so much more Western food than women do. "In Japan housewives still stay home," Dr. Sugimura said, "but men have many outside dinners and meetings, and food is Western style because it is easier and more convenient for the hotel or restaurant to prepare."

[16] And perhaps, as others have suggested, Western food, especially French and Italian, is seen as more sophisticated.

[17] The relation between colon cancer and a high-fat diet is pretty clear, Dr. Sugimura said. The relationship between breast cancer and fat is less so.

[18] A recent study of the cholesterol levels of Japanese children from ages 8 to 14 does not bode well for their future health. Children in urban areas have higher cholesterol levels than their American counterparts.

[19] "The Government is concerned; pediatric cardiologists are concerned," said Dr. Teruo Omae, president of the National Cardiovascular Center in Osaka. "They are warning that the situation is very risky and that children will have a greatly increased risk factor for heart disease."

[20] Over all, the mortality rate from heart disease has decreased somewhat, but the incidence of heart disease is rising. Dr. Omae said the impact of the Westernization of the Japanese diet on heart disease will probably not be clear for 20 years.

[21] The Japanese have embraced the worst aspects of the American diet and don't seem to know how to counteract their effects.

Source: Marian Burros, *The New York Times*, April 13, 1994.

Activity 4-17   Post-reading Questions

1. What is the author's overall judgment of the effect American and other Western food has on the diet of the Japanese? Where did you find this judgment?

2. What are two or three reasons that the Japanese have adopted more Western food?

3. Numbers: Skim the article for numbers (both in written and numerical form). What are at least three kinds of evidence given by these numbers?

4. Divide the article into four sections by drawing lines between them. Fill in the missing parts below as you make these divisions.

    Section 1   Paragraphs 1–5   introduction of topic

    Section 2   Paragraphs _____   examples of the young generation

    Section 3   Paragraphs 9–12   _____

    Section 4   Paragraphs 13–21   _____

5. Skim paragraphs 9 to 12 and note in the space provided whether consumption of the following items is going *up* or *down*.

    fat   _____

    grains/rice   _____

    milk   _____

    sodium   _____

    meat   _____

6. Skim paragraphs 15 to 21 for the effects of these dietary changes. Note whether these are going *up* or *down*.

    height and weight   _____

    cancer rate   _____

    death from strokes   _____

    cholesterol levels   _____

    infectious diseases   _____

    heart disease   _____

    death from heart disease   _____

In questions 5 and 6, you used cause and effect. We looked at those ideas in Chapter 3 as a part of explaining (explaining why). Cause and effect also play a strong role in providing support and evidence in evaluating.

Activity 4-18   Using Evidence to Support an Evaluation

In the space below each statement, name the kinds of evidence used.

1. "I eat hamburgers and french fries and drink a Coke two or three times a week, and cakes and pastries, but not every day," said Saori Yamaguchi, standing in front of a McDonald's.

   _____

2. A report from the Japanese Government released last month shows the impact of Western food.

   _____

3. A recent study of the cholesterol levels of Japanese children from ages 8 to 14 does not bode well for their future health.

   _____

4. Dr. Takashi Sugimura, president emeritus of the National Cancer Center in Tokyo, said that the striking rise in the cancer rate among men may be due to their eating so much more Western food than women do.

   _____

Activity 4-19   Using Appositives to Show the Credentials of a Source

Academic writers often quote or refer to the ideas of other people. To be persuasive, it is important to include information about the credentials of experts you quote or refer to, so your reader will trust their words and ideas. As you saw in Chapter 3, pages 82–83, appositives and non-restrictive adjective clauses can be used to give this important information.

1. Skim the reading and write the credentials of these people quoted in Reading 3 in the space provided.

Person Quoted	Credentials
Dr. Shuhei Kobayashi	_____
Dr. Teruo Omae	_____
Dr. Takashi Sugimura	_____

2. Other people are also quoted in this article. Who are they? Why are their credentials not given?

Activity 4-20   Using Comparisons to Give Evidence in Your Evaluation

When we evaluate, we often make comparisons with other things. Because of this, you will often find comparative and superlative language in written evaluations. In the article about the effect of Western food on the Japanese diet (Reading 3), several comparisons were made between the two.

1. Complete the missing parts below, filling in either the *criteria*, or the *comparison* between Western and Japanese food.

CRITERIA →	WESTERN FOOD →	JAPANESE FOOD
preparation [paragraph 5]		more difficult to prepare
   [paragraph 15]	more convenient for the hotel or restaurant to prepare	
sophistication [paragraph 16]		

2. Analyze the following three sentences. Circle the criterion in each sentence and underline the things being compared.

   a. Children in urban areas have higher cholesterol levels than their American counterparts.

   b. The Japanese continue to have the longest life expectancy of any nationality.

   c. The !Kung have a highly nutritional food supply that is more reliable than cultivated foods.

Activity 4-21   Using the Superlative to Give Evidence

1. Put the superlative form given below in the sentences based on the readings. Use each superlative only once.

    - the worst
    - the longest
    - the simplest
    - the trendiest
    - the most important

    a. The Japanese continue to have _____ life expectancy of any nationality.

    b. _____ adolescents eat fast food often and on some it is already showing, as they grow horizontally and vertically.

    c. Fast food is much cheaper than even _____ bowl of soup.

    d. They have embraced _____ aspects of the American diet.

    e. Food-getting is _____ activity among the !Kung.

2. Now, using the superlative, write five sentences comparing the food habits of the !Kung, college students, and the Japanese.

    The .

Activity 4-22   Using a Variety of Verb Tenses to Show Effects over a Period of Time

Readings 1 and 2 were examples of informational writing that used the present tense. Reading 3 used a variety of tenses because it not only told what Japanese people eat, but also how their diet has changed over time. In addition, it gives predictions for the future. To show this change over time, it is necessary to use various tenses. Refer to Section 8U in the GLR ⬤GLR to review the names of verb tenses.

1. Look in paragraph 10 of Reading 3 on page 107.

    a. Why is the past tense used in the first two sentences?

    b. Why is the present tense used in the last sentence?

2. Label the underlined tenses used in this sentence and explain why the tense changes:

    But the consumption of sodium, which once <u>amounted</u> to 20 grams a day, <u>has dropped</u> strikingly, to a little less than 13 grams a day.

3. With a partner, refer to number 4 in the post-reading questions on page 109 where you divided the article into four sections. Use these divisions to discover which tenses were used most in each section. (In many sections, more than one tense is used. Determine which one is used most frequently.)

	Content	**Tenses**
Section 1	_____	_past_____
Section 2	_____	_present_____
Section 3	_____	_both present_____
Section 4	_____	_both present_____

4. Explain how the content of each section influenced the choice of tense.

5. Look at numbers 5 and 6 in the post-reading questions on page 109 where you determined whether there was an increase or a decrease in food consumption and diseases. Write three sentences using that information. Use the present perfect tense, i.e., *has/have decreased, has/have increased.*

6. Look in paragraphs 19 and 20 of Reading 3 on page 108 to find the two examples of modals. Highlight these examples in the article. What degree of certainty does the modal *will* suggest?

LEARNER'S NOTEBOOK

Writing about the Effect of Changes

People often change what they eat when their life changes. Write about a time when your diet changed. Perhaps it changed when:

- you began college
- you became more health-conscious
- you started cooking for yourself
- you started or quit smoking
- you moved to a different culture
- your income increased or decreased
- you got married or had children
- your life became very busy

What is your evaluation of the effects this change had? Were they positive changes or negative changes? Why?

PUTTING IT ALL TOGETHER

FINAL WRITING ASSIGNMENT

Write an essay that gives an evaluation and includes information from at least one source. You may choose a topic related to nutrition or another evaluation topic approved by your teacher.

Plan

1. *Choose your topic.* Select one of the following ideas.

   a. If you are familiar with another culture whose eating habits have changed recently, evaluate the effects this changing diet has on the health of the population.

   b. Evaluate the nutrition of a particular group of people. It could be a specific group of college students, such as athletes, students who eat in residence halls, students who do their own cooking, or students from a particular country, or it could be people in different age groups, professions, or geographic regions.

   c. Evaluate the effects of fast food on a culture.

   d. Evaluate a restaurant, grocery store, or market.

   e. With your teacher's approval, choose another evaluation topic.

2. *Consider your audience and purpose.* Your audience is other students in the class (or another that you choose). Analyze the audience for your essay. What do they already know? What are their interests? How can you persuade them?

   Your purpose is to convince them to agree with your evaluation.

3. *Gather and organize your ideas.*

   a. Spend ten minutes writing about your ideas for your topic.

   b. Where will you gather information for your topic? What examples, research, facts, etc., can you give to support your criteria? Where can you find this information (interviews, journal articles, WWW)? Be sure to include at least one source in your paper with correct in-text and end-of-text references.

   c. Make a list of the criteria you will use. (You may discover other criteria as you research.)

   d. What do you think your overall judgment will be? (You may change your initial opinion after you do some research.)

4. *Think about organizing your essay.* Consider organizing your essay by stating your overall judgment in the introduction (as your thesis statement) and organizing your

body paragraphs by your criteria. Use one criterion per paragraph. Make a brief outline of the organization of your paper.

Sample Outline

Introduction	Tell what you will be evaluating. Name, define, or describe it, depending on your audience and purpose. Give necessary background information. Give your overall judgment in a thesis statement.
Body paragraphs	Topic Sentence 1: Criterion + judgment Supporting evidence*
	Topic Sentence 2: Criterion + judgment Supporting evidence*
	Topic Sentence 3: Criterion + judgment Supporting evidence*
	Topic Sentence 4: Criterion + judgment Supporting evidence*
Conclusion	Restate, perhaps with reference to supporting information, your overall judgment.

* Your supporting evidence in each paragraph can include facts, statistics, personal experience, quotations and ideas from reliable sources, examples, and description.

---

5. *Topic workshop.* Share your preliminary notes/outline with a partner.

   a. What subject will your partner be writing about?

   b. What is your partner's judgment about the topic? Is it stated well in the thesis statement?

   c. Do you think most people will agree or disagree with this judgment? Why might some people disagree? (Your answer could help the author present stronger support.)

   d. Examine the author's criteria. Are these important criteria to consider?

   e. Is there enough supporting evidence? What other interesting support could be added? What other resources could the author consult?

Write Your First Draft

Incorporate your partner's feedback from the topic workshop in your first draft. You will be able to revise and improve this draft to strengthen your evaluation.

Peer Response

1. Courtesy-edit. Read your own paper carefully to make sure your writing is clear. You want your partner to be able to read your ideas easily, so check for anything that would make it difficult for your partner to understand your paper. If some sentences are confusing, rewrite them now. Correct any problems with spelling, punctuation, and grammar that might confuse your reader.

2. Exchange your essay draft with your partner.

    a. Underline the thesis statement and topic sentences.

    b. Which is the best supported criterion in the essay? What makes this evidence interesting?

    c. Are you convinced by this evaluation? Tell your partner why or why not. How could the criteria or evidence be more convincing?

    d. Has the author integrated a source into the paper? Is this effective support? Should your partner use more support? Where?

Revise, Edit, and Proofread

1. Read your essay again. Is it a clear and convincing evaluation? Is it well-supported and organized? Check the overall essay organization and the organization of each paragraph. Is your writing cohesive? In addition, how will you use your partner's comments to help you make improvements?

2. Edit your essay for the following, and correct any errors. After you have edited for each of these features, check (✓) the box as a reminder that you have done that task.

    ❏ complete sentences

    ❏ correct sentence punctuation

    ❏ subject-verb agreement

    ❏ appropriate transition words and phrases to show logical relationships

    ❏ modals and other grammar to avoid over-generalization

    ❏ if you included any passive sentences, check the form of the verb

☐ if you used another person's words or ideas, check that you used reporting verbs and quotations correctly. Should you add information about the credentials of that person to show why a reader should believe him or her?

☐ if you used numbers, check the form and spelling

3. Make necessary changes and rewrite your essay.

4. Proofread your final essay draft.

Activity 4-23   Write a Memo

Write a memo to your teacher. Tell what changes you made in revising your essay and why you made them. How did each change improve your essay? What do you think is the strongest paragraph in your essay? Why?

Activity 4-24   Evaluating a Final Writing Assignment

1. Write a short evaluation of one of the final writing assignments you wrote for Chapter 1, 2, or 3. Be sure to:

   • state the title and topic of the assignment
   • give your overall judgment of your paper
   • suggest the grade you think you deserve

2. Choose two or three criteria to evaluate your essay:

   • overall organization   • correct grammatical structures
   • interesting ideas   • improvements from first to final draft
   • audience interest   • effective support/evidence/detail
   • use of sources

3. Give specific examples from your essay to support the criteria you choose. Convince the teacher of the grade you deserve.

● ●

L
O
O
K
I
N
G
A
H
E
A
D

Academic Assignments

You do not have to do these authentic assignments. However, analyzing them will give you a clearer understanding of types of assignments you will face in your under-graduate courses. For the two assignments below, with a partner or a small group of classmates,

• underline key words
• discuss possible organization of the answer

- discuss techniques for giving a good evaluation
- determine if there are questions you need to ask the professor about the assignment

Chemistry

Write a report about the experiment you did today. Use the following sections to organize your report:

Introduction: Describe the background to the experiment, what is to be found, and how;

Experiment: Present the various observations, measurement, and graphs required in the experiment;

Results and Conclusion: Report on how your raw data led to certain conclusions and **evaluate** the success of your experiment.

Marketing

The following project involves a one- to three-page paper.

Content Requirements

The purpose of this project is to identify a real, current example of product positioning. The organization may be nonprofit or profit-oriented; retail, wholesale, manufacturer, or a service provider; it may be a local, regional, or national brand; it may be a new product introduction, or repositioning of an existing product.

Your task is to:

(a) Identify the organization and the market segment being targeted (focus on one target market);

(b) Determine the probable approach(es) to positioning being employed;

(c) Gather evidence to support (a) and (b) above. This evidence may take virtually any form you choose, including (but not limited to):

news or magazine articles
copies of print ads
copies of press releases
interviews with company executives
photos of displays or outdoor advertising
samples of sales promotion material
direct mail pieces
audio or videotapes of ads
audio or videotapes of public service announcements

Use your imagination! Be sure to label all supporting materials with your name, the company or product name, and any appropriate reference, such as document name, title, company, time, place, date, etc.

(d) **Evaluate** the organization's strategy. Does its approach seem reasonable? Why or why not? Is the target market an attractive one? Why or why not? Are there changes you would recommend to the company? Why or why not?

Format Requirements

The text of the paper should be one to three pages in length (three page maximum), typed, double-spaced, one-inch margins, 10- or 12-pitch type.

Supporting materials (*c* above) should be attached and appropriately labeled. If you use news or magazine articles, attach a reference list, citing the author, title, name of publication, and date; you need not attach the articles themselves.

Chapter 5

*S*ummarizing and Responding

Mathematical Literacy

GOALS

WRITING
- summarize and respond to reading passages
- distinguish main ideas from supporting details and examples

GRAMMAR
- practice using reporting verbs and subject-verb agreement
- learn basic features of past time narrative

CONTENT
- read about mathematics, mathematics education, and the history of counting devices

ACADEMIC FIELDS
Mathematics
History

Sample Authentic College/University Writing Assignments

In your academic courses, you will use the skills you learn in this chapter to complete assignments like the examples below.

Business Management

You are required to read five articles related to this course in journals that are on reserve in the library. For each article, write a summary and then respond to the main ideas of the article. Show how the ideas relate to one of the business principles we have studied in class.

Art History

For your next three-page report, you will explore a major work of an Impressionist. At the beginning, summarize the focus and highlights of the artist's career. Then place the work you have chosen within that context.

GETTING READY

LEARNER'S NOTEBOOK

Warm-up Writing

What is the meaning of this quotation?

I have made this letter longer than usual, only because I
have not had the time to make it shorter.

Blaise Pascal (1623–1662)
French scientist, philosopher, and mathematician

Why would it take more time to write a shorter letter?

An Introduction to Summarizing

Summaries are shortened versions of a longer message. We often encounter summaries in our daily lives. For example, we may hear a 60-second news report on the
radio, which gives brief information on the most important news of the day. Before a
new episode of a series on TV, we may see a quick summary of what happened in the
previous episodes. We may summarize a movie, magazine article, or book we'd like a
friend to enjoy, or we might summarize details of our lives to tell others. We may send
postcards when we travel, summarizing the highlights of our vacation. And when a
classmate asks us "What happened in class today?" we quickly summarize the main
points covered.

In the working world, potential employees summarize their qualifications, such as
educational and employment background, on a resume or application form. On the job,
workers may be asked to give oral or written progress reports to summarize the work
that has been completed. And at many business meetings, minutes are read that summarize the business of the previous meeting.

Activity 5-1   Discussion

In a small group, think of specific situations when you have given, read, or heard summaries in your daily life during the past week. Why are these summaries necessary and
important?

Summarizing in Academic Work

Summaries are widely used in academic work. They are often found at the end of textbook chapters to help students review the key points. In addition, professors may give a brief summary at the end of a lecture or begin a class with a summary of what was previously covered. By reading a summary or abstract of an article you can quickly determine whether the article is a possible source in doing library research.

Students are also asked to write summaries. An effective student must be able to:

- summarize material and take notes while listening to lectures or reading texts
- summarize readings to include in reports, projects, papers, and assignments
- summarize text or lecture material to answer test questions
- summarize material and then write a reaction, analysis, or response

Summaries are shorter than the original message because they contain only the main ideas and main supporting ideas.

Elements of a Summary

1. **A summary contains only the most important information.**

   An effective summary answers the question: What are the main points of the original lecture, reading, or message? To answer this question, the summary gives the main ideas and main supporting ideas of the original message, so that the reader or listener does not have to go to the original source to understand it. The summary is complete within itself.

2. **A summary is concise.**

   Because a good summary contains only the essential information, it is considerably shorter than the original. Your job as the summary writer is to distinguish the main, essential information from the examples and detail, so you will know what to include in your summary. The length of the summary may depend on the assignment given or the length and difficulty of the original.

3. **A summary respects the author's original work.**

   A summary respects the author's original work by:

   - citing the author
   - objectively stating the author's ideas without additional ideas or interpretation
   - using the author's exact sentences only in the proper form of quotation

4. A summary follows an introduction/body/conclusion format.

A summary is not a loosely connected list of the main ideas. Whether it consists of one paragraph or several, it is structured with an *introduction*, a *body*, and a *conclusion*. As in all good writing, the ideas and sentences are smoothly connected by a variety of techniques, such as repetition of key words, pronoun reference, and transitional words and phrases.

| Activity 5-2   Analyze a Summary of Informational Writing |

The following is a sample summary from Reading 3 on pages 107–108 in Chapter 4.

In the article, "High-fat food is taking its toll in Japan," which appeared in *The New York Times* on April 13, 1994, Marian Burros reported that the Japanese people are experiencing deteriorating health from eating more and more Western food. A study by the Japanese government has shown that the increase in fat and calories of these foods has resulted in a higher risk for different kinds of cancer and for heart disease. As a result, medical professionals and the Japanese government are concerned about the long-term effects of this diet on their population.

1. Does this summary contain only the main ideas of the original article?

2. How does this summary compare in length to the original article?

3. What three pieces of information are given in the first sentence of the summary?

4. Whose opinions and ideas are given in the summary?

5. Does the summary read smoothly? How do the phrases "these foods" and "as a result" help connect the sentences?

How to Summarize a Reading Passage

In your academic course work, you will often write summaries of a reading passage, either for your self-study, or for tests or assignments. The following six steps will help you write a good summary. The first three steps involve reading and the last three primarily involve writing. Do not hurry to start writing. Read and understand well first.

1	2	3	4	5	6
Preview the reading.	**Read** for main ideas.	**Reread** for greater understanding.	**Take notes** and organize your ideas.	**Write** the summary.	**Revise** the summary.

As you read, concentrate on the main ideas. Remember that you will focus on the main ideas when you write your summary.

1. **Preview.** First, quickly look at and skim parts of the reading that are likely to contain main ideas: title, introduction, the first and last sentence of each paragraph, and the conclusion. Longer readings may also include subtitles, headings, pictures, charts, graphs, and key words in **bold** or *italics*. From this limited information, you can discover the general topic and ideas.

2. **Read.** Read the entire passage. Continue to focus on main ideas. Highlight, underline, or number the main ideas.

3. **Reread.** Read it again (and again, if necessary) for greater understanding.

4. **Take notes and organize.** Look back at what you highlighted, underlined, or numbered in the reading. Begin your notes.

5. **Write.** In your first sentence, cite the author, the work, and the main idea. For example, *According to [author] in the article "XXX,"; In the article "XXX," [author] states that . . .*

   In the body of the summary, use reporting verbs such as: The author *believes, states, reports, says, discusses, notes, concludes . . .*

6. **Revise.** Check your summary for meaning, conciseness, and grammatical accuracy. Make certain it has a clear introduction, body, and conclusion and that the sentences are smoothly connected.

Activity 5-3   Writing the First Sentence of a Summary

Three key pieces of information—the author, the work, and the main idea—are generally included in the first sentence of a summary. This information clearly identifies the source material for the summary. (See examples in number 5 above.)

Reporting verbs are needed to refer to the author's ideas in the first and future sentences of the summary. The most commonly used are *say/said, write/wrote.* Many times these are appropriate; however, you can often use a more precise reporting verb.

GLR   See Section 5B in the GLR for a list of many commonly used reporting verbs.

The information below is about reading selections in the earlier chapters of this text. Use this information to write the first sentence of a summary. Use a different reporting verb for each one.

1. **Chapter 1, Reading 3, page 15**

      Author: James Kalat

      Source: Textbook, *Introduction to Psychology*

      Main idea: How vicarious reinforcement and self-efficacy influence success

2. **Chapter 2, Reading 5, page 46**

      Authors: John Gardner and Jerome Jewler

      Source: "Evaluating Sources," in the textbook, *Your College Experience—Strategies for Success*

      Main idea: Six essential criteria for evaluating research sources

LEARNER'S NOTEBOOK

Summarize a Reading Passage

Write a 75–100 word summary of one of the readings in Chapters 1–4 of this textbook. You may choose one of the readings listed in Activity 5-3 or another reading. Follow the six-step process, being sure to put key information in your first sentence.

Grammar Preview

When writing a summary and response, it is important to identify which ideas belong to the author whose work you are summarizing and which ideas are yours. To make this distinction, you will practice using reporting verbs. In addition, you will review subject-verb agreement and learn about and practice the features of past time narrative.

> **GLR** Refer to Section 2 of the GLR for explanations and examples of past time narrative.

FOCUSING

The readings in this chapter are about the growing need for mathematical skills in our society, math anxiety, statistics, and the history of computing devices. Math is very important in higher education because every discipline or major requires some mathematical knowledge. However, you do not have to have a strong math background to read these articles.

READING 1   OPPORTUNITY ... TAPPING THE POWER OF MATHEMATICS (RESEARCH REPORT)

Activity 5-4   Vocabulary Matching

The following words are from Reading 1. With a partner, match the word on the left with the meaning on the right.

__f__ 1. ambiguity

____ 2. fundamental

____ 3. unconventional

____ 4. prerequisite

____ 5. remedial

____ 6. calculation

a. basic and necessary

b. designed to correct or cure

c. mathematical problem-solving

d. not usual

e. something that is necessary before something else can happen

f. something unclear because it has more than one meaning

Activity 5-5   Pre-reading Questions

1. **Preview.** First, quickly preview the reading. Spend one or two minutes reading the title, skimming the introduction and conclusion, and reading the first and last sentence of each paragraph.

    a. What is the main topic of the reading?

    b. What are some areas of the topic that will be covered?

    c. Did you learn anything else about the reading?

2. **Read.** Read the article. Pay special attention to the main ideas. Use a system for marking the main ideas: highlighting, underlining, or numbering. What are three of the most likely places to find main ideas in the reading?

    a. _____

    b. _____

    c. _____

3. **Reread.** Read again for greater understanding.

OPPORTUNITY . . . TAPPING THE POWER OF MATHEMATICS

Mathematics is the key to opportunity. No longer just the language of science, mathematics now contributes in direct and fundamental ways to business, finance, health, and defense. For students, it opens doors to careers. For citizens, it enables informed decisions. For nations, it provides knowledge to compete in a technological economy. To participate fully in the world of the future, America must tap the power of mathematics.   5

Communication has created a world economy in which working smarter is more important than merely working harder. Jobs that contribute to this world economy require workers who are mentally fit—workers who are prepared to absorb new ideas, to adapt to change, to cope with ambiguity, to perceive patterns, and to solve unconventional problems. It is *these* needs, not just the need for calculation (which is done mostly by machine), that 10 make mathematics a prerequisite to so many jobs. More than ever before, Americans need to think for a living; more than ever before, they need to think mathematically.

Yet, for lack of mathematical power, many of today's students are not prepared for tomorrow's jobs. In fact, many are not even prepared for today's jobs. Current mathematical achievement of U.S. students is nowhere near what is required to sustain our nation's 15 leadership in a global technological society. As technology has "mathematicized" the workplace and as mathematics has permeated society, a complacent America has tolerated underachievement as the norm for mathematics education. We have inherited a mathematics curriculum conforming to the past, blind to the future, and bound by a tradition of minimum expectations.   20

Wake up, America! Your children are at risk. Three of every four Americans stop studying mathematics before completing career or job prerequisites. Most students leave school
without sufficient preparation in mathematics to cope either with on-the-job demands for
problem-solving or with college requirements for mathematical literacy. Thus, industry, universities, and the armed forces are burdened by extensive and costly demands for remedial 25
education.

Today's mathematics opens doors to tomorrow's jobs. As successive waves of immi-
grants have used this country's educational system to secure better lives for themselves and
their children, so today's children the world over are using mathematical training as a plat-
form on which to build up their lives. America's children deserve the same chance.   30

Children *can* succeed in mathematics. Many do so in other countries and some do so in
this country. The evidence from other nations shows overwhelmingly that if more is expected in mathematics education, more will be achieved. Clear expectations of success by parents, by schools, and by society can promote success by students.

In today's world, the security and wealth of nations depend on their human resources. 35
So does the prosperity of individuals and businesses. As competitors get smarter, our problems get harder. Long-term investment in science and technology—both for businesses and
our nation—requires serious commitment to revitalizing mathematics education. It is time
to act to ensure that *all* Americans benefit from the power of mathematics.

Source: National Research Council, *Everybody Counts—A Report to the Nation on
the Future of Mathematics Education* (National Academy Press, 1989).

Activity 5-6   Post-reading Questions

Be sure you have completed steps 1 (preview), 2 (read), and 3 (reread) before you answer
these questions.

1. In a small group, discuss how you decided to mark the main ideas in the article. Did
    you highlight, underline, or number the main ideas? Why?

    a. Where did you find the main ideas?

    b. Was there a place that they usually appeared?

2. In one sentence, what is the main idea of this reading?

3. Fill in the spaces below by giving the main ideas and some supporting detail for each
    of the seven paragraphs in the article. For paragraph 1, the main ideas and some of
    the supporting details are given. Try to put this information into your own words.

Paragraph →	Main Idea	→ Some Supporting Details
1	People who know mathematics have many opportunities.	students → careers citizens → informed decisions nations → better competitors
2	More and more jobs require mathematical ability.	
3 and 4		low math achievement little desire to improve outdated math curriculum 3/4 of students lack preparation for college and jobs
5	Children need mathematics for their future.	
6		
7		

4. In summarizing, it is important to be able to distinguish the main ideas from the supporting details. This chart helped you separate the two. Which column will you use the most for your summary?

5. Who is the audience for this article? How do you know?

6. Look in paragraph 7 to find the sentence that states the author's purpose for writing. Underline it in the text.

7. In Chapter 4 you worked on the parts of a good evaluation. What is the author's overall judgment of mathematics education in the United States? What criteria and evidence are used?

LEARNER'S NOTEBOOK

Strategies for Finding Main Ideas

What strategies help a reader or listener find the main ideas of an article, lecture, or other work? What strategies work well for you when you are looking for main ideas?

Activity 5-7   Using Subject-Verb Agreement in Present Time Summaries

The previous reading about mathematics education was in the present tense, and so a summary would also be written in the present tense. When using the present tense, subject-verb agreement is important. For each of the following sentences from the reading:

1. Underline the main subject of the sentence.

2. From the verbs given below, choose the correct one for each blank. Be sure to use the correct form of the present tense.

   • be • be • have • have • make • show • stop • require • require

   a. Jobs that contribute to this world economy _____*require*_____ workers who are mentally fit.

   b. It is *these* needs, not just the need for calculation (which is done mostly by machine), that _____ mathematics a prerequisite to so many jobs.

   c. Mathematics _____ the key to opportunity.

   d. Current mathematical achievement of U.S. students _____ nowhere near what is required to sustain our nation's leadership in a global technological society.

   e. A complacent America _____ tolerated underachievement as the norm for mathematics education.

   f. We _____ inherited a mathematics curriculum conforming to the past, blind to the future, and bound by a tradition of minimum expectations.

   g. Three of every four Americans _____ studying mathematics before completing career or job prerequisites.

   h. The evidence from other nations _____ overwhelmingly that if more is expected in mathematics education, more will be achieved.

   i. Long-term investment in science and technology—both for businesses and for
       our nation—_____ serious commitment to revitalizing mathe-
       matics education.

   GLR   Refer to Section 3G for more information on subject-verb agreement.

Activity 5-8   Write a Summary

We are now at the last three steps of preparing a summary as shown on page 125. Use
steps 4, 5, and 6, given again below, to write a summary paragraph of Reading 1.

4. **Take notes and organize them.** You can refer to the chart you completed on
    page 130.

5. **Write.** Write a summary paragraph of this article. Refer to "Elements of a Summary"
    on pages 123–124.

6. **Revise.** Use the following checklist.

    ____✓ a. Did you include the author, work, and main idea in the first sentence?

    ____✓ b. Did you use your own sentences instead of the author's?

    ____✓ c. Did you give only the author's ideas and not your own?

    ____✓ d. Did you connect the ideas and sentences in your paragraph?

    ____✓ e. Did you check for meaning and grammatical accuracy?

An Introduction to Responding

   While a summary is objective and only includes the author's ideas, a written
response includes your own ideas and reaction to the reading.
   For some academic assignments, you will only be asked to write a summary. For others, you will be asked to respond to the reading. In an academic response, you will be
expected to develop an informed opinion and support your ideas with examples,
details, and facts, either from the reading or another source, just as you do in other kinds
of writing. You can not just give a general opinion, such as "I liked/hated this article" or
"I thought this was an interesting/boring article."
   There are several types of responses. Most commonly, you will be asked to *disagree*
or *agree*. For example, an assignment may ask you to agree or disagree with the main
idea of a reading passage, or ask you to choose some part of a reading to agree or disagree with. A second type of response may ask you to *compare* and/or *contrast* what you

have read with your own experiences or the experiences of others. For other response assignments, you may be asked to *apply* what you read to another situation, or to *evaluate* a reading. Remember that for all of these responses, you must provide adequate support for your opinion.

If you are asked to summarize and respond to an article, mark interesting parts of the article as you read. You may be able to incorporate these when you write your response.

A response paragraph may follow a summary paragraph.

Summary Paragraph
Response Paragraph

A longer response may take the form of an essay.

Introduction = Summary + Thesis Statement
Body Paragraph: Response
Body Paragraph: Response
Body Paragraph: Response
Conclusion

In your response paragraphs, you need to clearly show which opinions and ideas are the author's and which are yours. To do this, you can begin your response paragraph referring directly to the author or article.

- The author states that . . .
- According to the author, . . .
- In the article, "(Title)," . . .

This lets the reader know which part of the author's work you will be responding to. After this sentence, you can begin your ideas with sentences such as:

- However, I believe that . . .
- I agree with this because . . .
- In my experience, the author's point is . . .

Then you can continue your paragraph with support for your ideas. By doing this, you clearly separate the author's ideas from yours. The majority of the paragraph will be the support for your opinion.

Activity 5-9   Analyze a Response

Read the following response paragraph and then answer the questions that follow.

> The author of "Opportunity . . . tapping the power of mathematics" states that many students do not have the necessary math background to do well in the job market. However, I think that for lower level jobs, which often are jobs with little chance of advancement, workers don't need math skills. For example, grocery store clerks run the products over a scanner and the cash register figures out how much change the customer should receive. At many fast-food restaurants, the clerk can press a picture of a hamburger on the cash register instead of pushing numbered buttons for the price. Certainly, to get ahead, people need math, but I think our society has made it very easy for people to have a variety of jobs that require few or no math skills. Consequently, there is little incentive for some students to become well-educated in math.

1. In which sentence does the writer of this response begin to express her ideas? What words and phrases help separate the ideas of the two people?

2. What examples does the author give to support her opinion?

Activity 5-10   Write a Response

1. Write a one paragraph response to Reading 1. Respond to one of the following quotations from the article, or choose an idea of your own to respond to. In your topic sentence, agree or disagree with one of these quotations. Support your opinion.

   a. "More than ever before, Americans need to think for a living; more than ever before, they need to think mathematically."

b. "Most students leave school without sufficient preparation in mathematics to cope either with on-the-job demands for problem-solving or with college requirements for mathematical literacy."

c. "Children *can* succeed in mathematics. Many do so in other countries and some do in this country."

2. Now add this response to your summary of Reading 1.

READING 2   MATH WITHOUT FEAR (BOOK EXCERPT)

Many people have a fear of math. The author of the following reading discusses the effects of this "math anxiety."

Activity 5-11   Pre-reading Questions

1. Think about any math you have done in the last week outside of a math class. How do you use math in your academic classes, everyday life, and/or employment? As a group, try to list at least 15 ways on the chalkboard.

2. How has your ability or interest in mathematics influenced your choice of major or career?

3. Which fields of study require little or no mathematical ability? Which require the most?

4. Some people have anxiety about doing math. List possible causes and effects of this anxiety.

Causes   **Effects**

_____   _____

_____   _____

_____   _____

_____   _____

5. You will write a summary of the following article. Remember to follow the steps in the chart below. In addition, mark any place that interests you for your response to the article.

1	2	3	4	5	6
Preview the reading.	Read for main ideas.	Reread for greater understanding.	Take notes and organize your ideas.	Write the summary.	Revise the summary.

MATH WITHOUT FEAR

Math anxiety has major effects on men and women. It can create a cycle of fear and defeat for individuals with math problems. Anxieties about mathematics can lead to mental blocks and confusion when solving 5 a problem. These feelings of loss of control prevent the individual from making any progress. Failure to arrive at an answer creates even greater anxieties and fears. And so the cycle goes on and on, with anxieties 10 mounting at each step. If you believe that you will not be able to solve the problem before you even start, defeat is certain to follow.

Naturally, the most common result of 15 math anxiety is math avoidance. You stop taking math courses, choose jobs that involve little or no math, get someone else to do your taxes, have a friend check the restaurant bill, or assign math-related prob-20 lems to co-workers so that you won't have to reveal your inadequacy on the job.

What are the effects of this math avoidance? First of all, math avoidance will prevent you from ever developing better math 25 skills. You will always fear it, and daily tasks involving math or related skills will create more anxieties and will contribute to a low self-image.

In addition to lowering self-confi-30 dence, the math anxiety-avoidance cycle has other far-reaching consequences. As technology progresses, math avoidance becomes increasingly difficult. Daily tasks—determining gas mileage, figuring 35 out tips, interpreting utility bills, choosing insurance policies, understanding charts and graphs in newspaper articles—all involve math. It's really just not possible to pass on *all* math-related tasks to someone 40 else. We are constantly in need of math skills. Even a trip to the grocery store, with the various discounts and specials, can become an exercise in mathematical confusion. Personal finances, major purchases 45 such as buying a car, and choosing a retirement plan are all daily experiences that involve not only math skills but confidence in your ability to compare various collections of data (percentages, deductions, dec-50 imals, and so forth) in order to decide on a best purchase.

If math skills are necessary for day-to-day routines, they are becoming even more essential for a wide variety of jobs and for 55 career advancement. Careers previously thought to be people-oriented are relying more and more on math skills. Careers in management, the social sciences, counseling, law, business, and government work 60 are only a few of the fields requiring math skill. A degree in any of these fields requires advanced mathematics. Needed math skills may include reading computer printouts, using ratios and percentages, or 65 understanding statistical data. Higher paying jobs often demand an ability to use such skills. Thus, math avoidance also prevents many adults from career advancement or changes. 70

Finally, math avoidance also may be keeping you from participating in a whole range of activities. Hobbies such as photography and flying, doing your own electrical work or plumbing, or even solving a 75 puzzling problem can provide many rewards, including both pleasurable and financial ones. However, these activities do require math skills.

Source: Carol Gloria Crawford, *Math Without Fear* (NewViewpoints/Vision Books, 1980).

Activity 5-12   Post-reading Questions

Be sure you have previewed, read, and reread the article before you start the following questions.

1. Based on Reading 2, decide whether each statement is true or false. Put "T" or "F" in the space provided.

   _____ a. Math anxiety affects both men and women.

   _____ b. Math anxiety often leads to math avoidance, which can lead to more math anxiety.

   _____ c. If you have math anxiety, it is best to drop your math classes.

   _____ d. People need math skills and confidence to use them in their daily life.

   _____ e. People-oriented jobs require few or no math skills.

   _____ f. You might be able to get a higher-paying job if you have good math skills.

   _____ g. Many leisure-time activities also require math skills.

2. Correct the false statements to make them true.

3. Define each of these terms in your own words and give an example to explain each.

   Math anxiety is _____

   _____.

   Math avoidance is _____

   _____.

4. What is the *math anxiety-avoidance cycle*?

5. What are some of the effects of the *math anxiety-avoidance cycle*?

6. The author gives many uses for math. One paragraph is devoted to daily tasks, another to careers, and the last paragraph to hobbies. Below list several of the examples that the author gave for the first two categories. For the last category, "hobbies," give your own ideas for the math that is needed. Examples are provided.

Math for daily tasks	Math for careers	Math for hobbies
determining gas mileage	reading computer printouts	

7. In a short summary of Reading 2, would you include the examples from your list? Why or why not?

8. Underline each of the author's topic sentences. Notice how she uses these to hook two paragraphs together. What techniques does she use?

Activity 5-13   Write a Summary and Response

1. In a small group, discuss the main ideas of the reading. What did you highlight, underline, or number in the reading? Try to summarize the reading orally in a few sentences, getting feedback from your partners. Take notes to help you write a summary. Your summary should be a well-connected paragraph that includes the main ideas of this article.

2. Your response should be one or two paragraphs. Choose one of the following ideas:

   a. Do you agree with the author that math is important for our daily tasks, jobs, and hobbies? Do you think she exaggerates the importance of math?

   b. In your response, apply what Dr. Crawford has written about the effects of math anxiety to individual examples. Have you or others you know experienced these effects of math anxiety?

   c. Dr. Crawford discussed the effects of math anxiety. In your response, consider possible causes of math anxiety.

READING 3 STATISTICS—MATHEMATICAL MANIPULATIONS (BOOK EXCERPT)

Activity 5-14 Pre-reading Questions

1. What are statistics? When are they used? Are they always reliable?

2. How are statistics used in your field of study?

3. As a class, try to define the words in the first sentence of this reading.

4. Prepare to write a summary and response to this article. Review page 136 for the six steps to summary writing.

STATISTICS—MATHEMATICAL MANIPULATIONS

Means, averages, medians, percent, mode, percentile, graphs ... are all ways of manipulating numerical values. Take two numbers, 6 and 8. One can make various comparisons— the ratio 6:8, the fraction 3/4, the percent 75%. The moment one gathers numerical values in an attempt to describe a situation, one is beginning to delve into the realm of statistics. Whether helpful or misleading, statistics is almost always influential.   5

Used to predict various phenomena such as—

   a presidential candidate (Gallup poll)
   statistical performance (SAT scores)
   the status of the economy (inflation numbers, GNP growth numbers, unemployment
     figures, increases and declines of interest rates)   10
   the DOW (averages of the stock market)
   insurance rates
   demographic data
   weather prediction
   pharmaceutical analysis on the effectiveness and/or side effects of a medication   15
   gambling odds
   incidence of ocean waves and tides—

the domain of statistics is continually growing. When looking at the end result of any statistical analysis, one must be very cautious not to over interpret the data. Care must be taken to know the size of the sample, and to be certain the method for gathering the infor- 20 mation is consistent with other samples gathered. For example, if an exit poll in a particular election is done, the sample must be random and as large as possible. Imagine if the poll were only done in one neighborhood which was heavily weighted toward one side—a prediction based on such a small poll would be ludicrous.

Suppose a daily newspaper printed *"From a poll conducted by the Daily Enquirer, 75%* 25 *of those polled had contracted flu this year."* With this statement some people would jump to the conclusion that nearly 75% of the populace had contracted flu. The *Daily Enquirer* did not indicate the size of its poll. They may have asked only four people in their office and three of them had suffered from the flu. *No one should ever base conclusions without knowing the size of the sample and how random a sample it was.* But all too often such data 30 is not mentioned when the statistics are given—perhaps it is overlooked or even intentionally omitted.

Another method for altering statistics is to change the make-up of your sample. For example, suppose the method for measuring unemployment was based on the number of unemployed persons in civil and private industry jobs. Now suppose after the year 1980, 35 the statistics also include the armed services. This naturally enlarges the number of employed persons, since anyone who is in the armed services is employed. Thus, a comparison of unemployment statistics before 1980 with those as of 1980 is invalid.

With the introduction of computers and the ability to gather, sort and analyze large quantities of data quickly, statistical data and information should be more reliable as long 40 as the agency conducting the analysis is unbiased and would not attempt to manipulate the results. The influence and power of statistics is enormous. It can be used to persuade or dissuade individuals. For example, if individuals feel their vote will not change the final result, they may not make that extra effort to vote—especially if statistics are showing exit polls leaning in one direction several hours before the polls close.   45

Statistics is a very powerful and persuasive mathematical tool. People put a lot of faith in printed numbers. It seems when a situation is described by assigning it a numerical value, the validity of the report increases in the mind of the viewer. It is the statistician's obligation to be aware that data in the eyes of the uninformed or poor data in the eyes of the naive viewer can be as deceptive as any falsehoods.   50

Source: Theoni Pappas, *More Joy of Mathematics: Exploring Mathematical
Insights and Concepts (*World Wide Publishing/Tetra, 1991).

Activity 5-15   Post-reading Questions

1. What is the purpose of the first paragraph? What basic information does it give?

2. How does the author define statistics?

3. The author gave numerous examples of when statistics are used. What effect, if any, did this have on you, the reader? What are other examples you could give from your major field of study or your other interests?

4. In preparing to write a summary, you will separate the main ideas from the examples that support those main ideas. This reading is rich in examples; in fact, a large portion of it is examples and other supporting material.

   a. Draw a box around the examples given in this article. Start by drawing a box around the list in paragraph 2 of ten ways statistics are used. Then, look for the key expressions "for example" and "suppose." These both mark where an example begins. Draw a box around these examples, including the key expressions.

   b. Compare the boxes you drew with those of a partner. Did you find the same examples? For each example you found, tell what main idea it supports.

Activity 5-16   Write a Summary and Response

In a small group, discuss the main ideas of the reading. What did you highlight, underline, or number in the reading? Try to summarize the reading orally in a few sentences, getting feedback from your partners. Take notes to help you in writing the summary.

1. Now, write your own summary. Your summary should be a well-developed paragraph that includes the main ideas of this article.

2. Respond to the following topic:

   The author describes statistics as powerful, influential, and persuasive. Do you agree? Explain. (In thinking about your answer, you can refer to the list of ten examples in the reading.) Can you think of a particular incident when statistics were influential in your decision-making?

READING 4   EARLY COMPUTING DEVICES (BOOK EXCERPT)

The following reading describes the history of computing devices. It begins with counting on our hands and ends with working on computers. Like most accounts of history, it is written in the past tense. Your summary will also be in the past tense.

Within the reading, you will see the raised numbers [1] and [2]. These refer to notes giving additional information at the end of the article.

EARLY COMPUTING DEVICES

Our very first calculating device was and is our hands. As time passed, a hand number system developed for communicating among merchants and others who did not speak the same language. Even today 5 we see young students either counting or carrying on their fingers.

But when numerical figures began to exceed our ten fingers, new devices had to be explored. Here enters the stacking peb- 10 bles method. But still a person had to perform the major work of grouping and counting the stones. 15 Someone then came up with the idea of a portable pebble device which eventually gave rise to the abacus. Various types of abaci were used in China, ancient Greece and Rome. Abaci are still 20 used in many parts of Asia today. The Chinese first used bamboo rods for calculating (circa 542 B.C.) and their abacus entered the computing world around the 12th century. The abacus was considered 25 adequate for traditional calculations by merchants for centuries to follow.[1] As mathematicians tackled various problems that required either very large or very small numbers with complicated decimal work, 30 the abacus did not suffice and manual calculations were too time consuming and prone to errors. A new method had to be devised. In the 17th century, John Napier (Scotland) invented logarithms along with 35 a set of rods called Napier's bones. Mer-

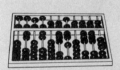

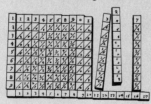

chants would carry a set of rods, made from ivory or wood, to perform their accounting. Without the discovery of logarithms, the slide rule would not have been invented 40 (circa 1620) by Edmound Gunter (England). With the mathematics of logarithms, comprehensive tables were also published so that complex computations involving powers, roots and difficult divi- 45 sion and multiplication became much easier and far less time consuming.

In 1642, at the age of eighteen, French mathematician Blaise Pascal built the first calculator, probably to aid him in the 50 accounting he was doing at his father's office. It could add and subtract, but did not become popular 55 from a commercial point of view since merchants could hire people to do the work for far less than the cost and maintenance of the machine. But it was an important step toward more sophis- 60 ticated devices. In 1673, German mathematician Gottfried Wilhelm von Leibnitz was able to devise a calculator that could also do multiplication and division. These machines were far from perfect, but they 65 were a very important beginning. They were continually improved and expanded, and ultimately evolved to the desk top calculator.

In the meantime, Englishman Charles 70 Babbage became very disenchanted with mathematical errors continually recurring in published timetables and charts, and decided to begin building a machine that could be programmed to process data to 75 preset specifications (circa 1812).

Unfortunately the technology of the time was not refined enough to produce the needed gears and cogs. Nevertheless, his work along with the computer program-80 ming work of Ada Lovelace[2] furnished the foundations for the modern computer.

The next major breakthrough came with population census taking. The 1880 census took 10 years to count manually. 85 By the time it was finished it was about time for the next census. In 1887 the U.S. Census Department announced a contest open to the public to develop a reliable and efficient system for taking the cen- 90 sus. Inventor Herman Hollerith entered a machine that processed information from punched cards using counter wheels and electromagnetic relays. He made the finals, but his machine met with much skepticism. 95 Each of the three finalists was given a trial run to perform. Hollerith's machine did the job in 5.5 hours and the nearest runner up's method took 44 hours. He won the contest and the job of the 1890 census, which his100 machine completed in only one month! Even so, this machine was not capable of storing data and acting on that stored data, as envisioned by Charles Babbage.

The 20th century has been the dawn of105 the modern computer. Within the decades of this century and with the improvement of technology—the use of electricity to power machines, the development and use initially of vacu-   110 um tubes and later the use and discovery of the transistor and the integrated cir-   115 cuit, the development of the LSI

(large-scale integrated) circuit on a silicon chip which made the personal computer feasible in size and price—computing120 devices have advanced enormously.

---

[1]Of course navigation required special types of calculating devices for charting courses by the stars. Here we find the ancient astrolabe and much later the sextant, 1757.

[2]As a tribute to the genius and work of Charles Babbage and Ada Lovelace, IBM built a working model of his Analytical Engine on which he and Lovelace (who furnished technical programming help and monetary support to Babbage) worked.

Source: Theoni Pappas, *More Joy of Mathematics: Exploring Mathematical Insights and Concepts.*

Activity 5-17   Discovering Features of Past Time Narrative

1. Past time narratives, like this one, can be used for historical accounts. This kind of writing often contains many proper nouns (John Napier, Blaise Pascal, Ada Lovelace, Charles Babbage . . .). Highlight the proper names of the people in this article and the pronouns that refer to these people. For additional information, see Section 2D on proper nouns in the GLR (GLR).

2. Past time narratives frequently use many time expressions, chronological organizers, to show when events happened. The most frequently used are dates, such as "in 1642." With a partner, circle at least four time expressions in the article "Early Computing Devices." Refer to Section 2C in the GLR (GLR) for more information on chronological organizers.

Creating Study and Research Summaries

In addition to summaries you write as academic assignments, you can use summaries for your own study and research purposes. Two common ways to do this are with graphic organizers and research note cards.

Graphic Organizer Summary

Creating a graphic organizer (see below) can help you group similar information for easy reference and study. It may also help you prepare to write a summary. First, you need to understand the basic organization of the reading and the types of information given. "Early Computing Devices" is organized chronologically, and contains key information about dates, counting devices, inventors and their countries of origin, and problems that led to a new invention. Knowing this, one can create a chart like the one below.

Activity 5-18   Completing a Graphic Organizer Summary

Organize the information in the reading by filling in the blanks.

When?	What?	Who? Where?	What problems were faced?
earliest	hands	XXX	difficult to use with large numbers
XXX	stacking pebbles method	XXX	a lot of work for a person to group and count
12th century	abacas	China, Greece, Rome	
17th century	logarithms and Napier's bones		
circa 1620	slide rule		
1642		Blaise Pascal (France)	too costly to operate
1673	calculator for multiplication and division		
1812	programmable machine		
1887	elec card	Herman Hollerith (U.S.)	can't store data
20th century	modern computer	xxx	What do you think?

Once it is completed, you can use this type of summary to help you study for tests or prepare written assignments.

<hr>

Activity 5-19   Write a Paragraph Summary

1. Depending on the length of your summary, you will include different amounts of information. Rank the information in your graphic organizer summary from what you think is the most important (1) to what you think is least important (5). Be prepared to explain your choices.

    _____ Date

    _____ Invention

    _____ Name of inventor

    _____ Inventor's country of origin

    _____ Problems that led to a new invention

2. Write a one-paragraph summary of the article, "Early Computing Devices." Compare this summary with those written by other members of your class. Revise your summary.

    Note: You will not write a response to this reading. Generally, responses are written to readings that contain authors' ideas and opinions, but Reading 4, about early computing devices, contains historical facts.

Research Summaries

When you gather information from a variety of sources, you should be summarizing as you work. One way to organize this information is to use index cards (3x5- or 4x6-inch cards).

For example, if you were writing on the methods of census-taking, you could find some information in Reading 4 about how the 1880 census was taken. You could summarize this information on an index card, and later use it in your paper. In addition to the summary itself, it is important to write the source of your information (author, title, publisher, year) so that you may include it later in your paper's bibliography of your sources.

At the top of the card in the activity below, you will see the title "1880 census-taking." By giving your card a title, later you will be able to identify it quickly when you have many different cards with information from a variety of sources.

Activity 5-20   Creating a Summary While Gathering Information

Write a short summary of the information about this census from Reading 4. Instead of putting information that identifies the source in the first sentence of your summary, put it at the bottom of the card.

1880 census-taking

Summary:

Source:

Activity 5-21   Write Your Math Autobiography

At the beginning of some academic courses, professors may give you an assignment to write about your background. This type of assignment varies according to the subject, professor, and course. Sometimes you will be asked to write about prior coursework and experience you have had that is related to the course. Sometimes you will be asked to write about your attitudes, or goals, or provide general information about yourself. This kind of assignment helps the professor understand the background of all the students in the class.

Write your math autobiography. Write at least two connected paragraphs, describing your experience with mathematics. Some possible topics are listed below but you do not have to write about all of these or follow this particular order. You may also choose other areas you are interested in.

Brainstorm first by listing the topics that interest you the most. Below each heading, write your ideas. After you review these areas, decide on the main point or topic sentence for each of your paragraphs.

Possible topics include:

- childhood experiences with math
- reasons for liking or disliking math
- math courses you have taken
- math teachers who influenced you positively or negatively
- the emphasis of math in your high school or college curriculum
- the importance of math to your daily life and your career plans

Notice that some of these choices will require you to write a past time narrative. Review Section 2 in the GLR (GLR) before you begin writing.

Activity 5-22   Summary of a Peer's Paragraphs

1. Read your partner's paragraphs.

2. Write a short summary of his or her work.

3. Show your summary to your partner. Work together to be sure it expresses the main ideas of the paragraphs.

PUTTING IT ALL TOGETHER

FINAL WRITING ASSIGNMENT

Your essay will be a summary and response. First, you will select a reading, then summarize it and write a response.

Plan

1. *Choose what you will summarize.* Some possibilities are:

   a. an article related to mathematics or mathematical literacy

   b. an article about another kind of literacy, such as computer, geographical, cultural, scientific, or media literacy

   c. three to five pages from a textbook in your major

   d. a two- to five-page article in a current news magazine

   e. another source approved by your teacher

Begin to write about the topic you will choose and about your interest in that topic. How will you find a reading about your topic?

2. *Consider your audience and purpose.* Your audience is other students in the class who have not read your article. Your purpose is to summarize the article so that your classmates will be able to understand the main points of the original. Your response should relate clearly to the original.

3. *Gather and organize your ideas.* Find and read your source, following Steps 1, 2, and 3 (preview, read, reread). Then do Step 4 (take notes and organize your ideas.)

Sample Outlines

Introduction: One to three paragraphs of summary.
Body: One to three paragraphs of response.
Conclusion: One paragraph.

Depending on your topic, you may decide to have a longer summary than response or have a short summary followed by a longer response. Your final essay should be at least four paragraphs and at least two double-spaced typed pages.

---

4. *Topic workshop.* First give your partner an oral summary of your reading. Then share your preliminary summary and response notes with your partner.

Questions for peer reviewer:

a. What are the main points that the author will be responding to?

b. What support does the author plan to use in the response?

c. Examine the author's support. Is there enough to support the response? Can you think of another example to add?

Write Your First Draft

As you write, be sure to distinguish between the ideas in the summary and your own ideas and opinions in the response.

Peer Response

1. Courtesy-edit. Before you exchange your paper with your partner, read your own paper carefully to make sure your writing is clear. You want your partner to be able to understand the main ideas of the article you chose to summarize. Does your summary present these main ideas clearly? If some sentences are confusing and need re-wording or additional information, do that now. Make sure spelling, punctuation, and grammar are correct.

2. Exchange your draft with a partner.

    a. Does the summary appear complete? Why or why not?

    b. In the response, is it clear which opinions belong to the author of the original source and which opinions belong to the response writer?

    c. Is the response well supported? Can you think of other support that could be added?

    d. Do you think you would like to read the original article that is being summarized? Explain.

Revise, Edit, and Proofread

1. Read your essay again. Does it say what you want it to say? Use your partner's comments to make improvements.

2. Edit your essay for the following and correct any errors that you find. After you have edited for each of these features, check (✓) the box as a reminder that you have done that task.

    ❏ complete sentences

    ❏ correct punctuation

    ❏ spelling and correct pronoun reference if you used any proper names

    ❏ verb tense choices

    ❏ appropriate transition words and phrases showing logical or chronological relationships

    ❏ reporting verbs

3. Make necessary changes and rewrite your essay.

4. Proofread your summary and response by reading it aloud and listening for errors. Make necessary corrections.

LOOKING AHEAD

Academic Assignments

You do not have to complete the following authentic assignments. However, analyzing them will give you a clearer understanding of the types of assignments you will face in your undergraduate courses.

After you read the following assignments, discuss the questions that follow.

(This assignment calls for writing a summary and response.)

Adult Education

As lifelong learners, one of the most important skills we need is knowing how to find sources of information on adult education that most of us know little about. By using ERIC or the Education Index, find an article on some facet of adult education or lifelong learning that interests you. Read it and write a two- to three-page summary and response to the article.

DISCUSSION

1. Are there any questions you would need to ask the professor before you began this assignment?

2. How could you narrow the topic before you begin your search?

3. What problems might you encounter?

4. How much time would you allow yourself?

5. What factors would influence the time it takes you to complete the assignment?

(For this assignment, a summary is required as one part of a longer class project.)

Urban Water Management

A major part of the class effort will be directed toward a research paper and oral presentation. The goals of the exercise are first, to study a particular topic of interest in enough detail to become an expert, and, second, to convey to the class, in the form of a summary abstract and a brief oral presentation, the most important aspects of the subject you choose.

Due dates

February 10: Submit a one-page proposal for your topic, with objectives and scope of the paper. I will comment on them and return.

March 31: Submit a one-page summary abstract of your paper and oral presentation. Include in the one page any diagram that helps illustrate your topic. These will be collected, copied, and distributed to the class as reference material.

April 7: Oral presentations begin. I will provide a schedule and copies of the summary abstracts. Each oral presentation, including questions, will be five to ten minutes. We will schedule about four per class period. An overhead projector or a slide projector is available by advance arrangement.

April 24: Written papers due. They should be well-presented in a format similar to a journal article submission. This means it should include a clear objective, good presentation of facts, a conclusion, and references. Length should be about five to ten single-spaced pages or equivalent.

DISCUSSION

1. Are there any questions you would need to ask the professor before you began this assignment?

2. How could you narrow the topic before you began your search?

3. What are problems that you might encounter?

4. How much time would you allow yourself?

5. What factors would influence the time it takes you to complete the assignment?

6. How would your oral and written presentations differ?

Chapter 6

Arguing

Issues in Grading

GOALS

WRITING
- express and support an opinion
- understand both sides of an issue
- refute opposing arguments
- learn ways to organize an argu-mentative essay

GRAMMAR
- practice the grammar necessary to state opinions and persuade others

CONTENT
- learn about issues in grading in the American educational system

ACADEMIC FIELD
Education

Sample Authentic College/University Writing Assignments

In your academic courses, you will use the skills you learn in this chapter to complete assignments like these:

Economics

Read and think about the following statement:

> The government has the capability of creating either a shortage or a surplus of any good at any time.

Do you agree or disagree? Convince me.

Political Science

Write a five- to seven-page paper (double-spaced) on whether or not marijuana should be legalized. In your paper, address how legalizing marijuana would affect health and economics. Cite at least three different sources in your argument. Use APA format for citations and reference list.

GETTING READY

Warm-up Writing

In your learner's notebook, write about a time when you persuaded someone to agree with your opinion. Was your argument oral or written? Was it easy or difficult? What strategies did you use to persuade the other person?

An Introduction to Argument

The goal of argument is persuasion. We want others to accept our point of view, and we have good reasons why they should. Sometimes gentle persuasion is enough. We may be able to easily persuade our friend to go to a movie instead of the gym or to go to one restaurant instead of another. Other times, we work harder to convince teachers to extend a deadline for an important project, bosses to give us a day off, or banks to give us a loan.

In all of these situations, we need to give logical reasons. In order to be convinced, these people may ask, "Why should I do that?", "Can you give me some good reasons?", or simply "Why?" Our arguments are not always successful, but we have a stronger chance if we express our opinions clearly, respect opposing viewpoints, and provide strong evidence to support our position.

You have gained many of the skills necessary for argumentative writing in previous chapters of this book. You have practiced forming a clear opinion and providing support and evidence for each essay you have written. What is new in this chapter is learning to anticipate opposing viewpoints (the opinions of people who do not agree with you). Although we have talked before about audience, remember that in argumentative writing, your audience may not agree with your opinion. Your purpose is to persuade this audience that your ideas are valuable.

We will look at four major aspects of argumentative writing:

- forming your opinion
- acknowledging and refuting your opponent's opinion
- supporting your opinion with evidence
- stating your opinions in appropriate language

Forming an Opinion and Expressing It Clearly

You must know exactly what you believe before you can convince others to agree with you. You must be able to state that opinion clearly in the thesis statement of your essay.

EXAMPLES

A clear opinion: Students should receive pass/fail grades in their ESL classes.
A fact: Some students want to receive letter grades in their ESL classes, but other students want pass/fail grades.

The first sentence is an opinion, an idea some people would agree with and others would disagree with. The second sentence is a fact that is not arguable.

To test whether a statement is an arguable point, form a question using *should*. For example, "Should students receive pass/fail grades in their ESL classes?" The answer is "yes" for some people and "no" for others. Therefore, this is an arguable point. Make sure that your question can be answered with both yes and no. If almost everyone would choose the same answer, it is probably not an arguable point.

Activity 6-1   Expressing and Supporting an Opinion

With a partner, choose six of the following categories and express your opinion about each. Write a question using *should*, and then answer it with yes or no. For each question, give three reasons to support your opinion. If you and your partner have the same opinion about a topic, work together on that item. If you have different opinions about a topic, each of you can write a separate opinion and supporting reasons. Notice how the general category—television—is made more specific in the question.

EXAMPLE   TELEVISION

Question: Should adults spend more time watching television?
Answer: Yes, because

Reasons: 1. television has high entertainment value.

          2. watching TV is relaxing.

          3. watching the news on TV is easier than reading a newspaper or news magazine.

1. Cigarettes

    Question: _____

    Answer: _____ because

Reasons: 1. _____

2. _____

3. _____

2. Immigration

Question: _____

Answer: _____because

Reasons: 1. _____

2. _____

3. _____

3. Drug use

Question: _____

Answer: _____because

Reasons: 1. _____

2. _____

3. _____

4. Requiring seat belts and/or air bags in cars

Question: _____

Answer: _____because

Reasons: 1. _____

2. _____

3. _____

5. Censorship on the Internet

Question: _____

Answer: _____because

Reasons: 1. _____

2. _____

3. _____

6. Physician-assisted suicide

Question: _____

Answer: _____because

Reasons: 1. _____

2. _____

3. _____

7. Use of credit cards

Question: _____

Answer: _____because

Reasons: 1. _____

2. _____

3. _____

8. Using disposable items: diapers, razors, tableware, cameras, etc.

Question: _____

Answer: _____because

Reasons: 1. _____

2. _____

3. _____

Activity 6-2   Choosing Your Strongest Reason

1. Share your ideas for Activity 6-1 with another pair of students. On which general categories do you agree? On which do you disagree?

2. For each of the categories you chose, circle the most convincing reason you wrote. Be prepared to explain why you think it is your strongest reason.

LEARNER'S NOTEBOOK

Analyzing Your Answers

What was easy or difficult about Exercise 6-1? Which general categories were the easiest for you? Which were the hardest? Why?

Obstacles to Forming Opinions and Support

You may have had difficulty forming an opinion about some of the items in Activity 6-1. Look again at the ones you didn't choose, which are probably the ones you thought were most difficult. There are several possible reasons why these were difficult for you.

First, you may need more *knowledge* about an issue to form an opinion. In fact, you may never have thought about that issue before! The solution is to do some research to understand the topic better. Once you have this background knowledge, it will be easier to form an opinion and give your reasons to support your opinion.

Lack of *interest* is another possibility. It is natural to be more interested in some issues than others. In many cases, though, the more knowledge you have about a topic, the more interested in it you become. Often you can find some aspect of the topic that will interest you.

Another reason is that your educational, cultural, or family *background* may have given you few opportunities to express and support your opinions. In fact, expressing your opinion may have been considered rude or inappropriate because of your age, gender, or status. It is also possible that the style of argument you are most familiar with is quite different from the one you will be expected to use in your college or university work in the United States. With practice, you will be able to add a new style of argument to the one you already have.

Activity 6-3   Discussion

1. In academic work, students are often expected to form opinions and support them orally and in writing. How might a professor perceive a student who can not meet this expectation?

2. If you are familiar with another culture, what techniques are used in that culture to persuade others?

3. It is important to be able to express your opinions. It is also important to maintain some flexibility in your thinking, to "keep an open mind." Why? When?

4. Look again at the general categories in Activity 6-1. For each item, list people—potential audiences—who would be concerned about that topic. In the example, the people interested in the topic "television" might be parents, educators, advertisers, and TV viewers.

LEARNER'S NOTEBOOK

Discussion Follow-up

Choose one of the first three discussion questions in Exercise 6-3 above. Write your response to the question and your reaction to your classmates' ideas.

Acknowledging and Refuting Opposing Arguments

Not everyone will have the same opinion you do. If they did, there would be no argument! While it is important to state and support your opinions, you must also understand the opposing opinions if you plan to convince your opponents to give up their opinions and accept yours. You *refute* their opinions; in other words, you show that their opinions are not as strong or as valid as yours.

These two sides of an argument are often called *pro* and *con*. The pro arguments are positive; they answer the *should* question with yes. The con arguments are negative; they answer the *should* question with no.

Activity 6-4   Making a Pro/Con List

Issue 1: In the United States, should restaurant customers give wait staff (waiters and waitresses) a 15% tip for ordinary service and a higher tip for exceptional service?

Role play. In a small group, have one person play each of the following roles: waiter or waitress, restaurant owner, and two or more restaurant customers (one with limited funds and one with abundant funds). Assume these roles and discuss the issue, trying to persuade others in your group to accept your arguments.

1. Who had the strongest arguments? Who was the most convincing? Why?

2. Complete the pro/con list below with points brought up in your role play.

Pro Arguments	Con Arguments
a. _Wait staff depend on tips for income._	a. _Restaurants should pay their staff more._
b. _____	b. _____
c. _____	c. _____
d. _____	d. _____

Issue 2: Should cities impose an 11:00 P.M. curfew for people under 18 years old?

Role play. In a small group, have members take the role of a teenager, a parent(s), a teacher, or police officers. Discuss the issue, trying to convince the others of your viewpoint.

1. Who had the strongest arguments? Who was the most convincing? Why?

2. Complete the pro/con list with points brought up in your role play.

Pro Arguments	Con Arguments
a. _____	a. _____
b. _____	b. _____
c. _____	c. _____
d. _____	d. _____

Issue 3: Choose your own issue and roles to discuss.

Issue: Should _____

_____

Roles: _____

1. Who had the strongest arguments? Who was the most convincing? Why?

2. Complete the pro/con list with points brought up in your role play.

Pro Arguments	Con Arguments
a. _____	a. _____
b. _____	b. _____
c. _____	c. _____
d. _____	d. _____

Analyzing Your Group Work

What did you learn in your group work that will help you become more persuasive?

Audience

The more you know about the people who hold opposing viewpoints, the better. Not all audiences are alike. Some may be uninformed about or unaware of the issue, and may need considerable background information. Other audiences may hold opposing opinions, but, if you present a rational argument, they will be easily convinced. The most difficult audiences are those who are very opposed to your opinions. They may feel so strongly about their opinion that it is unlikely that they will change their minds. They can be called "hostile" audiences.

You need to know about your audience's educational background, age, career, political beliefs, economic status, organizations they belong to, and other opinions they may hold. By learning this information, you can understand your audience's position and better present your argument to this specific group of people.

Activity 6-5   Describing Your Audience

With a partner, use your imagination to describe characteristics of the people (audiences) in Issues 1, 2, or 3 in Activity 6-4. In each case, describe their age, interests, educational background, and economic status. What other information about each person would be helpful to learn in order to persuade them about your opinion?

Supporting Your Opinion with Evidence

As in all writing, you need to support your main ideas with strong evidence. In argumentative writing, this evidence is crucial. Without solid and reliable evidence, you will have difficulty persuading your opposition. There are three main types of evidence that help you support your argument.

Personal Experience

You, or someone you know, may have experience relevant to your topic. When using personal experience, be sure that this experience is generalizable. In other words, make sure there is a good possibility that other people could have this experience or at least understand it. For some arguments, you may use a lot of personal experience as evidence, while for other topics you will rely more on other types of evidence.

Facts and Statistics

Depending on your topic, you may need to present historical or scientific facts, statistics and other numerical data to support your argument. Be sure your facts and statistics are current and from reliable sources. For example, in writing about the current world population, population figures from 1998 would provide better evidence than statistics from 1960.

Quotations and Support from Experts

Your argument can be strengthened by quotations and support from experts. "Experts" may be defined as people who are very knowledgeable about the topic because of their research or their professional or personal experience. For example, if the topic relates to a medical condition, you could get valuable information from medical doctors and researchers, and also from people who have that condition. When using quotations and other support from experts, use proper citing and quoting techniques.

GLR	See Section 5G of the GLR for more information on referencing systems.

Activity 6-6 Developing Supporting Evidence

In a small group, choose at least four of the opinions from the six listed below. Your group can either agree or disagree with the statement. Then brainstorm to develop specific evidence—personal experience, facts, statistics, quotations and support from experts—that you could use to support your opinion.

EXAMPLE

Should people who have gotten three speeding tickets have their driver's licenses taken away?

Sources of evidence:
- personal experience of getting two speeding tickets
- experience of others who have gotten speeding tickets
- number of accidents caused by speeding drivers
- the age group that gets the most speeding tickets
- quotations from police or insurance agents

1. Should college athletes finish an undergraduate degree before they join professional teams?

2. Should the government spend more money for AIDS research?

3. Should mandatory retirement age be set at 60 to allow more young workers to join the labor force?

4. Should new businesses be taxed less in their first two years of operation than established businesses?

5. Should students prove proficiency in a second language before they are allowed to get an associate or undergraduate degree?

6. To relieve prison overcrowding, should criminals who have committed nonviolent crimes be released?

LEARNER'S NOTEBOOK

Activity Follow-up

1. Identify two experts to interview about one of the questions in Activity 6-6. Write a brief description of these experts (occupation, age, interests, etc.) and list five questions you could ask each of them.
2. Identify the most hostile audience for one of the questions in Activity 6-6. Why are they so hostile? How could you attempt to persuade them?

Stating Your Opinions in Appropriate Language

When you state your opinions, you need to consider your audience. You need to use appropriate language and an appropriate strength to your argument so that you convince your audience without alienating them. The language you choose can help you vary the strength of your statements and avoid faulty reasoning.

Your readers will be convinced by logical, rational argument, not by emotional appeals, so you must be careful of faulty reasoning—*logical fallacies*. The following are some of the most common fallacies and should be avoided.

Hasty Generalization

Arriving at an opinion quickly without much evidence.

EXAMPLES

Two of my friends failed that class, so the professor is unfair.

Everyone I talked to thought it was a workable plan, so we should adopt it immediately. (The writer talked to only three people.)

Solution: Get enough evidence to present a convincing argument.

Stereotype

A generalization applied to people or to a particular group of people, often using words like *always, everybody, all, nothing, never, only.* When these are used, or even when they are just implied, readers will find the claim unbelievable because they can probably think of at least one case in which the generalization or stereotype isn't true.

EXAMPLES

[All] College freshmen spend more time partying than studying.

Every adopted child wants to find his or her biological parents.

It is unsafe for [all] people over the age of 70 to drive.

Either/Or

Oversimplifying the argument, so it seems that the choices between the ideas are very limited.

EXAMPLES

Motorists can either wear seatbelts or die on the highways.

You can study hard or flunk out of college.

There is only one thing to do: raise taxes.

Solution: Be sure to consider all rational outcomes before making a concluding statement.

Ad Hominem

Attacking or insulting a person instead of rationally confronting the issues.

EXAMPLE

Bill is totally uneducated and uninformed and should not be allowed to express his opinion.

Solution: Confront the issue rather than the speaker.

Grammar Preview

In this chapter, you will learn to use many of the grammatical structures you have already studied to present a strong argument. You will review and practice grammatical structures to help you control the strength of generalizations in your argument, as well as modals and present tense to vary the strength of your opinions. You will also see how past tense can be used to give examples in an argumentative essay.

FOCUSING

The readings in this chapter are about the issue of grades and grading in the American educational system. In these readings, you will see how the authors form an argumentative opinion, how they address opposing viewpoints, and how they use evidence to support their arguments. Before we begin, develop your own ideas and opinions about grades. These ideas may change or become more developed as you react to the readings.

Activity 6-7   Group Discussion

1. How important do you think your grades are to you? To your friends? To your parents? To college admissions committees? To your academic department? To scholarship committees? To your current or future employer?

2. In addition to grades, what are other "indicators of success"?

3. Are high grades always the result of hard work? Explain.

4. Explain the possible relationship between grades and

   academic stress   self-esteem
   cheating   self-destructive behavior
   choice of major field of study   future success
   future income level   life satisfaction
   standardized test scores
       (like the ACT, SAT, and TOEFL)

5. Complete the following list of the pros and cons of grades.

   Pro Arguments   **Con Arguments**

   a. Grades can help motivate some   a. Students can become more interested in

   students.   grades than in learning.

b. _____   b. _____

   _____   _____

c. _____   c. _____

   _____   _____

d. _____   d. _____

   _____   _____

READING 1   LEARNING AND GRADES (SURVEY)

Answering the questions in this survey will help you think more about the issue of grades. The following reading is part of a questionnaire, LOGO II, designed to show students' attitudes towards learning and grades.

Directions: Please read each of the following statements. Indicate how frequently your behavior coincides with the action described using the following rating scale:

1. Never

2. Seldom

3. Sometimes

4. Often

5. Always

_____   **1.** I do optional reading that my instructors suggest even though I know it won't affect my grade.

_____   **2.** I try to make time for outside reading despite the demands of my coursework.

_____   **3.** I try to get old tests when I think the instructor will use the same questions again.

_____   **4.** I will withdraw from an interesting class rather than risk getting a poor grade.

_____   **5.** I get irritated by students who ask questions that go beyond what we need to know for exams.

_____   **6.** I stay after interesting classes to discuss material with the instructors.

_____   **7.** I discuss interesting material that I've learned in class with my friends or family.

_____ **8.** When looking at a syllabus on the first day of class, I turn to the section on tests and grades first.

_____ **9.** I participate in out-of-class activities even when extra credit is not given.

_____ **10.** I buy books for courses other than those I am actually taking.

_____ **11.** I borrow old term papers or speeches from my friends to meet class requirements.

_____ **12.** I cut classes when confident that lecture material will not be on an exam.

_____ **13.** I try to keep all my old textbooks because I like going back through them after the class is over.

_____ **14.** I try to find out how easy or hard an instructor grades before signing up for a course.

_____ **15.** I'm tempted to cheat on exams when I'm confident I won't get caught.

_____ **16.** I browse in the library even when not working on a specific assignment.

Source: Ohmer Milton, Howard R. Pollio, and James A. Eison, *Making Sense of College Grades: Why the Grading System Does Not Work and What Can Be Done About It* (Jossey-Bass, Inc., Publishers, 1986).

Activity 6-9   Grade-oriented vs. Learning-oriented Responses

Some of the items in the survey above are designed to focus on students who are learning-oriented and some are focused on grade-oriented students. In the margin, put an "L" next to the items that are focused on learning, and a "G" next to items focused on grades. Check your answers with another student. Do you agree?

Activity 6-10   Tally Your Responses

Tally your numbers to see if you are more grade-oriented or learning-oriented. Remember that you do not have to be one or the other. It is possible to be both highly grade-oriented and learning-oriented.

LEARNER'S NOTEBOOK

Analyzing Your Grade- and Learning-Orientation

Summarize the results of your survey. Do you think you are more grade-oriented or more learning-oriented? Are there times when you are more grade-oriented, and times you are more learning-oriented? Explain.

Activity 6-11   Writing Assignment

1. Choose one of the following statements to agree or disagree with. In a short paragraph, start by giving your opinion in the topic sentence. Then give at least two reasons for your opinion and support your reasons with examples and detail.

   a. It is better to get an A in an easy course than to get a B in a more difficult course.

   b. Teachers should give extra credit work for students who want to raise their grades.

   c. Potential employers are often unconcerned about an applicant's college grades.

   d. College transcripts should report + and – grades (for example, A+, A-, B+, B-, C+).

   e. Teachers should fail more students (give more F's).

2. When you are finished with your paragraph, write one paragraph expressing the opposite viewpoint on the same topic. Imagine that you are the opposition and express those opinions as your own. Be sure to give at least two reasons for this opinion and support your reasons with examples and detail.

3. Reread your paragraphs and make necessary corrections to prepare for Activity 6-12.

Activity 6-12   Peer Review

1. Read your partner's paragraphs and answer these questions.

   a. Does the author express a clear opinion?

   b. Does the author give at least two reasons to support this opinion?

    c. How does the author support these reasons? With facts? Personal experience? The ideas of experts?

    d. Which of the two paragraphs is more convincing? Why?

2. Share your answers with your partner. Use this feedback to revise the paragraphs.

READING 2   HOLD YOUR HORSEPOWER (MAGAZINE ARTICLE)

Activity 6-13   Pre-reading Questions

1. What are at least five reasons a student might receive a failing grade in a course?

2. Should high school students have part-time jobs? If so, what should they do with the money they earn?

3. What are some advantages and disadvantages of students having part-time jobs?

4. Notice the title of the reading. *My Turn* is the name of a weekly column in *Newsweek* magazine. The actual title of this *My Turn* column is "Hold Your Horsepower." What do you think this means?

- Preview the reading.
- Read actively. Highlight points of the author's argument. Put a question mark in the margins next to words or ideas you do not understand.
- Review.

MY TURN: HOLD YOUR HORSEPOWER

The pressure on high-school students to keep up the car payments can lead to falling grades.

    Folks in the small Michigan town where I grew up revere the work ethic. Our entire culture lauds those who are willing to work their tails off to get ahead. Though there's nothing wrong with hard work, I suggest that our youngsters may be starting too young—and for all the wrong reasons.

    Increasingly I identify with Sisyphus trying to move that stone. There are more mornings than I would like to admit when many of my students sit with eyes glazed or heads slumped on their desks as I try to nurture a threatening-to-become-extinct interest in school. These are not lazy kids. Many are high-achieving 16- and 17-year-olds who find it tough to reconcile 7:30 a.m. classes with a job that winds down at 10:30 p.m. or later.

    "What's wrong?" I asked a student who once diligently completed his homework assignments. He groggily grunted an answer. "I'm tired. I didn't get home until 11 p.m." Half the class nodded and joined in a discussion about how hard it is to try to balance schoolwork, sports and jobs. Since we end up working most of our adult life, my suggestion to the class was to forgo the job and partake of school—both inter- and extracurricular.

"Then how do I pay for my car?" the sleepy student, now more awake, asked. Click. The car. That's what all these bleary eyes and half-done papers are about. My students have a desperate need to drive their own vehicles proudly into the school parking lot. The car is the teenager's symbolic club membership. I know because I've seen the embarrassed looks on the faces of teens who must answer "No" to the frequently asked "Do you have a car?" National Merit finalists pale in importance beside the student who drives his friends around in a shiny new Ford Probe.

My own son (a senior at the University of Michigan) spent a good part of this high-school years lamenting our "no car in high school" dictate. When he needed to drive, we made sure he could always borrow our car. Our Oldsmobile 88, however, didn't convey the instant high-school popularity of a sporty Nissan or Honda. Our son's only job was to do as well as he could in school. The other work, we told him, would come later. Today I see students working more than the legally permitted number of hours to pay for their cars. I also see once-committed students becoming less dedicated to schoolwork. Their commitment is to their cars and the jobs that will help them make those monthly car payments.

Once cars and jobs enter the picture, it is virtually impossible to get students focused on school. "My parents are letting me get a car," one of my brightest students enthused a few months ago. "They say all I have to do is get a job to make the payments." *All.* I winced, saying nothing because parents' views are sacrosanct for me. I bit my cheeks to keep from saying how wrong I thought they were and how worried I was for her schoolwork. Predictably, during the next few months, her grades and attitude took a plunge.

I say attitude because when students go to work for a car, their positive attitude frequently disappears. Teachers and parents are on the receiving end of curved-lip responses to the suggestion that they should knuckle down and do some schoolwork. A job and car payments are often a disastrous combination.

These kids are selling their one and only chance at adolescence for a car. Adults in their world must help them see what their children's starry eyes cannot: that students will have the rest of their lives to own an automobile and pay expenses.

Some parents, I know, breathe a sigh of relief when their children can finally drive themselves to orthodontist appointments and basketball practice. This trade-off could mean teens' losing touch with family life. Having a car makes it easy for kids to cut loose and take part in activities far from home. Needing that ride from Mom and Dad helps to keep a family connection. Chauffeuring teens another year or two might be a bargain after all.

What a remarkable experience a school day might be if it were the center of teens' lives, instead of that much-resented time that keeps them from their friends and their jobs. Although we may not have meant to, parents may have laid the groundwork for that resentment. By giving kids permission to work, parents are not encouraging them to study. Parents have allowed students to miss classes because of exhaustion from the previous night's work. By providing a hefty down payment on a $12,000 car and stressing the importance of keeping up the payments, they're sending a signal that schoolwork is secondary.

The kids I'm writing about are wonderful. But they are stressed and angry that their day has too few hours for too much work. Sound familiar? It should. It is the same description adults use to identify what's wrong with their lives.

After reading this, my students may want to hang me in effigy. But perhaps some of them are secretly hoping that someone will stop their world and help them get off. They might also concede that it's time to get out of the car and get on mass transit. For students in large metropolitan areas, public transportation is the only way to get around.

Adults should take the reins and let teens off the hook. We must say "no" when we're implored to "Please let me get a job so I can have a car." Peer pressure makes it hard for kids to turn away from the temptation of that shiny four-wheeled popularity magnet. It's up to the grown-ups to let kids stay kids a little longer.

The subject of teens and cars comes up in my home as well as in my classroom. My 15-year old daughter gave me some bone-chilling news yesterday. "The Springers got Suzi her own car!" she announced. "All she has to do is make the payments."

I smiled and went back to correcting the essays that would have been lovely had their authors had some time to put into constructing them. The payment, I told myself after my daughter went grudgingly to begin her homework, may be greater than anyone in the Springer family could possibly imagine.

Source: Lyla Fox, *Newsweek*, March 23, 1996 (Fox teaches at Kalamazoo Central High School, Kalamazoo, Michigan).

Activity 6-14   Post-reading Questions

1. What is the author's main argument? Where did she state it?

2. Do you agree with her argument? Why or why not?

3. Who is her audience? How do you know?

4. Complete the following statements from the author's point of view. In other words, say what you think the author would say.

   a. These students are intelligent, but . . . *they are lazy*

   b. Students should concentrate on . . . *school work*

   c. Students who are making car payments . . *work too hard*

   d. When parents stress the importance of making car payments, . . . *They make their kids go to work*

   e. Family life . . .

   f. Most of my students probably won't like my arguments, but some . . .

   g. Parents should . . .

5. What types of evidence does the author use to support her argument? Does she use personal experience, facts and statistics, or quotations and support from "experts"? Find an example of each type of evidence she uses.

Activity 6-15   Making a Pro/Con List

Issue: High school students should not be making car payments because this pressure prevents students from concentrating on their studies.

Role play. In a small group, have at least one person play each of the following:

- car salesperson
- student making car payments
- student's parents
- the student's employer
- teacher

Assume these roles and discuss the issue, trying to persuade the others in your group to accept your arguments.

1. Who had the strongest arguments? Who was the most convincing? Why?

2. Complete the pro/con list with points brought up in your role play.

Pro Arguments	Con Arguments
a. _____	a. _____
b. _____	b. _____
c. _____	c. _____
d. _____	d. _____

Activity 6-16   Controlling the Strength of Generalizations in Your Argument

1. Review Section 6B in the GLR (GLR) and answer the following questions.

   a. What are generalizations?

   b. Why is it important to control the strength of generalizations?

   c. What are three common ways to control the strength of generalizations?

2. The following sentences are taken from Reading 2. Circle the word(s) in each sentence that control the strength of the generalization. Remember that without these words, the generalization would most likely be too strong to be accurate.

   a. Though there's nothing wrong with hard work, I suggest that our youngsters may be starting too young—and for all the wrong reasons.

   b. Many of my students sit with eyes glazed or heads slumped on their desks . . .

   c. Although we may not have meant to, parents may have laid the groundwork for that resentment.

   d. When students go to work for a car, their positive attitude frequently disappears.

   e. A job and car payments are often a disastrous combination.

   f. This trade-off could mean teens' losing touch with family life.

   g. What a remarkable experience a school day might be if it were the center of teens' lives . . .

   h. But perhaps some of them are secretly hoping that someone will stop their world and help them get off. They might also concede that it's time to get out of the car and get on mass transit.

3. Identify what type of word(s) controlled the strength of the generalizations in items *a* to *h* above. Were they modals? Adverbs of frequency? Quantifiers?

4. Write six generalizations about students and grades, using the ways indicated to control their strength.

   Frequency adverbs

   a. _____

   b. _____

   Quantifiers

   a. _____

   b. _____

   Modals

   a. _____

   b. _____

Activity 6-17   Stating Opinions with Modals and Present Tense

1. The author of Reading 2 gave some strong opinions. One way she expressed them was with the use of modals.

EXAMPLE

Adults in their world *must* help them see what their children's starry eyes cannot: that students *will* have the rest of their lives to own an automobile and pay expenses.

Find two more of the author's opinions expressed with modals in lines 132–135. Describe the strength of these opinions.

2. The author gave even stronger opinions by using the simple present tense. In the following example, she presented an opinion as a fact.

EXAMPLE

For students in large metropolitan areas, public transportation is the only way to get around.

Find two more of the author's opinions expressed using the present tense in lines 102–116 from the reading. Why did she use these strong opinions?

Activity 6-18   Using Past Time Examples

In argumentative writing, specific examples help make the argument stronger. Some of these examples may be in the past tense. After giving such an example, an author often relates this past time example to the present argument. Notice how the writer uses specific examples, often in the past, to strengthen her argument in paragraph 5 of the article.

1. Underline the verbs in this paragraph.

2. Circle the word in that paragraph that signals the end of the past time example and the beginning of the present time example.

3. Why was this example important to her argument?

> **GLR**   Refer to Section 2 for more information on past time narratives.

LEARNER'S NOTEBOOK

Summary Writing

Write a paragraph summarizing this article. Your first sentence should give the author, the title of the article, and the main idea of the article. After you finish your summary paragraph, write a paragraph of response.

READING 3   GRADES IN NON-MAJOR COURSES (STUDENT ESSAY)

In the following essay, Tolleif Onarheim, a student at the University of Wyoming, presents his ideas about another grading controversy regarding pass/fail grades (instead of letter grades like A, B, C) for non-major courses.

Activity 6-19   Pre-reading Questions

1. Have you ever taken a pass/fail or credit/no credit course? What types of courses are sometimes graded this way?

2. Are most students motivated to work hard in a pass/fail course? Why or why not?

GRADES IN NON-MAJOR COURSES

Almost every student here at the University of Wyoming is required to take several courses which have little or no relevance to their field of study. Why is it that these non-major classes are graded, and added to the GPA, as if they were ordinary major classes? I think that a pass/fail grading system would be more just. The students have chosen their major and should consequently prioritize these courses, and not have to worry about grades 5 in irrelevant and often time-consuming courses.

The drawback with pass/fail classes, many will argue, is that the students will simply not work hard enough. This will of course be true in many cases. But so what? The students are responsible individuals who must be allowed to make their own choices. If they want to specialize in their major field, they should have the possibility to do so. However, such spe- 10 cialization requires the student's full attention. In order to do well, most people simply do not have the capacity to put in enough hours in non-major fields. It could be considered patronizing to tell students they must take a certain course, when it is not in their major and they have no interest in it. Still, I think most students would work fairly well in order to learn the subject. The students have, just by attending university and paying the tuition, 15 shown themselves worthy of being treated as responsible young adults.

Another argument for having ordinary grades in non-major classes is to prevent students leaving the university with a degree but a narrow academic width. Society needs people with broad knowledge. However, there is little chance of this happening in my view. At least I don't think the grading system will affect it. There are, of course, some individuals with a 20 very specific aim for their education, who refuse to learn anything else than exactly what they are majoring in. This group of people, who after all are in the minority, would not work for grades above a minimum passing-grade anyway.

The most important reason why non-major classes should only be graded pass/fail is that the university should respect the students' choice of study. When someone chooses a 25 major, the university should do its utmost to accommodate the decision, considering the size of the tuition. As in other commercial services offered in society, students should expect to get value for their money. When the purpose of the education is, for instance, to become an

engineer, it is not fair to require that courses without engineering relevance be taken on an
equal basis as the major courses.   30

Another aspect is the effect on the Grade Point Average (GPA), which is printed on the
transcript. This score is very important because most higher education institutions, and
many potential employers, look at this when evaluating an application. A student, who may
have done excellently in his or her major courses, may have the GPA lowered by non-rele-
vant grades.   35

Another argument for a pass/fail system is the fact that society has changed over the
years. What may have been a desirable goal for academics many years ago, may not be the
same today. Our society has become very complex and people need to perform tasks with a
high degree of specialization. One simply can't learn much about everything if one is to be
good enough in one's major.   40

I conducted a mini survey in a scientific manner among thirteen of the Norwegian students. Most of the Norwegians gave a very clear position on the issue. The people might not
be exactly representative, for the university as a whole, but it gives at least an indication of
the international student's views. As Torstein Molvik said it, "It's a drag. I can't see the use
of it. It should not be necessary to go so in-depth to get good grades. The courses in Political 45
Science and English, which are my non-majors this semester, are skills I'll develop while
living in the U.S."

Table 1 gives the result of the inquiry. It was conducted on the 4th and 5th of November
during an international student organization meeting here in Laramie. As the numbers show,
there was a strong agreement with the pass/fail grading system. A noteworthy detail is that 50
most would not object to an increase in the requirements to pass in such a grading system.

Question	Yes	No
Are you in favor of a pass/fail grading system in non-major courses?	13	0
Would you work less if you were given a pass/fail grade in a non-major course?	4	9
In such a system, should a passing grade be equal to a D?	4	9
Equal to a C?	7	6
Equal to a B?	2	11

Table 1

A compromise, which I think most people could accept, is to have a passing require-   60
ment somewhere between a C and B. This would ensure that some effort would have to be
put into the class in order to pass. It would not distract the students too much from the more
important major courses.

In addition, students who wanted ordinary grading could perhaps receive them on a voluntary basis, if they applied before the course began. This should then only be done in cases 65
where the course would be of some special interest to the student in his or her future plans.

By Tolleif Onarheim, Jr.

Activity 6-20   Post-reading Questions

grade   *Yes, because it all the same,*

1. What is the author's main argument in this reading? Do you agree or disagree with this position? Why?

2. What types of evidence did he use to support his argument?

3. Are you persuaded by this essay? Do you believe in and respect the ideas of the author? Why?

4. Onarheim quoted another student, Torstein Molvik, as an authority on the subject of grades and majors. However, he did not give us any information about that student's credentials as an expert. What could he have added to make Molvik's opinion even more believable?

5. Outline Onarheim's essay by writing the following:

   A. Thesis statement _____

   B. Con arguments and Refutation

      1. _____

      2. _____

   C. Pro arguments

      1. _____

      2. _____

      3. _____

   D. Survey results _____

   E. Conclusion (What is his recommendation?) _____

6. Circle at least five cohesion devices Onarheim used to connect sentences and paragraphs. Start by looking at his topic sentences. What paragraph hooks does he use?

Argumentative Essay Organization

There are several ways to organize an argumentative essay, but two common types of organization will serve you well for many different topics, purposes, and audiences. First, decide what your main points and the main points of your opposition will be. A pro/con chart, such as you made earlier in this chapter, will help you see what material you have to organize.

Plan 1 works best for arguments that have one or two major counterarguments. Writers refute the opposition early in the essay and then spend most of their time presenting their pro arguments strongly. By the time the readers reach the conclusion, they are convinced by the strength of the pro arguments and their evidence.

Pro	Con
X will be safer	X costs more
X will be more efficient	
X will be easier	

PLAN 1

Introduction	Like most academic essays, start with an introduction and end with a conclusion. The introduction and conclusion together will be about 10% of your essay.
Background Paragraph (optional)	For some topics, you may have a background paragraph following the introduction. This paragraph is often necessary for a complicated topic.
Con Arguments and Refutation	Give the con arguments and refutation before your pro arguments. This will only be about 20% of your essay.
Pro Argument 1	The majority of your essay (about 70%) is devoted to your pro arguments. In your first pro argument paragraph, put your strongest pro argument.
Pro Argument 2	You will probably have three or four pro argument paragraphs.
Pro Argument 3	
Pro Argument 4 (optional)	
Conclusion	Your conclusion will summarize, recommend, predict, and/or offer a solution.

The next organizational plan, Plan 2, works well if your pro/con lists are nearly equal, or if you have opposing and parallel arguments, as in the lists below.

Pro	**Con**
X costs less	X costs more
X will be helpful	X will be harmful
X will be more efficient	X will be less efficient
X will be easier	X will be harder

PLAN 2

Introduction	See Plan 1.
Background Paragraph (optional)	See Plan 1.
Con Argument 1 with Pro Argument Refutation	Your essay will be about 70% pro arguments and only 20% con arguments and refutation. However, both kinds of argument will be in each paragraph, instead of separated into different paragraphs as in Plan 1.
Con Argument 2 with Pro Argument Refutation	Begin each body paragraph with a counter-argument, and then follow that argument with a transition and your topic sentence (e.g., "However, . . .").
Con Argument 3 with Pro Argument Refutation	Continue each body paragraph with pro-arguments and evidence that • refutes the con argument • proves the pro argument in that paragraph
Con Argument 4 with Pro Argument Refutation (optional)	You will probably have three or four body paragraphs.
Conclusion	Your conclusion will summarize, recommend, predict, and/or offer a solution.

PUTTING IT ALL TOGETHER

FINAL WRITING ASSIGNMENT

Write an argumentative essay on one issue concerning grading, another issue in education, or an issue approved by your teacher.

Plan

1. *Choose your topic.* Choose your own topic or select a topic such as:

   a. grade inflation

   b. overimportance of grades

   c. emphasis on grades leads to cheating

   d. pass/fail grades instead of letter grades

   e. incentive programs for better grades (students receive prizes or money for good grades)

   f. grades and college athletes

2. *Consider your audience and purpose.* Your audience for this essay is someone who does not agree with your opinion. You must select and describe this audience. Your purpose in this essay is to persuade your audience that your ideas are valuable.

3. *Gather and organize your ideas.* For this essay, you will conduct either an interview with an authority or a survey with a group of students. You will also use one or two secondary sources (books, newspapers, magazine articles, or the Internet). You may use one article from this chapter as a source. Your essay will be about three to four double-spaced typewritten pages. In addition, you will have a title page and a reference page. You may also include a page with your interview questions or your survey.

   a. Choose your topic and begin to collect ideas and sources for your essay.

   b. Select and describe your audience. Be specific about approximate age, education and interests, and reasons for your audience's negative attitude about your opinion.

4. *Topic workshop.* With a small group of classmates, share your selected topic. Ask your group to help you make your pro/con list for your argument, and help your group members with their pro/con lists. Make a list of any questions you might have about the assignment to ask your teacher.

Write Your First Draft

Write your arguments as clearly as possible, but remember that you will be able to revise this first draft to make your ideas more persuasive.

Peer Response

1. Courtesy-edit. Before you exchange your paper with your partner, read your own paper carefully and correct problems in meaning, spelling, and grammar that might confuse your reader. This will make your paper more readable and also make the peer response easier and more beneficial.

2. Exchange your draft with your partner and respond to these questions.

   a. What is the thesis statement? Underline it.

   b. Which organizational plan did the author use?

   c. Are there any logical fallacies? If so, how could the reasoning be improved?

   d. What evidence did the author use to support the argument? What other evidence could be added to make a more convincing argument?

   e. As a hostile reader, were you persuaded by your partner's essay? Why or why not? Did the author acknowledge counterargument(s)?

Revise and Edit

1. Read your paper again. How will you use your partner's comments to help you make improvements? Make any changes needed to improve your argumentative essay.

2. Edit your paper for the following, and correct any errors that you find. After you have edited for each of these features, check (✓) the box as a reminder that you have done that task.

   ☐ verb tense choices

   ☐ subject-verb agreement

   ☐ appropriate transition words and phrases to show logical or chronological relationships

   ☐ appropriate language for strength and tone (adverbs of frequency, modals, quantifiers)

   ☐ proper quotation and citation forms

3. Make necessary changes and rewrite your essay.

Peer Response

1. Exchange revised drafts with a partner. Read just the introduction of your partner's essay draft. Does it introduce the topic adequately? Does it give some background information about the topic? Does it state the thesis of the essay?

2. From the introduction, what do you expect the essay to be about? How do you expect it to be organized?

3. Is there a background paragraph in the essay immediately following the introduction? If so, does it provide adequate information for the audience about the topic? What additional questions do you have?

4. If there is not a background paragraph, should there be one? What questions might the author answer for the audience?

5. Read the conclusion of your partner's essay draft. Does it fulfill the expectations you had from the introduction? Why or why not? Use specific detail from your partner's essay draft to support your ideas.

6. Discuss one suggestion to improve that essay with your partner.

Revise, Edit, and Proofread

Make any final changes to your essay before you turn it in to your teacher.

LEARNER'S NOTEBOOK

Problem and Solution

Analyze one problem you encountered as you drafted this essay. Then describe the solutions you used to solve that problem.

Peer Review Memos

Author Memo. At the end of your essay, list the revisions you made after the peer response workshop in class. How did your classmate(s) help you improve your essay?

Reader Memo. Read your classmate's essay and the author's memo at the end of the essay. Then write a memo describing why a hostile audience might be persuaded by the essay. Give specific examples from your classmate's essay to support your ideas.

Academic Assignment

LOOKING AHEAD

You do not have to write the following research paper. However, analyzing this assignment will give you a clearer understanding of some types of assignments you will face in your undergraduate courses.

Read the following assignment and discuss the questions that follow.

Political Science

Research Paper: Education in the United States: What Is Wrong with the System?

For years the United States led the world in education. In recent decades, the U.S. has fallen behind other industrialized nations in educating its youth. There is general agreement that there are many problems with our educational system. However, the solutions to these problems are controversial. Educational reform theories present two different solutions:

- Should the United States try older ideas such as going "back to the basics"?
- Should the country adopt a system like another country's?

In this paper, you will research these solutions, argue for one of the solutions (or develop a completely new solution) and then give your recommendations about how your solution will work.

Organization

1. Background must be given in order to evaluate the current situation. When do you think the U.S. lost its edge? Could this have been preventable? (Hindsight is always better than trying to look into the future. Be reflective and think!) 30 points.
2. Research the educational reform theories. Would these theories work in real schools, or, if already tried, did they work (in part or as a whole)? 60 points.
3. Compare our educational system with the educational system of one other country. What are the similarities and differences? 35 points.
4. After researching the reform theories and looking at the educational system of another country, decide which of the two solutions is the best. Or, if you think that neither will work, come up with a totally new idea. (Personal arguments are strongly encouraged.) 35 points.
5. Finally, write your conclusion. Include your opinions and your recommendations. 30 points.

References

1. You are required to use *at least* two periodicals in your paper.
2. You are required to use three additional references. On reserve at the library are books that can help you do research for this paper.
3. Use MLA format.

Grading

1. Points will be deducted for grammar and spelling errors and improper citations.
2. Points will be deducted for not following the outline given above.
3. Points will be added for good evidence and persuasiveness.

DISCUSSION

1. What is the purpose of this assignment?

2. What is not clear about this assignment? Make a list of what you will need to know in order to complete the assignment successfully.

3. How might you ask the professor about this assignment? Write three questions you might ask the professor.

4. Who is the audience for this assignment?

5. With a partner or a small group of classmates, discuss the educational system in another country that you are familiar with. How does it differ from the U.S. secondary school system? Make a list of similarities and differences.

6. With a small group of classmates, discuss the issue(s) in this assignment. Make a pro/con list for each one of the solutions given in the assignment. Which solution would you and your group choose? Why?

Synthesizing

Consumer Decision-Making

GOALS

WRITING
◆ practice answering test questions
◆ review each chapter focus:
  instructing, explaining, evaluating,
  summarizing and responding, and
  arguing

GRAMMAR
◆ use the grammar learned throughout this text in answering test
  questions

CONTENT
◆ learn about consumer decision-
  making and consumer lifestyles

ACADEMIC FIELDS
Business
Marketing

Sample Authentic College/University Writing Assignments

In your academic courses, you will use the skills you learn in this chapter to complete essay test questions, which require at least a paragraph answer. You often write these answers under time pressure.

Anthropology

Explain how cultural boundaries, relative values, and the view of cultures as organic wholes serve as obstacles to cultural change.

History of English

What effects will electronic communication have on written English? Will these effects be greater than those resulting from the invention of the printing press? Argue your position.

Politcal Science

Summarize the progression of the presidential nominating process from the early days of the United States up to today's reformed nominating system. Be sure to include differences and the merits of each system. The three main areas you should include are Congressional Caucus System, Brokered Convention System, and the reform era after 1968.

 CNN video support is available for this chapter.

GETTING READY

Warm-up Writing

There are many different types of test questions: multiple choice, true/false, identification, short-answer, and essay questions. Choose one of these types of test questions, perhaps the one you feel most comfortable and successful in answering, and describe the best ways to prepare for and succeed in answering this type of question.

Synthesizing Information to Answer Test Questions

A Review of Synthesizing

Throughout your education and this textbook, you have synthesized information. In other words, you have selected information from several sources and combined it with your own ideas. You have gathered information from personal experience, reading, and interaction with others. This has included:

- your prior knowledge and experience
- textbook reading
- sources in the library and on the WWW
- interviews with others
- informal discussions
- classroom lectures

After gathering your information, you have selected what is best for your purposes and used it to support your ideas in your written assignments. In other words, you have gathered and used information that supported your main ideas, thesis statement, or topic sentences.

For most written assignments, this writing process lasts several days or even weeks. You will have time to think about your ideas, find good supporting materials, talk to others about your topic and your writing, think, write, and revise. You may have access to a computer, dictionaries, and advice and feedback from others.

Synthesizing in Written Tests

For an in-class written test, you have a limited amount of time (perhaps as little as an hour) to write. You use the information that you have synthesized from your class notes, textbook reading, additional course readings, class discussions and lectures. However, for most tests, you cannot consult these sources during the test—this information must all be in your head.

You will be asked to do different things. For some test answers, you will be asked to *restate* information. This may include definitions, facts, and formulas. You do not add your own ideas; you restate them as they were in your text or notes. Other questions will ask you to use the information you've learned—to *analyze information* or to *apply the information* to a particular situation. In studying and synthesizing information for tests, you do more than simply memorize information. It is important to understand connections and relationships, since many questions ask you to use what you know in new ways.

To be successful with these different types of questions, you must know the material well before the test and work efficiently during the test. You must understand what is expected of you from the question, what to include in your answer, and how to organize that information. Then you must write carefully because you most likely will not have time to revise or rewrite your answers although you should take a few minutes to check and proofread your work.

To write effective essay test answers, first you must thoroughly know and be able to use the material that you will be tested on. In addition, you must:

- understand the question (what is expected of you)
- write clear, well-organized, and concise answers
- work under time pressure

LEARNER'S NOTEBOOK

Difficult Test

Describe the most difficult test you have ever taken. Why was it difficult? What kinds of questions did it include? Did the questions ask you to restate information or analyze or apply the information? If you were going to take the test again, how would you study differently?

Understanding Test Questions

On a written test, you need to be able to identify and understand the focus words in the questions, such as *argue, contrast, describe,* and *explain,* which help guide your answer. Other valuable clues about the organization or grammatical structures can sometimes be gained from the question.

SAMPLE TEST QUESTION

Explain how the development of agriculture changed the way humans lived.

In this question, the focus words are *explain how.* The expected answer would be to describe or explain how X (agriculture) changed Y (the way humans lived). Other clues that you could gain from the question are that your answer would probably be written in the past tense, and could follow a chronological order.

Question Words

The most common question words are *who, what, where, when, how,* and *why.* These words frequently appear in test questions. Often *who, where,* and *when* ask for a specific piece of information, such as a name, a place, or a date, so these are more frequently used in short-answer questions. The words *what, how,* and *why* are more frequently used for questions that demand a more complex answer.

Question	Type of Answer
What	definition, description, or explanation
How	explanation of a process or procedure
Why	analysis, cause, or effect

In addition to these words, the following list contains commonly used focus words that guide you in responding to test questions. You will recognize several of these from the chapters in this text: Instructing, Explaining, Evaluating, Summarizing and Responding, and Arguing.

FOCUS WORDS IN TEST QUESTIONS

Analyze	Divide something into its parts, evaluate these parts, and explain them
Argue	Present the reasons for one side of a position
Comment	Give your own opinion
Compare	Look at the qualities or characteristics of things and show their similarities and differences
Contrast	Point out the differences
Define	Give the meaning of a term
Describe	Tell in detail the characteristics or qualities of something or some event
Discuss	Present the various sides of a argument and its key questions
Explain	Tell how or why
Evaluate	Give a judgment based on accepted criteria, looking at both positive and negative points
Prove	Show that something is true based on facts
Respond	Give your opinion or reaction
Summarize	Tell briefly, covering all the key points but omitting details and examples

Activity 7-1   Analyzing Academic Assignments

Look again at the examples of test questions in the academic assignments at the beginning of this chapter on page 185.

1. Circle the focus words that will help guide your answer.

2. In a small group or as a class, discuss the clues that you get from each question that would help you in your answer.

   a. How will the question words guide your answer?

   b. What is the possible organization for your answer?

   c. Are there any other clues that tell you something about the grammar to use in your answer?

3. For additional practice, analyze the academic assignments at the beginning of several chapters in this text.

Activity 7-2   Predicting Test Questions

In this activity, you will write a summary and response. Before you begin, return to Chapter 5 to review the six-step process for summary writing and the information about writing a response.

1. Write a short summary paragraph of Reading 3—"How to Predict Test Questions," in Chapter 2 on page 39. Remember to give identifying information in your first sentence.

2. Write a paragraph of response to this article. Do you agree with this advice? Which advice is most helpful? Do you disagree with some of the advice? Can you give any other helpful advice?

Grammar Preview

In this final chapter, you will review major features of the grammar of academic writing covered throughout the textbook. As you learn more about how to answer test questions, you will have opportunities to practice sentence types, verb tenses, logical and chronological organizers for cohesion, definitions of terminology, and analysis of academic vocabulary.

FOCUSING

The readings in this section are taken from introductory marketing textbooks. They present information about consumers, the decisions they make, and their lifestyles. Marketers can use this information to advertise their goods to consumers in the most appealing ways.

These readings will be the basis for practice with test questions, so it is important to read each selection carefully. At the end of each reading, you will find exercises and a variety of short writing assignments that prepare you to understand the vocabulary and organization of textbook readings and prepare you to take written tests.

READING 1   CONSUMER DECISION-MAKING (MARKETING TEXTBOOK)

In the first reading, you will learn about the five steps consumers take in deciding what they will buy.

Activity 7-3   Pre-reading Questions

1. Consider the criteria people use to evaluate their purchase and the time it takes to buy the following items:

    a. a candy bar

    b. a pair of jeans

    c. a piece of sports equipment

2. When are people most likely to research a purchase before they buy it?

3. Have you ever bought something that you were later not happy with? Explain why.

    Directions for Reading

    - Preview. Look carefully at the chart and the headings.

    - Read actively. As you read, circle vocabulary terms that are defined in the reading.

    - Review.

CONSUMER DECISION-MAKING

Figure 7.1 shows an outline of the major steps buyers go through in the purchase process. This process has been termed by some as the consumer's "black box." That is, it represents the invisible activity that goes on in the consumer's mind as he or she makes a buying decision. The process is a series of responses to various internal and external stimuli. Some of these stimuli are initiated by marketers, such as advertising or a call by a salesperson; some   5 have other sources. Some marketer-dominated stimuli are successful in moving the consumer toward the marketer's product and some stimuli may actually accomplish the opposite effect.

Figure 7.1 The Process for Making Buying Decisions

While a variety of titles exist for each stage in the process, a representative list would include:

(1) Need recognized.   10
(2) Information search accomplished.
(3) Alternatives compared.
(4) Decision made and implemented.
(5) Satisfaction/dissatisfaction realized.

Need Recognized   15

A consumer recognizes a need (or want) when something that he or she requires is found lacking. Some marketers call this "problem recognition." Events or conditions that stimulate need arousal vary. You may experience hunger pangs during your noon marketing class and realize that you need to purchase some lunch. Or you may visit with a fellow student and find out that his computer has graphics capabilities and hard-drive capacity far   20 superior to your old 1982 model. Another possibility is that you read an article in *Consumer Reports* that explains several new features available in the latest cameras.

Finally, you may be influenced by marketer-dominated sources. Suppose you read an advertisement about a line of shampoo and conditioner products that help preserve the "permanent" curl for which you paid a beautician dearly. Or your favorite sporting goods store   25 is running a sale on ski boots.

In each of these cases, the discrepancy between what you have and what you need or want may lead you to begin the decision-making process that results in a purchase. In some cases, the need arises naturally from physiological conditions; in other cases, the influences come from sources external to you. As you can see from the above examples, sometimes a   30 need is triggered by simply finding out that a product is available that offers "better" features than the product you already have.

Information Search Accomplished

Information search can be internal or external. Internal search relies on the buyer's memory and prior experiences for matching problems with possible solutions. If you want   35 lunch, you may think about various restaurants and pick one that you have enjoyed in the past. You may have also learned which ones to avoid through past experience.

Another possibility is to rely on external information by asking one of your friends to recommend a good restaurant. For a special occasion, you might even go so far as to read restaurant reviews in the local paper.   40

External sources for different product categories include friends and family; marketer-dominated sources, such as advertising, brochures, packaging, or salespersons; and unbiased sources, such as *Consumer Reports*. The extent of your search will depend on such factors as the importance of the decision to you, the amount of risk involved, how familiar you already are with the product category and the alternative brands, how many different information   45 sources are available to you, and how much time you want to spend making the decision.

Alternatives Compared

The number of brands that a consumer actually considers in making a purchase decision is called the *evoked set.* Some brands, while known, are not deemed worthy of consideration; other brands may be unknown to the consumer. Certainly marketers' objectives include 50 getting their brands into the consumer's evoked set.

Evaluative criteria refer to those features that the buyer uses to make a choice between brands. These include perceived quality, price, size, convenience, durability, color, and reputation (company and brand).

Evaluative criteria vary from one market segment to another; in fact, this variation may 55 be the basis for benefit segmentation. For example, one group may want automobiles that are moderately priced, offer good gas mileage, and retain their resale value better than other models. Another group's criteria may include leather seats, climate control, sporty design, and interior leg room. Of one thing we can be certain: Consumers will pay special attention to those features and benefits that satisfy their particular needs. 60

However, alternatives are also evaluated using criteria that are suggested by marketers in their advertisements. Choice of an airline might be influenced by pointing out safety record, on-time arrivals, or baggage security. Thus marketers' objectives should encompass both achieving enough visibility to get into the evoked set and influencing which criteria that consumers use to evaluate brands. 65

Decision Made and Implemented

Once consumers have identified unmet needs, searched for information, and used that information to evaluate various brands, they are ready to make a purchase decision. At this point, buyers have formed intentions but have not yet carried out those intentions.

As suggested earlier, consumers' search and evaluation processes may lead them to 70 postpone or cancel the purchase. Perhaps no satisfying brands are offered anywhere on the market; perhaps none of the local retailers carry the preferred brands. Sometimes customers decide that they have other priorities for their limited financial resources, and sometimes interpersonal influences, such as friends or family, dissuade buyers from making an intended purchase. 75

Often consumers will purchase a second-choice brand if their first choice is unavailable. Occasionally customers will choose an alternative brand because they do not want to shop where their preferred brand is carried. The point is that a variety of influences may thwart the ultimate purchase, even if a prospective customer has the intention of buying a given brand. It is at this stage that accessory attributes may be most important in capturing the 80 sale: such attributes as warranties, maintenance, delivery terms, and installation.

Satisfaction/Dissatisfaction Realized

After the purchase is completed, the customer's post-purchase evaluation begins. How a consumer evaluates the satisfaction (or dissatisfaction) of a particular purchase will determine whether the next buying cycle will result in the same brand choice. 85

A common aspect of the post-purchase stage is the *cognitive dissonance* that many buyers experience. Cognitive dissonance means that the buyer is not entirely satisfied with the purchase, and discomfort results. Perhaps the chosen brand did not perform as the customer was led to believe it would. Perhaps after making the purchase the customer found the brand at a much lower price elsewhere.   90

These are common examples of post-purchase dissonance, but sometimes feelings are more complex. Even a buyer who would make the same decision again may regret the loss of some attributes that were associated with another brand. Cognitive dissonance results when buyers conduct an extensive search and in the end experience both positive and negative feelings toward any given choice. Once a choice is made, the rejected alternatives as 95 well as the negative consequences of the brand selected must be rationalized.

A buyer who has to purchase a new car as a result of a car accident, for example, may regret the use of her funds even though she knew she had to replace the wrecked car. Another buyer may feel guilty for spending so much money; and another may lose satisfaction when friends fail to admire the new product as much as the buyer had anticipated.   100

Marketers should take these opportunities to solidify and strengthen buyer satisfaction with their brands. By providing additional information and encouragement during this phase, marketers enable buyers to work out their dissonance in positive ways.

Source: Marjorie J. Cooper and Charles Madden, *Introduction to Marketing*
(New York: HarperCollins Publishers, Inc., 1993, 47–50).

Activity 7-4:   Post-reading Questions

1. What three methods did the authors use to help the reader understand the organization of this reading? How are these helpful in reviewing the reading?
   compare, implemented, evaluated

2. Without looking at the reading, try to write down the five steps in the process of making buying decisions. Then explain this process to a partner orally, referring to the reading if necessary.

3. The authors used a wide variety of examples in this reading. Give three examples. How did the authors signal these examples?
   chronological order, italic, subheading

4. Did the authors make these examples relevant to college students, the intended audience for this introductory textbook? Give specific examples.

Activity 7-5   Predicting Test Questions

With a partner, discuss possible test questions that could come from this reading. You can refer to the list of Focus Words for Test Questions on page 189 to help develop your questions. Write your three best questions. Discuss their answers.

1. _____

2. _____

3. _____

Activity 7-6   Understanding Vocabulary for Test Questions and Answers

Reading 1 introduced and explained many new vocabulary words, a common feature of introductory textbooks. This new terminology may appear in test questions, and you may need to include it in your answers. Some textbooks use a specific typeface to indicate these key terms. For example, some use **bold** type, while others may use *italics*. Many textbooks also contain a glossary of key terms at the back of the book.

Analyze how the author explained the new terminology in Reading 1 listed below.

1. Number each paragraph in Reading 1.

2. Work with a partner to write a definition and an example for each of these terms. Look for clues within the paragraph for the definition. Try to write your own examples.

Paragraph 1   internal stimuli
Definition   _inside want to de st._
                   _____
Example   _____
                   _____

Paragraph 1   external stimuli
Definition   _outside want to do St._
                   _____
Example   _I_____
                   _____

Paragraph 1   marketer
Definition   _person who looks at market._
                   _____
Example   _____
                   _____

Paragraph 3   "problem recognition"
Definition   _recognize problem_

Example

Paragraph 6   internal information
Definition   _inside infor_

Example   _feeling_

Paragraphs 7–8   external information
Definition   _outside info_

Example

Paragraph 9   evoked set
Definition

Example

Paragraph 10   evaluative criteria
Definition   _judgement on standard_

Example   _news paper._

Paragraph 12   intentions
Definition

Example

Paragraph 15 post-purchase evaluation
Definition _judgement use after purchase._

Example _____

Paragraph 16 cognitive dissonance
Definition _____

Example _____

Activity 7-7   The Grammar of Definitions

In Activity 7-6, you saw several different ways that terminology can be presented and learned that not every definition follows the basic pattern of X = Y. Understanding different ways that words are used and defined is important to test-taking. The material in this section will also help you to recognize definitions and to write definitions on tests.

Before you begin this activity, review the information in the GLR GLR , Section 4, "Writing Definitions."

1. Circle the word being defined in each definition below. Underline the definition.

   a. Figure 7.1 shows an outline of the major steps buyers go through in the purchase process. This process has been termed by some as the consumer's "black box." That is, it represents the invisible activity that goes on in the consumer's mind as he or she makes a buying decision.

   b. A consumer recognizes a need (or want) when something that he or she requires is found lacking. Some marketers call this "problem recognition."

   c. The number of brands that a consumer actually considers in making a purchase decision is called the _evoked set._

   d. _Evaluative criteria_ refer to those features that the buyer uses to make a choice between brands.

   e. Cognitive dissonance means that the buyer is not entirely satisfied with the purchase, and discomfort results.

2. Which definitions are the most direct? Explain.

3. What patterns, if any, do you see in these definitions?

4. What strategies would you use to learn these definitions so that you are able to use them on a test? What strategies would you use if you knew you would only have to restate the definition? How would they differ if you knew you would have to use analysis or application of this material?

Activity 7-8   Cohesion Devices

In the reading, "Consumer Decision-Making," the audience was being introduced to this material. Therefore, it was important for the authors to be clear and logical in how they present the new material. To do this, they used many words and phrases to help connect one idea to the next. These cohesion devices will also help you to logically connect and organize your ideas in your test answers.

1. Look at the section under the heading "Needs Recognized." Highlight or underline the following words and phrases:

    a. *Or, Another possibility, Finally*

    b. *In each of these cases, In some cases, In other cases,*

    c. *As you can see from the above examples,*

2. What is the purpose of each of these groups of words in this section?

3. In a small group, select another one of the five main sections of Reading 1. What words or phrases help connect the ideas in the paragraph? Highlight these words and phrases. Explain their purpose.

Activity 7-9   Discussing Test Questions

1. The following test questions relate to the chapters and writing purposes we have studied in this textbook. With a partner, try to answer them orally. Refer to Reading 1 in this chapter if necessary.

Instructing	Give *advice* to consumers about how to do a thorough external information search for a major purchase.
Explaining	*Explain* cognitive dissonance. What is it? When is it felt?
Evaluating	*Evaluate* the decision-making process to buy a pen and a new car in terms of information search and comparison of alternatives.
Summarizing	*Summarize* the five-step consumer decision-making process that is presented in Reading 1.
Responding	Do you *agree* with the thesis of this article? Do you think most people go through this process?
Arguing	The most important stage for advertisers and marketers is clearly the first one—Need Recognized. Do you agree or disagree? *Support* your argument.

2. Which of these questions asks you to restate information from the reading? Which questions ask to analyze or apply the information from the reading?

Beginning Your Answer Directly

When you write an introduction to an essay or a longer piece of writing, your introduction can start with general statements that grow gradually more specific into your thesis statement. However, in a timed test question answer, you do not have time to gradually lead to your main point. Your professor expects that you will begin directly with your main point/topic sentence/thesis statement.

By taking words and ideas from the question, your answer will begin directly. As the example below shows, many times you can restate the ideas in the question in your first sentence.

EXAMPLE

Test Question: Describe the process that goes on in a consumer's mind after a purchase is made.

Your first sentence can begin: After a purchase is made, a consumer . . .

Activity 7-10   Answering Test Questions

1. What would your first sentence be for the questions in Activity 7-9? Write these sentences.

2. Answer two of the test questions given in Activity 7-9. Write a one-paragraph answer for each. Use your first sentences from number 1 above.

3. Analyze your paragraphs.

_____ Did you begin directly?

_____ Are your answers clear, logical, and cohesive?

_____ Did you proofread and correct any grammatical errors?

4. With a partner or in a small group, compare your answers. Tell which paragraph you think is your best answer and explain why. Get feedback from your peers.

READING 2   SELECTED CONSUMER LIFESTYLES (MARKETING TEXTBOOK)

The following reading, taken from a marketing textbook, describes seven types of consumer lifestyles. Marketers use this kind of information when they are targeting their products to a particular audience.

Activity 7-11   Pre-reading Questions

1. How would you describe your buying habits? Do you make impulsive purchases? Do you purchase only what is absolutely necessary?

2. What kind of research do advertisers do to understand their target markets? What kind of information do they want to know about people?

SELECTED CONSUMER LIFESTYLES

Many distinct consumer lifestyles are expected to continue. Seven of these are discussed here: family values, voluntary simplicity, getting by, "me" generation, blurring of gender roles, poverty of time, and component lifestyle.

In some households, family values have a great impact.

With a *family values* lifestyle, emphasis is placed on marriage, 5 children, and home life. According to "survey after survey, traditional relationships among parents, children, and siblings are identified as more important than work, recreation, friendships, or status. Researchers have been asking about families for over half a century, and the results have always been that family takes priority over 10 everything else in their lives."[1] This lifestyle encourages people to focus on children and their education; family autos, vacations, and entertainment; home-oriented products; and so on.

Yet, as previously noted, the traditional family is becoming less representative of all households—particularly in the United States. 15 Thus, marketers need to be very careful in appealing to those who say they follow a family values lifestyle: "The link between strong family ties and overall happiness indicates that family should be more important than anything else. But, the truth is that many if not most Americans will sacrifice traditional family ties for activities 20 they claim are less important. It is common for Americans to let the pursuit of more individualistic goals interfere with their family life, even when doing so is clearly contrary to their own self interest."[2] Marketers should also keep in mind that a family values lifestyle remains the dominant one in many countries outside the United 25 States. For instance, in Italy, less than one-third of women are in the labor force and the divorce rate is about one-eleventh that of the United States.

Voluntary simplicity is based on ecological awareness and self-reliance.

Voluntary simplicity is a lifestyle in which people have an ecological (environmental) awareness, seek material simplicity and 30 durability, strive for self-reliance, and purchase more inexpensive products. In short, it is a plainer, more basic lifestyle. It grew out of the 1960s and 1970s, when people first became aware that many natural resources were being depleted and continued into the 1980s due to high inflation and unemployment. Today, many people are 35 concerned about the environmental effects of the way they live and the purchases they make; and some are choosing more modest lifestyles.

Consumers with this lifestyle are apt to be cautious, conservative, and thrifty shoppers. They do not buy expensive cars and fur 40 coats, do hold on to major purchases (such as cars and major appliances) for longer periods, are not dazzled by optional product features, and infrequently visit restaurants or go on prepackaged vacations. They like such activities as going to a park or taking a vacation by car, are more concerned with a product's durability than its 45 appearance, and believe in conservation of scarce resources. There is also an attraction to rational appeals and no-frills retailing.

Getting by is a frugal lifestyle that is pursued by people because of their economic circumstances. As with voluntary simplicity, those who are "getting by" seek material simplicity and durability, strive 50 for self-reliance, and purchase inexpensive products. They, too, partake of a plain, basic lifestyle. However, unlike with voluntary simplicity, people who follow a getting by lifestyle do so because they must. In less-developed and developing countries, most people fall into this lifestyle category; a much smaller proportion do in indus- 55 trialized countries (except during recessions and industry consolidations).

People with this lifestyle are generally cautious. They are attracted to well-known brands (because their perceived risk is very low), are not adventuresome in trying new goods and services, rarely 60 go out (but do rent videos), and take few vacations. They also look for bargains, whenever possible, and tend to patronize local stores. Consumers with this lifestyle rarely believe they have any significant discretionary income.

For certain consumers, there remains an interest in a more self- 65 oriented lifestyle, that of the *"me" generation*. This lifestyle stresses being good to oneself. The me-generation concept is popular with some people because of their interest in self-fulfillment and self-expression. It involves less pressure to conform, as well as greater acceptance of diversity. It places less emphasis on obligations, 70 responsibilities, and loyalties.

Consumers with this lifestyle are interested in staying young and taking of care of themselves. They stress nutrition, exercise, weight control, and grooming. Expensive cars and apparel are bought, and full-service stores are patronized. These consumers are more 75

Marginal notes:

When their economic circumstances are tough, people place greater emphasis on getting by.

The "me" generation stresses self-fulfillment.

concerned with a product's appearance than its durability, and some place below-average importance on conservation, especially if it will have a negative effect on their lifestyle.

Blurring gender roles involves men and women undertaking nontraditional duties.

Because a larger number of women are now in the labor force, more men are assuming the once-traditional roles of their wives, and vice versa, thus *blurring gender roles.* For example, 80

> Men are doing more shopping and housework, but only because women are making them change. Women still decide most household purchases, unless they're high-priced items. Women are disillusioned by the "new man," but there's hope for young and affluent men, who are more 85 likely to share household work and value romance. Knowing how men are changing—and how they aren't—is the key to targeting them. Meanwhile, more and more women are learning how to buy cars, program VCRs, and use power tools.[3]

Generally, these are the household tasks men perform most fre- 90 quently: taking out the garbage, washing dishes, cooking, vacuuming, doing the laundry, and cleaning. About 30 percent of all food-shopping dollars are spent by male consumers. These activities are expected to continue during the next decade.

A poverty of time exists when a quest for financial security results in less free time.

For many households, the prevalence of working women, the 95 long distances between home and work, and the large number of people working at second jobs contribute to less, rather than more, free time. The *poverty-of-time* concept states that for some consumers the quest for financial security means less free time because the alternatives competing for time expand. According to a Coca- 100 Cola Retailing Research Council study, a typical U.S. household now has 14 hours per week for true leisure-time activities—compared with 26 hours in 1973.[4] As the prices of housing, medical care, higher education, cars, food, and other items continue to go up in the future, even more households will require two incomes and, perhaps, 105 a second job for the main earner.

Their poverty of time leads these consumers to greater use of time-saving goods and services. Included are convenience foods, quick-oil-change services, microwave ovens, fast-food restaurants, mail-order and telephone retailers, one-hour photo processing, and 110 professional lawn and household care.

With a component lifestyle, consumer attitudes and behavior vary by situation.

Today, more people are turning to a *component lifestyle,* whereby their attitudes and behavior depend on particular situations rather than an overall lifestyle philosophy. With a component lifestyle, consumers may take their children with them on vacations (family 115 values), participate in trash recycling programs (voluntary simplicity), look for sales in order to save money (getting by), enroll in continuing education classes ("me" generation), share such household chores as food shopping (blurring gender roles), and eat out on busy nights (poverty of time).

1. Norval D. Glenn, "What Does Family Mean?" *American Demographics* (June 1992), 30.

2. Ibid., 34.

3. Diane Crispell, "The Brave New World of Men," *American Demographics* (Jan. 1992), 38, 43.

4. *Wetterau Incorporated 1990 Annual Report,* 15.

Source: Joel R. Evans and Barry Berman, *Marketing,* 7th Ed. (Prentice-Hall, Inc., 1997).

Activity 7-12   Post-reading Questions

1. What is the main idea?

2. Who is the audience for this reading? How do you know?

3. How many sources did this author cite? See endnotes. What information is given in each endnote?

4. How would this information help marketers and those developing new products?

5. How is this reading organized? What devices does this marketing textbook use to highlight key ideas?

6. With a partner, write three items that each group would be likely to buy. Explain why you think these items are representative of this consumer lifestyle. Give your answers without referring to the reading.

   a. family values

   b. voluntary simplicity

   c. getting by

   d. "me" generation

   e. blurring gender roles

   f. poverty-of-time

   g. component lifestyle

7. Compare your answers with another group of students. How are your lists similar and different?

Activity 7-13   Predicting Test Questions

With a partner, discuss possible test questions that could come from Reading 2. You can go back to Focus Words for Test Questions on page 189. Write your three best questions and discuss their answers.

Activity 7-14   Supporting Extended Definitions

In Reading 2, extended definitions were given to explain these seven consumer lifestyles. Each began with a one-sentence definition, which served as the topic sentence for the paragraph(s) of definition.

1. Highlight or underline the sentence where each of these lifestyles is defined.

    Example for the first category: With a *family values* lifestyle, emphasis is placed on marriage, children, and home life.

2. What key information about that lifestyle is given in each of the sentences you highlighted or underlined?

3. Now, with a partner, notice how additional information is given in the supporting sentences of each paragraph. Discuss which definition(s) is/are supported with:

    a. a quotation

    b. a research study

    c. historical information

4. In studying for a test, are the definition sentences and supporting sentences in a paragraph equally important?

Activity 7-15   Discussing Answers to Test Questions

1. The following test questions relate to the chapters and writing purposes we have studied in this text. With a partner, discuss:

    a. a possible first sentence for your answer

    b. the answer

    c. possible organization for a written answer

    Instructing   Give *advice* to people in the *poverty of time* lifestyle about three types of products that will help them save time.

    Explaining   *Explain* what a *family values* lifestyle is. What are some difficulties in defining this market?

Evaluating	Which consumer lifestyle(s) do you *consider best* for a) the environment, b) the economy, and c) you?
Summarizing	Briefly *summarize* the lifestyles of *voluntary simplicity* and *getting by*. Discuss their main similarities and differences.
Responding	Choose one of the lifestyles defined in the reading. What are the advantages and disadvantages of this lifestyle? Would you choose this lifestyle? *Why or why not?*
Arguing	Choose one of the lifestyles. Should U.S. consumers be educated to adopt it? *Why or why not?*

2. Which of these questions asks you to restate information from the reading? Which questions ask to analyze or apply the information from the reading?

Activity 7-16   Writing Answers to Test Questions

1. Write possible first sentences for the answers to the six questions in Activity 7-15.

2. Answer two of the questions in Activity 7-15. Write a one- to two-paragraph answer for each one. Use your first sentences from number 1 above.

3. Analyze your paragraphs. Go back to the reading to see if you answered the questions well.

   _____ Did you begin directly?

   _____ Did you include the necessary information?

   _____ Are the answers clear, logical, and cohesive?

   _____ Did you proofread, add cohesion, and correct grammatical problems?

4. With a partner or in a small group, compare your answers. Tell which you think is your best answer and explain why. Get feedback from your peers.

Preparing for Timed Written Essay Exams

There are several different types of tests. For a take-home test, students often have several days to complete their answers, and the instructor's expectations for depth of answers, length, and word processing are generally different than for in-class tests. There are two kinds of in-class tests: open-book and closed-book. Both are taken under time pressure. During an in-class open book test you can often use your textbook and notes. This can be helpful if you have already studied well and know where to locate key material in your text or notes. In-class closed-book tests are the most common. The following suggestions apply to this kind of test.

Studying Before the Test

If you have done active reading before the test, you can go back to your notes and study what you've highlighted, underlined, or numbered in your text without rereading everything. You'll be able to spend more time reviewing the main points instead of reading all the material again. One way to review is to write a list of possible essay questions and compare your list with someone else in the class. Then practice writing answers for these questions. (Just be sure that when you get to the test, you don't write the answer to the question you *thought* would be on the test, when it is actually a different question.) In addition, take advantage of any review session the professor offers or any study guide. Both give strong indications of what might be on the test. Keep your eyes and ears open.

Taking the Test

1. **Assess.** Before you write any answers, read all of the questions carefully. Circle key words in the questions to help you focus on what you have to do.

   Divide up the time you have for each question. For example, if you have 90 minutes for three questions, allot yourself about 25 minutes for each question so you will have some time left to review your work. (Wear a watch!)

2. **Take quick notes to organize your thoughts.** After you read the questions, in the margin of the test paper make a quick list of information you will include in the answer. After you have generated your list, organize the information by grouping or numbering your items. Eliminate any irrelevant ideas.

   The temptation with a timed essay test is to begin writing without taking these preliminary quick notes. However, these notes will free your mind to concentrate more on the form and style of your answers. You can concentrate more on your English.

3. **Begin writing.**

   a. *Start with the easiest questions.* This will give you a boost of confidence and help you warm up your mind and your writing skill. In addition, you might spend less time on the easy questions so that you can devote more time to difficult questions. Be sure to write legibly and work within your time limit for the question. While you are working on these easy questions, your unconscious mind will help you prepare for the other questions you have previewed.

   b. *Begin your short-answer or essay test answers with a thesis statement or topic sentence.* Due to your time limits, there will be no time for a gradual introduction. Instead, start with a direct thesis statement or topic sentence. In many cases, this can be a restatement of the test question. By restating the question in your first sentence, you will help focus your answer. Then add the necessary examples, details, and evidence to support your main idea.

   c. *Write organized answers.* Connect your ideas with transition words and phrases (i.e., *next, as a result, after that, consequently*) to show the relationships between your ideas. Don't just scribble down the ideas from your notes in random order.

4. **Revise and Proofread.** Be sure you save some time to check over your work. Your professors do not want you to recopy your answers because that would take time away from your thinking and writing. But they do expect you to reread your answers before you turn them in, and make neat corrections, such as crossing out unnecessary words, adding necessary transitions, and correcting spelling and grammar.

PUTTING IT ALL TOGETHER

FINAL WRITING ASSIGNMENT

Your final writing assignment for this chapter is a written test on the materials from Readings 1 and 2.

1. Give a brief definition of each of these terms.

   a. internal and external information searches

   b. evaluative criteria

   c. *component* lifestyle

   d. cognitive dissonance

   e. *blurring gender roles* lifestyle

2. Describe a purchase that you or someone you know made using the terms in the five step process in Reading 1, "Consumer Decision-Making." Start with "recognizing a need" and continue through the five steps.

3. Explain two reasons why cognitive dissonance may occur after a purchase. How can it be reduced?

4. Contrast the purchases typically made in a *voluntary simplicity* lifestyle with those made in a "*me*" *generation* lifestyle. Explain both the kind of purchases made and the primary reason for these purchases.

5. What part do advertisers play in need recognition? Give a few examples of needs that have been created or recognized due to advertising.

Evaluating Your Answers

On a real written test, you would have time to proofread your answers, but not enough time to critically evaluate and rewrite them if necessary. However, since this was only a practice test, we will evaluate your answers.

Peer Review

In a small group, compare your answers.

_____ **1.** Did the writer answer the question? Reread the question and the source material to be sure.

_____ **2.** Did the writer start directly with a clear topic sentence?

_____ **3.** Are cohesion devices used effectively?

_____ **4.** Is new terminology used correctly in the answers?

_____ **5.** Did the writer use his or her own words?

Revise

Review the readings if necessary. Rewrite your answers and give them to your teacher.

• •

L O O K I N G   A H E A D

Academic Assignments

You do not have to write the answers to these authentic test questions. However, analyzing them will give you a clearer understanding of the types of assignments you will face in your undergraduate courses.

For each of the following questions:

1. Circle the focus words that will help guide your answer. Some questions contain more than one.

2. In a small group or as a class, discuss the clues that you get from each question that would help you in your answer.

   a. How will the focus words guide your answer?

   b. What is the possible organization for your answer?

   c. Are there any other clues that tell you something about the grammar to use in your answer?

   d. What would be a direct first sentence for your answer?

Business

Describe the preliminary steps entrepreneurs take in forming a small business. Be sure to summarize the contents, focus, and importance of the business plan in your response.

Speech Communication

What are three barriers to effective listening? How can you, as a speaker, help reduce or eliminate each of these three barriers?

World Geography

Explain how the development of agriculture changed the way humans lived.

Business Management

Discuss the issue of comparable pay for comparable work. Give and support your opinion on this issue.

Economics

Property tax is often considered a bad tax. Do you agree or disagree? Present your argument—for or against—on the grounds of equity and efficiency.

Systematics and Ecology

Should genetically engineered organisms be introduced into natural ecological systems?

Chemistry

Discuss the process involved in testing pollution that is caused by carbon monoxide.

Agronomy

As a manager of a cattle operation, you have found *brucellosis* in your herd. Explain the means of eradicating this disease and preventing its occurrence. Describe how each of these is effective.

History

What were President Truman's other options regarding the war in the Pacific? What would have been the impacts of, and reasons supporting, those options?

Nutrition

Analyze the relationship of fatty acids and cholesterol to heart disease.

Grammar and Language Reference

The examples in this section are based on the readings in the textbook or on academic textbooks used in U.S. universities.

CONTENTS

Section 1 Grammar Common to All Types of Academic Writing

1A Sentences

In your academic work, you will read and write using four basic sentence types: simple, compound, complex, and compound-complex. Understanding how to use these sentence types will help you express your ideas and the relationships among your ideas clearly and logically.

Three important terms are often used to talk about sentence structure: sentence, independent clause, and dependent clause.

1. A **sentence** contains a subject and a verb.
2. An **independent clause** is a complete sentence; it can be used alone.
3. A **dependent clause** is not a complete sentence. It must be combined with an `
   independent clause to make a complete sentence.

SIMPLE SENTENCES A **simple sentence** must have at least a subject and a verb. Another name for a simple sentence is **independent clause.**	
In these examples of simple sentences, the **subject** is underlined once and the **verb** is underlined twice.	Mathematics <u>is</u> the key to opportunity. Today's mathematics <u>opens</u> doors to tomorrow's job.
Notice that the subject and verb each can be more than one word. Simple sentences can be long and complicated, but they have only **one subject and one verb.**	The influence and power of statistics <u>is</u> enormous. <u>You</u> <u>may have</u> also <u>learned</u> which ones to avoid through past experience. <u>Most students</u> <u>leave</u> school without sufficient preparation in mathematics to cope either with on-the-job demands for problem-solving or with college requirements for mathematical literacy.
Sometimes writers use **short simple sentences** for dramatic effect.	<u>Wake up</u>, America. <u>Your children</u> <u>are</u> at risk.

COMPOUND SENTENCES

To make a **compound sentence,** you combine two or more independent clauses. You can combine them using: 1) **a comma and a coordinating conjunction,** or 2) **a semicolon.**

In these examples, two independent clauses are joined with a **comma and a coordinating conjunction.** The most frequently used coordinating conjunctions are *and, but, or,* and *so.* Notice that the comma is written at the end of the first sentence.	<u>Quick and easy meals are</u> most attractive to students, so <u>the microwave plays</u> a major role in students' lives. <u>Infant mortality would be</u> high, <u>malnutrition would be</u> rampant, and <u>the elderly and infirm would be abandoned.</u>
You can use a **semicolon** in place of the comma + coordinating conjunction. However, semicolons are not used as much in academic writing as the comma + coordinating conjunction. You should avoid using large numbers of semicolons in your writing.	<u>These sources may</u> not <u>be</u> as relevant as others; <u>they may be</u> dated, or <u>they may be</u> inaccurate.
Compound sentences are used when the writer wants to emphasize a **balance** or **parallelism** between two ideas or pieces of information. Notice how the writers of the examples use parallel structure for dramatic effect.	More than ever before, Americans need to think for a living; more than ever before, they need to think mathematically. The government is concerned; pediatric cardiologists are concerned. Many people exercise far too little, but many others exercise far too much.

COMPLEX SENTENCES

To make a **complex sentence,** you combine **an independent clause** and a **dependent clause.**

Complex sentences are frequently used in academic writing. Most academic writing is made up of complex sentences with a few simple, compound, or compound-complex sentences used for special purposes.

Another term for a **dependent clause** is **subordinate clause.** There are three main types of dependent clauses: adverbial clauses, relative clauses, and noun clauses.	**When you become sleepy in class,** the problem might be lack of oxygen.
Adverbial clauses behave like adverbs, giving information about *when, where, why,* or *how.* Notice that an adverbial clause can come either at the beginning or the end of a sentence.	I don't spend much time reviewing the readings **because it would take too long.** **When material from reading assignments also is covered extensively in class,** it is likely to be on the test. You can't take Western Civ **until you are either a junior or a senior.**
Relative clauses combine with nouns to make complex noun phrases. *restrictive & nonl*	Give the file or document a name **that you can easily recognize and remember.** *who, which, such as* I get irritated by students **who ask questions.**
Noun clauses work like nouns in sentences. They are often used as direct objects and sometimes as subjects of sentences.	Bowes recalls **that she was much more comfortable talking to people through a computer screen.** You may experience hunger pangs during your noon marketing class and realize **that you need to purchase some lunch.**

<table>
<tr><td colspan="2">COMPOUND-COMPLEX SENTENCES
A compound-complex sentence joins two independent clauses (thus forming a compound sentence) and at least one dependent clause.</td></tr>
</table>

This example sentence shows how **two independent clauses** and **one dependent clause** combine to form a compound-complex sentence. In each example the subject is underlined once and the verb twice. The examples show how the two kinds of clauses are connected. Note that *athletes who overdo it* is a noun phrase with a relative clause.	Minor problems with equipment, such as worn-out running shoes or a new tennis racket, won't bother the average recreational athlete, but they can cause big problems in athletes who overdo it. Minor problems with equipment, such as worn-out running shoes or a new tennis racket, won't bother the average recreational athlete. They can cause big problems in athletes who overdo it.

1B   Using Numbers

The following are general rules that are often followed in academic writing. Different academic fields use numbers in different ways, so you may need to ask your teacher for advice and look at the ways that numbers are used in your textbooks and class handouts.

Numbers as Words. Numbers from one to ten are usually written as words rather than numbers if they do not represent precise measurements. Generally, numbers that can be written in one or two words are given in words rather than in numbers.	Breathe deeply **three** times. !Kung adults spend between **twelve and nineteen hours** per week in the pursuit of food.
Age and **time** are generally given in numerical format.	These students are high-achieving **16- and 17-year-olds** who find it tough to reconcile **7:30 a.m. classes** with a job that ends at **10:30 p.m.** or later.
Exact Numbers are written as numerals. Exact numbers include exact counts, exact sums of money, technical measurements, decimals, fractions, and percentages.	By providing a hefty down payment on a **$12,000** car and stressing the importance of keeping up on the payments, parents are sending a signal that schoolwork is secondary. <div align="right">Continued</div>

Percentages. Use numerals, and spell out the word *percent*. However, some academic disciplines prefer the use of the symbol % as in the second example, which is from an accounting textbook.	Japanese consumption of fat rose from **8.7 percent** of calories in 1955 to **25.5 percent** in 1992. In this text, we will use a combined rate of **7.5%** on the first $70,000 of annual earnings and a rate of **15%** on annual earnings in excess of $70,000.
Mixed Types in One Sentence. When a sentence involves both shorter and longer numbers, use numbers for all of them rather than mixing the two styles.	…only **17** of the **223** local species of animals known to the !Kung are hunted regularly.
Large Numbers. Notice that *24 million* is easier to read than *24,000,000* in the context of the first example. However, in other settings the numerical version would be preferred. Compare the second example from the 1994 financial statement of the Walgreen Co., as quoted in an accounting textbook.	A recent study from Nielsen Media Research based on more than **4,200** telephone interviews of randomly selected households in the U.S. and Canada, found that **11 percent** of the population **16 years** and older, or **24 million** people, use the Internet. On August 31, 1994 and 1993, inventories would have been greater by **$393,568,000** and **$388,464,000** respectively, if they had been valued on a lower of first-in, first-out (FIFO) cost or market basis.

Section 2 Past Time Narrative

2A Overview

Past time narrative is used in fiction, but also in several other types of writing in which the writer tells a story about something that happened in the past. Past time narrative is used to write biographies and autobiographies, case studies, and history. It can be used to write about the history of different professions as well as the history of a country or a period of time. For example, introductory textbooks often include some information about the history of the discipline, such as the history of accounting or of chemistry.

Past time narrative writing requires you to use several grammatical features that are frequently found in this type of writing. These features include • **past time verbs,** • **chronological organizers,** • **proper nouns,** and • **personal pronouns.** This short sample of past time narrative shows how these grammatical features interact with each other in this type of writing.	Lisa Bowes had a wonderful life as a student at Humboldt State University in California. Every day she chatted with her pal Johan from Sweden. She'd discuss movies and her favorite hobby, quilting, with girlfriends from California. And, for about a year, she flirted with her special friend Jason from Pennsylvania. There was only one problem. Bowes had hardly a friend on campus.

2B Past Tense Verbs

The **simple past tense** is the most frequently used verb in past time narratives. It is used to tell the basic story of the narrative. It is also used to give facts about the past and about things that happened in the past. This sample is from a U.S. history textbook.	In 1519, an extraordinary soldier named Hernan Cortez **landed** on the coast of Mexico with 508 soldiers, 200 Indians, some Africans, seven small cannons, and 16 horses. He **landed** at what is now Vera Cruz and **was attacked** by the Tabascan Indians, whom the Spaniards **devastated** with their cannons at the loss of only two of their own men.
Past Progressive is used to emphasize the ongoing nature of some past event—that it happened over a period of time. Past progressive can also be used to write about two past time events that happened at the same time.	Pascal built the first calculator, probably to aid him in the accounting he **was doing** at his father's office.

Continued

Past Perfect. Remember that this verb combines *had* with the past participle of the verb.	Before he landed in Mexico, Cortez **had heard** of Tenochtitlan, the capital of the Aztec Empire, and of Aztec riches.

2C   Chronological Organizers

An important feature of narratives is the use of **chronological organization.** This means that the story is told in the sequence in which it occurred, following the chronology of the events. Chronological organizers are adverbial **words, phrases,** and **clauses** that help the reader understand the sequence of events and how they are related to each other in time.

Words: • *first* • *next* • *then*	Our very **first** calculating device was our hands. Someone **then** came up with the idea for the abacus. Abaci are **still** used in many parts of Asia today.
Phrases: • *after that* • *at first* • *before that* • *in/before/after 1642* • *at that time* • *100 years ago* • *last week/month/year* • *ever since* • *since the beginning of the century*	**In 1642,** Blaise Pascal built the first calculator. **In the meantime,** Charles Babbage became very unhappy about the mathematical errors that recurred in published timetables and charts.
Clauses: • *until you graduate from college* • *when he was young* • *while they are in school* • *before they began* • *after it was introduced*	*As* **time passed,** a hand number system developed for communication among merchants. *When* **numerical figures began to exceed our ten fingers,** new devices had to be explored.

2D   Proper Nouns

Narratives of all sorts use proper nouns to name the people, places, companies, and events involved in the story. Learning about the forms of names and how they are used in writing can be difficult for writers from other countries and cultures that have different ways of forming and using names. The emphasis here is on learning about using names as they are presented in academic materials.

Generally, a person's **full name** is given first.	Englishman **Charles Babbage** became very disenchanted with mathematical errors continually recurring in published timetables and charts.
Later in the passage, the person is often referred to by a **shorter form** of the full name. When the name combines a first name with a last or family name, the last or family name is used for the short version.	Even so, this machine was not capable of storing data and acting on that stored data, as envisioned by **Babbage**.
Of course, people are also referred to by using the appropriate **personal pronoun.**	Nevertheless, **his** work furnished the foundations for the modern computer.

Many other forms of names can be found in academic materials, especially in history materials. You will need to notice carefully how these names are used so that you can use them accurately in your own writing, especially on tests that cover the material. Here are some examples of names from a U.S. history textbook.	**Full Name** **Short Version**
	Christopher
	  Columbus Columbus
	George
	  Washington Washington
	Henry VIII Henry
	Henry VII Henry

2E   Personal Pronouns

Narratives can have numerous nouns that are used to refer to particular people, places, events, ideas, and objects. You must choose the correct **personal pronoun** to refer to these nouns, so the reader knows exactly to what or whom the pronoun refers. Pronoun reference is especially important when you are writing about an event that involves two or more people.

Personal pronouns have a **subject** form, an **objective** (object) form, and one or more **possessive** forms.	**Subject** forms:	*I, you, he, she, it, we, they*
	Objective forms:	*me, you, him, her, it, us, them*
	Possessive forms:	*my/mine, your/yours, his, her/hers, its, our/ours, their/theirs*
Pronouns must match nouns in **number.** Singular pronouns refer to singular nouns (as in the first example) and plural pronouns (second example) refer to plural nouns. This matching is true for proper and for common nouns.	**Pasta** in all shapes and sizes is a popular meal. **It's** easy, cheap, filling, and versatile.	
	Once **consumers** have identified unmet needs, searched for information, and used that information to evaluate brands, **they** are ready to make a purchase decision.	
Pronouns must also match the noun in **gender.**	**Lisa Bowes** had a wonderful life as a student at Humboldt State University in California. Every day **she** chatted with **her** pal Johan from Sweden.	
In this example, the subject of the sentence "the consumer" could be either masculine or feminine. Both *he* and *she* are used to refer back to this subject.	It represents the invisible activity that goes on in the consumer's mind as **he or she** makes a buying decision.	
Because academic writing so often refers to concepts and processes, the pronoun *it* is frequently used.	**Mathematics** is the key to opportunity. For students, **it** opens doors to careers. For citizens, **it** enables informed decisions.	

Section 3 Informational Writing

3A   Overview

Informational writing is found throughout the textbooks used in your academic courses. You will use this type of writing to state facts, data, theories, and definitions.

All of these features work together to make up the informational writing style as shown in this short sample. • The most important feature of informational writing is the use of **long, complicated noun phrases.** • **Generic nouns** are used to talk about groups rather than about individuals. • Many pieces of informational writing use **logical organizers** to show the relationships among sentences. • **Passive sentences** are often used because this style focuses on processes and theories rather than on people and actions. • Finally, **present tense verbs** are frequently used to make general truth statements. • Since present tense is used, **subject-verb agreement** is a feature of informational writing.	People's persistence or lack of persistence in coping with a difficult task is strongly influenced by their sense of self-efficacy. For example, kidney patients undergoing dialysis treatment are advised to curtail their fluid intake sharply. Patients who are confident they can follow the instructions generally restrict their intake and respond well to the treatment. Those who confess that they "can't tolerate frustration" generally yield to temptation, go on drinking fluids, and soon die.

3B   Complex Noun Phrases

Complex noun phrases put a lot of information into a sentence, so they are the most common characteristic of academic writing. These complex noun phrases take several forms, but each complex noun phrase contains a **main** or **core noun.** Other words can come either before or after this central noun. The central noun in the phrases is in **bold** type. Three common complex noun phrase structures are given below.	1. **lack** of persistence in coping with a difficult task 2. their **sense** of self-efficacy 3. kidney **patients** undergoing dialysis treatment 4. **patients** who are confident they can follow the instructions 5. **those** who confess that they "can't tolerate frustration"

Continued

Noun + prepositional phrase	lack **of persistence** sense **of self-efficacy**	
Noun + relative clause	a student **who has studied hard and has done well on several exams.**	
In **noun + noun,** the first noun is used like an adjective, but it remains a noun in form.	role models bullet train chicken nuggets trade practices a noodle restaurant	key ingredients world economy math anxiety computer printouts dialysis treatment

3C   Generic Nouns

In informational writing, we often use **generic nouns** to communicate about groups of people or classes of things rather than about particular objects or people. We do this when we are making generalizations or giving definitions. Generic nouns have four major types illustrated below.

Plural noun without an article can be used to refer to classes or groups.	**Atoms** are the building blocks of all matter. **Researchers** found that compulsive shopping correlates with low self-esteem.
A or *an* + **singular noun** is used to refer to one member or one example of a type. The meaning is about general types and not about particular instances. *A* or *an* with a singular noun is often used in definitions, such as in the last example.	**A minor injury** can easily develop into a serious condition. **An athlete** should not exercise to extremes. **A business transaction** is an economic event or condition that directly changes the entity's financial position or directly affects its results of operations.
The + **singular noun** is often used in technical writing.	**The computer** can practically fill a life. **The abacus** was considered adequate for traditional calculations by merchants for centuries to follow.
Noncount nouns are used without an article for this type of generalization.	**Addiction** stems from a bigger problem, such as **low self-esteem.**

3D   Logical Organizers

In contrast to narrative writing with its chronological organization, informational writing is organized in some logical manner. Recognizing the logic behind particular writing is a challenge for writers who come from different cultural and linguistic backgrounds. This chart provides a reminder of the vocabulary that you can use to indicate the **logical relationships** among the sentences in your writing.

Meaning	Coordinating Conjunctions	Subordinating Conjunctions	Transition Words	
addition	and		also additionally furthermore	in addition moreover
cause/result	so	if when	therefore thus as a result	as a consequence consequently for this reason
choice	or nor		instead	on the other hand
comparison (similarities)			also as well as both … and	by comparison similarly likewise
concession	yet	although even though	nevertheless despite	in spite of
condition		if unless even if		
contrast (opposites)	but	whereas while	however instead nevertheless	on the other hand in contrast on the contrary
emphasis			in fact undoubtedly	indeed as a matter of fact
example			for example for instance	as an example as an illustration
reason/cause	for	because as since		
summary or conclusion			after all all in all finally overall	in conclusion in closing in summary in sum
time		then when before while after since until		

3E   Passive Sentences

Passive voice is a common feature of academic writing done in scientific and technical fields. In addition, **passive sentences** can be used in all other types of academic writing.

Different academic disciplines have very different attitudes toward passive sentences. In your English composition courses, you may be told to avoid passives. In courses such as biology, chemistry, sociology, and business, you may find numerous passive sentences. You need to find out which style is preferred in each course and to work within that style.

Many verbs can have either an active or a passive form. Sentences 1 and 2 are **passive sentences** from the sample at the beginning of this section. Sentences 3 and 4 are **active sentences** using the same information. Although they have many words in common, active and passive sentences are very different. Sentence 1 is focused on "people's persistence"; sentence 3 is focused on "people's sense of self-efficacy." Sentence 2 focuses on kidney patients while sentence 4 is about their doctors.	**Passive Sentences** 1. People's persistence or lack of persistence in coping with a difficult task **is** strongly **influenced** by their sense of self-efficacy. 2. For example, kidney patients undergoing dialysis treatment **are advised** to curtail their fluid intake sharply. **Active Sentences** 3. People's sense of self-efficacy influences their persistence or lack of persistence in coping with a difficult task. 4. Doctors advise kidney patients undergoing dialysis treatment to curtail their fluid intake sharply.
Passive sentences can be used when you write about • **things**—rather than the people who use them • **processes**—rather than the people who did them • **history of a company or a sport or a country**—rather than the people who were involved In the first example, the writer is interested in the abacus rather than in the people who used it, so the abacus is the subject and the verb is passive. In the second example, the focus in on the food rather than on the people who might eat that food. The last two sentences are focused on soccer and Jamestown, rather than on the people who founded them.	The abacus **was considered** adequate for traditional calculations by merchants for centuries to follow. Three bagels a day may not be very nutritious, but bagels **can be consumed** while running for a bus. Soccer **was founded** in England in the late 19th century. In 1607, Jamestown **was founded.** In 1608, Plymouth **was founded** by a group of religious refugees from England. These settlers **are known** to us as the Pilgrims.

Continued

These sentences show how passive sentences are used in accounting and psychology. In these sentences, the writers are focusing on **processes and concepts** rather than on actions.	Accounting **may be defined** as an information system that provides reports to various individuals or groups about economic activities of an organization or other entity. You might think of accounting as the "language of business," because it is the means by which most business information **is communicated.** The term *psychology* comes from two Greek words, *psyche*, meaning the soul, and *logos*, referring to the study of a subject. These two Greek roots **were** first **put** together to define a topic of study in the 16th century, when *psyche* **was used** to refer to the soul, spirit, or mind.
Notice that there are a number of passive phrases that are frequently used in academic writing, especially in **definitions.** Also, materials that include charts, tables, pictures, and other graphics often use words such as *shown, defined, called,* and *located* that are used repeatedly in scientific and technical textbooks.	Accounting **may be defined** as ... The electron beam is produced by an assembly **called** an electron gun, **located** in the neck of the tube. The assembly **shown** in Figure 16.24a consists of a heater (H), a cathode (C), and a positively charged anode (A).

3F   Present Tense Verbs

Present tense verbs are a common feature of informational writing. Present tense verbs can be used in many different settings and can even refer to future time in sentences such as "The new store opens at 10 a.m. on March 14."

Simple present tense verbs are often used for generalizations. These generalizations can be made both about personal and non-personal information.	"I **eat** hamburgers and french fries and **drink** a Coke two or three times a week …" There **are** at least a thousand McDonald's in Japan today.
Present progressive verbs are used with action verbs to show that something is ongoing at the present moment. While this form is frequent in conversational English, it can also be found in writing about things that are happening now.	They **are warning** that the situation is very risky and that children will have a greatly increased risk factor for heart disease. Today's children the world over **are using** mathematical training … to build up their lives.
Present perfect verbs are not nearly as common in academic writing as the simple present tense. Present perfect verbs are used to make a connection between the past and the present. The present perfect is often used to introduce a topic and to show how the past is related to the present.	The decrease in salt consumption **has** strikingly **reduced** the number of deaths from stroke and from stomach cancer.

3G   Subject-Verb Agreement

Present tense verbs are so common in academic writing that student writers have many opportunities to apply the rules of **subject-verb agreement.** In these examples, the subject is underlined one time and the verb two times.

Subject-verb agreement is a relationship between a subject and a verb. The subject requires a particular form of the verb. Plural subjects require a simple form of the verb (sentence 1). Singular and non-count subjects require changes in the verb (sentence 2).	1. As competitors get smarter, our problems get harder. 2. The computer helps withdrawn young people reach out, make friends, and learn to interact.

Continued

STRATEGIES FOR SUBJECT-VERB AGREEMENT

Strategy 1. Learn to find the main subject word. You must know if the main subject noun is singular, plural, or noncount.

Strategy 2. Remember that **subject-verb agreement** occurs with
- simple present tense
- present and past of *be* (*am/is/are* and *was/were*)
- present perfect verbs (*has/have*)
- present and past progressive verbs (*am/is/are* and *was/were* with the present participle)
- present perfect verbs (*has/have* with the past participle)

Strategy 3. Generally, if the subject has *s*, it is a plural subject, and the verb will **not** have *s*. A singular subject or noncount subject requires *s* for the verb.

Strategy 4. Generally, any subject that is not clearly plural is treated as singular. Infinitives are treated as singular: "To study is to learn." Clauses are treated as singular: "That he studied hard was shown in his high grades."

| **Strategy 5.** Remember that some nouns end with *s* but are not plural. These include words such as *mathematics*, *economics*, and *news*. | <u>Mathematics</u> <u>is</u> the key to opportunity. |

SUBJECTS THAT REQUIRE VERBS WITH *S*

Singular count nouns	<u>A computer</u> <u>gets</u> "hung up" so that no matter what you do, absolutely nothing changes on the screen.
Singular pronouns *he, it, she*	<u>She</u> <u>spends</u> her free time engaged in such activities as going out with her roommates or watching television with friends.
Singular proper nouns	<u>Bowes</u> <u>recalls</u> that she was much more comfortable talking to people through a computer screen.
Noncount Nouns	<u>Communication</u> <u>has created</u> a world economy in which working smarter is more important than merely working harder.
Infinitives	<u>To buy a car in high school</u> <u>seems</u> like too big a burden for most students.

Continued

Gerunds are *ing* forms of verbs used like nouns.	Successfully <u>gathering</u> information <u>involves</u> more than just locating enough sources.
False plurals are nouns that look plural but are **non-count.** *linguistics physics* *mathematics news*	<u>Mathematics</u> <u>is</u> the key to opportunity.

VERBS THAT REQUIRE *S* WITH CERTAIN SUBJECTS	
Simple present tense	<u>A degree</u> in any of these fields <u>requires</u> advanced mathematics. Thus, <u>math avoidance</u> also <u>prevents</u> many adults from career advancement or changes.
Be	<u>Cereal</u> <u>is</u> another staple in the undergraduate kitchen. Like it or not, <u>numbers</u> <u>are</u> an important part of our life. <u>Hollerith's 1890 calculator</u> <u>was</u> not capable of storing data. <u>Her friends</u> <u>were</u> on the computer and not on campus.
Because *be* requires subject-verb agreement, **progressive and passive** verbs change to agree with their subjects.	<u>Careers</u> previously thought to be people-oriented <u>are relying</u> more and more on math skills. Pascal built the first calculator, probably to aid him in the accounting <u>he</u> <u>was doing</u> at his father's office. <u>Abaci</u> <u>are</u> still <u>used</u> in many parts of Asia today. <u>The abacus</u> <u>was considered</u> adequate for traditional calculations by merchants for centuries to follow.
Present Perfect	<u>Communication</u> <u>has created</u> a world economy in which working smarter is more important than merely working harder. <u>Times</u> <u>have changed</u>.

Section 4 Writing Definitions

4A Overview

Academic writing includes many **definitions** for terminology that students are expected to understand and use in their own writing. Your textbooks in many university courses will contain numerous technical definitions that must be learned and used accurately in your writing.

Textbooks will often mark this important vocabulary in **special print.** Sometimes the words will be given in **bold type** or in *italic type.* Vocabulary that you need to know is also sometimes listed in special review sections at the end of each chapter. Generally, your university instructors will expect you to recognize that these are important words that you are supposed to learn and use in your writing.	**Accounting** may be defined as an information system that provides reports to various individuals or groups about economic activities of an organization or other entity. The term *psychology* comes from two Greek words, *psyche,* meaning the soul, and *logos,* referring to the study of a subject. These two Greek roots were first put together to define a topic of study in the 16th century, when *psyche* was used to refer to the soul, spirit, or mind.
Textbook materials can be organized around the **presentation of definitions** for important terminology. See how this was done in Chapter 7, Reading 2, "Selected Consumer Lifestyles." In that reading, seven defined terms provide the organizational structure for the reading.	1. Family Values Lifestyle 2. Voluntary Simplicity Lifestyle 3. Getting By Lifestyle 4. "Me" Generation Lifestyle 5. Blurring Gender Roles Lifestyle 6. Poverty-of-Time Lifestyle 7. Component Lifestyle

4B   Understanding the Grammar of Definitions

Students are expected to learn and use many new words in each of their university classes. This work will be easier if you understand the way that **definitions** are structured so that you can more easily memorize them and repeat them accurately in your own writing, especially on tests but also in other required writing assignments. Definitions of terminology are often presented in the following formats where X = the term and Y = the definition.

X is Y	Psychology is the science of behavior and mental processes.
X means Y	Addiction to a drug means that the individual is physically dependent on the use of the drug.
X refers to Y	Evaluative criteria refer to those features that the buyers use to make a choice between brands.
Y is called X. Someone calls Y X.	The number of brands that a consumer actually considers in making a purchase decision is called the *evoked* set. A consumer recognizes a need (or want) when something that he or she requires is found lacking. Some marketers call this *problem recognition.*
X is Y or Z. This is usually an extended, lengthy definition. See Chapter 7, Reading 1 for a complete definition of internal and external information searches.	Information search can be internal or external. Internal search relies on … External sources …

4C   Recognizing Definitions: Indirect Presentation

While some writing makes definitions easy to recognize, other materials can present definitions more indirectly. Some of these definitions will need to be restated to make them into
full definitions. A possible restatement is given for each definition. Other ways of restating
them are also possible.

Format Style	Authentic Definition	Possible Restatement
The term is followed by **examples** that suggest a definition. Sometimes *for example* or *such as* are used; sometimes they are not included.	Naturally, the most common result of math anxiety is math avoidance. You stop taking math courses, choose jobs that involve little or no math, get someone else to do your taxes, have a friend check the restaurant bill, or assign math-related problems to co-workers so that you won't have to reveal your inadequacy on the job.	**Test Questions:** What is math avoidance? What does math avoidance involve? **Answer 1:** Math avoidance is living your life so that you do not have to use mathematics. **Answer 2:** Math avoidance is the development of a series of techniques to avoid having to use mathematics or having to show that you cannot use mathematics well.
The definition is placed near the term and put in **parentheses.**	… the development of the LSI (large-scale integrated) circuit …	**Test Question:** What does LSI refer to? **Answer:** An LSI is a large-scale integrated circuit.
The definition is given as an **appositive.** This style is frequently used in history textbooks.	The first American religious revival, the Great Awakening, broke out almost simultaneously in several colonies.	**Test Question:** What was the Great Awakening? **Answer:** The Great Awakening was the first American religious revival. It started at almost the same time in several colonies.
The definition is set off with a **dash.** This example is from an accounting textbook.	Even small businesses have several bank accounts and one or more *petty cash* funds—small sums of cash kept on hand for making small disbursements.	**Test Questions:** What are petty cash funds? How are petty cash funds used? **Answer:** Petty cash funds are small amounts of cash kept on hand by a business for making small disbursements.

4D   Recognizing Definitions: Vocabulary

Key **vocabulary** can help you see when a definition will be given. You can use this vocabulary for definitions in your own writing.

Format Style	Authentic Definition	Possible Restatement
The definition is given after the term and set off from the term with the word *or*.	"Fiscoholism," **or** the need to spend money to create a mood, may not do serious harm to those with unlimited funds, time, and closets.	**Test Question:** What is "fiscoholism"? **Answer:** "Fiscoholism" is the need to spend money to create a mood.
The definition is introduced by a phrase such as *for example, by example, for our purposes*, or some other similar phrase.	A drug can have a medical or a legal definition. **But for our purposes,** a drug is any chemical substance that changes mood, perception, or awareness.	**Test Question:** What is a "drug" as defined by the authors of our textbook? **Answer:** A drug is any chemical substance that changes mood, perception, or awareness.
The definition is introduced by a passive phrase such as *is said*. Other such phrases include • *called* • *is called* • *is defined as* • *is known as*	An individual **is said to be** psychologically dependent on a drug when the nonuse of it causes the person to have severe feelings of distress.	**Test Question:** What does it mean to say that a person is "psychologically dependent on a drug"? **Answer:** A person is psychologically dependent on a drug when the nonuse of it causes the person to have severe feelings of distress.

4E   Complex Noun Phrases in Definitions

A common pattern for a definition is: **noun to be defined +** **verb** (often a form of *be*) + **category** (classifying noun phrase), with **details** that separate the noun from other nouns in the same category.	<u>A drug</u> <u>is</u> any chemical substance that changes mood, perception, or awareness. subject of the sentence: noun to be defined a drug verb: a form of *be* is complex noun phrase with a relative clause: classifying noun phrase any chemical substance **that changes mood, perception, or awareness**
The following examples from an accounting textbook follow this common pattern.	Accounting is the system that measures business activities, processes that information into reports and financial statements, and communicates the findings to decision makers. An asset is an economic resource that is expected to be of benefit in the future. A certified public accountant (CPA) is a licensed accountant who serves the general public rather than one particular company.

Section 5 Reporting Other People's Words and Ideas

5A   Overview

One of the basic tasks students face is to report the **words and ideas of other people** in their own writing. In project papers, book reports, summaries of required reading, and other types of writing, you are expected to use the words and ideas taken from other people's writing. To do this effectively, you must understand and use the verbs of reporting, correct punctuation, and an appropriate referencing system to give the sources of these words and information.

5B   Verbs of Reporting

The following words can be used to report the words or ideas of a person or a research report. While in spoken language we often use the verb *say/said,* in academic writing we have a wider range of choices for more exact meanings and for stylistic variety.

admit	confirm	insist	report	tell
anticipate	consider	mention	say	think
argue	deny	point out	state	understand
believe	doubt	recall	stress	warn
claim	find	recommend	suggest	write

5C   Noun Clauses with Verbs of Reporting

The basic grammar for *verbs of reporting* requires a noun clause as the direct object. Notice that the formality of academic writing requires the use of "sequence of tense."	noun clause as direct object She <u>said</u> that she was an accounting major.
Sequence of tense means that the verb in the clause changes to match the verb in the main verb phrase. Also, pronouns have to be changed to fit the new context. Generally, the verb changes happen in the following patterns: • simple present tense becomes simple past tense • simple past tense becomes past perfect • *will* becomes *would*	Her actual words: "I am an accounting major." She said that she was an accounting major. Her actual words: "I studied in France before coming to the U.S." She told us that she had studied in France before coming to the U.S. Her actual words: "I will work for a bank when I graduate." She reported that she would work for a bank when she graduated. <div align="right">Continued</div>

However, sequence of tense is often not followed if the writer thinks that the change would alter the meaning of the reported words. For example, simple present tense is often kept for statements of generalizations. And *will* is often kept for future time meanings since the change to *would* could imply that the meaning is conditional.	She reported that she will work for a bank when she graduates. She said that she is an accounting major.

5D   Examples of Noun Clauses with Verbs of Reporting

The examples in Section 5C were created to show the grammar in a simple and clear way. The following are authentic examples that are like the ones that you will find in your academic reading and be expected to use in your academic writing.

Notice that the writer chose to keep the verb in **simple present tense** in the reported sentence. This tense form emphasizes the **general truth meaning.** The noun clause is in **bold.**	As reported in *the Journal of Consumer Policy* in 1990, researchers found **that compulsive shopping correlates with low self-esteem as well as anxiety.**
Here is another example in which the writer decided to use **simple present tense** for the reported generalization. The noun clause is in **bold.**	A recent study from Nielsen Media Research found **that 11 percent of the population 16 years and older, or 24 million people, use the Internet.**
Here the writer is reporting a **conditional statement** with *if.* The noun clause is in **bold.**	A report by the Japanese Government released last month shows the impact of Western food. It warns **that if the Japanese continue to increase their consumption of fat, which rose from 8.7 percent of calories in 1955 to 25.5 percent in 1992, they risk a much higher rate of chronic diseases.**

5E   Punctuation: Exact Quotations

Basically you are required to use quotation marks to indicate exact words taken from another person. **Quotations** can take many forms in academic writing. Several of these are illustrated here as models for your own writing. One type of quotation involves giving the words spoken by someone in an interview. The other major type of quotation involves using wording taken from written sources.

This quotation follows the pattern often used to give the **spoken words** someone used in an interview. The name of the source is given; the reporting verb *say* is used; and the exact words are put in quotation marks. The examples show three possible ways to organize such a quotation depending on where the **name + verb** is placed.	**Kandell says,** "It may give them a false sense of security." "It may give them a false sense of security," **Kandell says.** "It may give them," **Kandell says,** "a false sense of security."
This quotation is from an article about the use of portfolios in teaching writing from the journal *English for Specific Purposes.* It is typical of the way that academic writers include materials from **written sources.** Notice that the quotation includes a **reference to the reference list** at the end of the article and page number for the location of the words in the original source.	With this approach, **Hamp-Lyons (1991) explains,** "Some portfolios are simply a collection of responses to several essay prompts, usually in different modes ... and others incorporate drafts and other process data in addition to final products" **(p. 262).**
Long quotations of 40 words or more from another written source are presented in "block style" without quotation marks, but separated by indenting and spacing from the rest of the material. Look at the format for this type of block in the second paragraph of Reading 2, Chapter 7. Notice that the source of the information is given in an endnote in this textbook. In other academic writing, the reference comes at the end of the chapter.	Men are doing more shopping and housework, but only because women are making them change ... Women still decide most household purchases unless they're high-priced items. Women are ...[3] [3]Diane Crispell, "The Brave New World of Men," *American Demographics* (January 1992): 38, 43.

5F   Using Non-Restrictive Relative Clauses and Appositives

You will often need to give brief summaries of the **credentials and background** of the authorities you are quoting or citing. **Non-restrictive relative clauses** and **appositives** can be used to show why a person is a reliable source of information. Notice that the information may include a person's professional title or other credentials.

A **non-restrictive relative clause** gives additional information about a noun. In this example, the proper noun, *James G. Garrick, MD*, is completely identified and no additional information is required to tell who he is. The non-restrictive relative clause is used to give additional information about his credentials. Non-restrictive relative clauses are separated from the noun and the rest of the sentence with commas.	According to James G. Garrick, MD, **who is the director of the Center for Sports Medicine at Saint Francis Memorial Hospital,** excessive exercisers are people who work out or run two to three hours a day and won't back off despite pain and injury.
An **appositive** is a non-restrictive relative clause that has been reduced by removing the relative pronoun and the verb. This grammar is often used to give background information about people quoted as authorities. The first example shows how the non-restrictive relative clause in the first section of this chart was changed to make an appositive. The other examples are from other readings in this textbook.　　This reduction can only happen when the verb is a form of *be*.　　Dr. Garrick is the director of the Center …　　Dr. Kobayashi is the director of Japan's Institute …　　Mr. Najewicz is a computer science major …	According to James G. Garrick, **MD, director of the Center for Sports Medicine at Saint Francis Memorial Hospital,** excessive exercisers are people who work out or run two to three hours a day and won't back off despite pain and injury.　　"Diet is related to the change in economic growth," Dr. Shuhei Kobayashi, **the director of Japan's National Institute of Health and Nutrition,** said earlier this month in Tokyo.　　Chris Najewicz, **a computer science major at the University of Maryland,** spends between five and seven hours each weekday on the computer.

5G   Reference Systems

Different academic disciplines use somewhat different systems to give information about the sources for materials quoted, paraphrased, and summarized in writing. You need to find out the system that you are supposed to use in each class that you take. After you have selected your major field, you may need to get more detailed information about the discipline's reference system. **Reference systems** are used when you prepare papers, book reports, project reports, and other writing done for course requirements. Generally, adherence to these systems is not expected when you are writing examinations in class. However, it may be expected on "take-home" examinations, so be sure to ask about reference format when you are assigned a take-home exam.

Whatever the system, you will be expected to give details about the sources for your information and for any quotations that you use. These details will generally include

- *author(s)*
- *title of the publication*
- *publication date*
- *city of publication*
- *publishing company*

You should give this information in two places in your paper: (1) within the paper as a brief reference attached to the words or information you are using, and (2) at the end of the paper, a complete reference in a list with all other sources. The examples here use the system developed by the American Psychological Association (APA). The APA system is used by many disciplines in the social sciences.

Technically, the patient suffered from a condition called *visual agnosia,* an inability to recognize objects through sight. As **Sacks (1987)** put it, "Visually, he was lost in a world of lifeless abstractions" **(p. 15).**

Sacks (1987) tells us to look in the reference list to find an author with the last name Sacks who published something in 1987. The note **(p. 15)** tells us that this quotation is on page 15 of the publication.

Information:
Author: O. Sacks
Publication date: 1987
Title of the book: *The man who mistook his wife for a hat.*
City of publication: New York City
Publishing company: Harper & Row

As it appears in reference list at end of paper:

Sacks, O. (1987). *The man who mistook his wife for a hat.* New York: Harper & Row.

5H   A Note on Plagiarism

Plagiarism is using another person's words or ideas as if they were your own. This is not acceptable because in U.S. academic culture, writers "own" the words and ideas in their writing. Plagiarism is avoided by using two basic methods: 1) explaining where you got the wording or information and 2) punctuating your writing carefully to show which wording came from your source and which wording you created yourself. By doing this, you will avoid the serious consequences of plagiarism, which could be failure on the assignment or of the course.

Generally, plagiarism is an issue only in project papers, reports, research, summaries, and other writing that you do outside of class and then give to your teacher. You are not usually expected to give complete references in classroom tests and other timed writing when you are working from your memory. On such a test, you might be expected to associate a famous idea or product with its creator, but not to give the detailed references expected in outside-of-class writing.

However, when you write outside of class, you are expected to follow the U.S. academic practice of giving information about sources and of punctuating quotations correctly.

Section 6 Stating Opinions and Trying to Persuade

6A   Overview

All writers are trying to be persuasive. We all want our readers to understand our ideas and to believe that our writing is correct. When students write for a teacher, they are trying to persuade the teacher that they know the material. Being persuasive is a common feature to much of the writing done throughout the university.

To be persuasive in academic writing, student writers need to analyze their audience and to learn to write in ways appropriate for the academic setting. A basic characteristic of most academic writing is the careful tone through which the writer persuades the reader that he or she is not making claims that are too general for the evidence. Another feature often found in academic persuasion is the use of conditional statements to present cause-result statements. This section illustrates how academic writers use these features to create persuasive writing.

6B   Controlling the Strength of Generalizations

Adverbs of frequency, quantifiers and other words of measurement, and modal auxiliaries can help you avoid exaggerated claims by controlling the strength of your generalizations.

CONTROLLING THE STRENGTH OF GENERALIZATIONS: ADVERBS OF FREQUENCY	
Adverbs of frequency are those words that are used to indicate how often something happens. They range from *always* at the top of the scale to *never* at the bottom of the scale. *always* *frequently* *often* *usually* *generally* *sometimes* *seldom* *rarely* *never* Academic writers often use one of the adverbs of frequency to limit the strength of a claim. Think about what the sample sentences would mean without the adverb. Remember that words as strong as *always* or *never* are seldom used in academic writing because they are so strong.	They **often** have no use for the goods they carry home, and may not even open the packages. These are common examples of post-purchase dissonance, but **sometimes** feelings are more complex.

CONTROLLING THE STRENGTH OF GENERALIZATIONS: QUANTIFIERS AND OTHER WORDS OF MEASUREMENT	
Another technique used by academic writers is using **quantifiers and other words of measurement** like those below to make more exact statements. Academic writers seldom use words like *all* or *none* or *no* because they make such strong generalizations. *most* *some* *a lot of* *a great deal of* *a number of* *many* *a few* *few* *a little* Analyze the ways that these words are used in the examples. How would the meaning of the sentences change if they were removed?	**Some** college students spend as much as half of every day online. For **most**, addiction stems from a bigger problem, such as low self-esteem.

CONTROLLING THE STRENGTH OF GENERALIZATIONS: MODAL AUXILIARIES		
In academic writing, **modal auxiliaries** are often used to give possible explanations for situations, events, or actions. Writers frequently use modals when they draw conclusions about research. The modals have different **shades of meaning** based on the strength of the writer's belief in the explanation or conclusion.		
could *may* *might*	The writer gives a reasonable **explanation.** However, other explanations are possible. *May* is used frequently in academic writing for this purpose.	When you become sleepy in class, the problem **might be** lack of oxygen. Addicted shoppers **may feel** elated as they purchase but depressed afterward.
can	*Can* expresses **a possibility.** It also means that an action is allowed.	When shopping becomes an addiction, it **can destroy** lives. Predicting test questions **can do** more than get you a better grade on a test.
should *ought to*	The writer gives a good explanation and expects that it is **highly likely to be true.**	He works until 10:30 p.m. and takes only about 30 minutes to get home. He **should be** home no later than 11 p.m.
must *have to*	The writer gives a **very strong explanation** with little room for doubt.	Since he gets home from work at 11 p.m. and has a class at 7:30 a.m., he **must be** too tired to do all his homework carefully.
will	The writer has almost no doubt. This is a **statement of certainty** or a promise. This use of *will* is not about future time but about every time. You can usually substitute a simple present tense verb for the same meaning.	The debt **will be** real. Questions that only require a Yes or No answer **will not give** you new ideas for your writing. Finally, be on the look out for these words: this material **will be** on the test.
simple present tense	The writer is sure about the explanation. There is **no doubt** at all.	Our culture **is geared** to consumption; indeed, from early childhood we **are exposed** to ads urging us to buy.

6C   Giving Advice Using Modal Auxiliaries

Academic writing can include recommendations and advice. The writer must select modals to show the strength of this advice. The strength of the advice depends on the power relationship between the writer and the reader: The writer needs to have high enough status or appropriate academic standing to give strong advice to the reader.

can *could*	This is the **weakest** level of advice. The writer means only that these are the possible choices and does not really push for a particular choice.	You **can use** simple exercises to be more alert in class.
may *might*	The writer is **suggesting choices** and options. Readers may choose to accept the advice or to reject it. Sometimes a writer will use one of these modals even when she or he strongly believes in the advice in order to be polite and not "pushy."	You **might propose** storing credit cards in a safe deposit box or canceling them. Keeping a diary of purchases **may** also **be** helpful.
should *ought to*	The writer believes that this is very good advice or the writer believes that this action is the responsibility of the reader. This advice is **strongly recommended** but the punishment for not doing it is not very severe.	No one **should** ever **base** conclusions on research without knowing the size of the sample and how random a sample it was. You **should make** an appointment with your subject person well in advance of the actual meeting date.
must *have to*	The writer means that the action is **required** and that no choices are given. The writer implies that the punishment for not taking the advice is severe.	To participate fully in the world of the future, American **must tap** the power of mathematics.
will	This is the **strongest possible advice**. In fact, it is so strong that few people can use this modal to give advice because few people have the power to make such strong statements to other people. This use of *will* is almost never found in academic writing except, perhaps, in quotations. Because of that, no examples are used in this textbook.	

Continued

command forms	The next higher step in strength is the command.	Straighten your spine. Take a deep breath. Tense the muscles in your body. Breathe deeply three times.

6D   Conditional Sentences

Conditional sentences are created using an *if*-clause and a main clause. The *if*-clause gives the cause. The main clause gives the result. Various verbs can be used depending on shades of meaning required to be persuasive and exact.

Conditional sentences can be used to give advice. The main clause is a **command.**	If it's no big deal, then **don't worry** about it. If copies of previous exams are available, **use** those to predict questions.
The main clause can have different **modals** depending on the strength of the information. In the first example, *must* means that the rules for doing statistical studies require a random sample. In the second example, *will* means that the writer's evidence strongly predicts the result.	If an exit poll in a particular election is done, the sample **must be** random and as large as possible. The evidence from other nations shows overwhelmingly that if more is expected in mathematics education, more **will be achieved.**

6E　Using *Would* in Persuasive and Argumentative Writing

Would has a **conditional meaning** even when it is not used with an *if*-clause. When writing about proposed changes and other types of recommendations, writers often use this modal in sentences to show the results of their suggestions.

Chapter 6, Reading 3, is an essay by a student at the University of Wyoming who wants to have pass/fail grades for non-major courses. Since he is making a suggestion, he cannot predict that the university **will** accept his ideas. The whole essay has a **conditional meaning,** even though he does not use very many *if*-clauses. The major problem for writers working with conditional topics is to be consistent in the use of conditional verbs and not slip into using *will* rather than *would*.	I think that a pass/fail grading system **would be** more just. Still, I think most students **would work** fairly well in order to learn the subject. This group of people, who, after all, are in the minority, **would not work** for grades above a minimum passing grade anyway. A noteworthy detail is that most **would not object** to an increase in the requirements to pass in such a grading system. This compromise of setting the passing grade somewhere between a "C" and "B" would ensure that some effort **would have to be put** into the class in order to pass.

Section 7 Interactive Communication in Writing

7A　Overview: Speaking vs. Writing

In conversations, we often ask questions, refer to the other people in the conversation as *you*, and talk about *I* and *we*. There are many other characteristics that make a conversation different from writing, including using fragments, using contractions, taking turns, being able to have eye contact and to interact with the other people immediately, having short amounts of time to put together your words, and using informal vocabulary.

Writers sometimes use features of **conversational grammar in academic writing.** This style reaches out to the reader and attempts to interact with the reader. Very frequently you will find academic writers using questions and also the pronouns *you, we,* and *I*. Notice how this writer combines questions and personal pronouns with otherwise formal academic writing. He even uses a short answer form for one of his questions.	**You** watch an Olympic diver win a gold metal for a superb display of physical control. Presumably **you** would like to earn an Olympic medal too; so, because of this vicarious reinforcement, **you** should go out and try to make some spectacular dives into a pool. **Do you? Probably not. Why not? Why does that vicarious reinforcement fail to motivate you to engage in imitative behavior?**

7B   Using Questions in Academic Writing

In spoken language, people ask and answer many questions. Questions can be used for many purposes, such as getting information, making suggestions, and seeking clarification. Usually, one person asks a question and another person answers it as part of a discussion or conversation.

In writing, use of questions differs from their use in speaking in these ways: (1) the writer both asks and answers the questions; (2) the purpose of the questions is often to help structure or organize the writing; and (3) the questions often signal key points or key pieces of information.

The questions used in writing are sometimes those that the writer expects an **active reader** to ask.	The question here is: How much is too much?
Sometimes the question is used **to begin a section** of writing. Questions can be used as topic sentences or thesis statements. Look at pages 21 and 102 to see how these questions are used in context.	What do college students buy with their food money? What makes a champion? What has been learned from studying gold medalists?
Questions can be used **to structure** an entire piece of writing. Look at page 15 in the reading from a psychology textbook to see how these questions are used by the author.	How do you decide whether or not to take this step? Might vicarious learning lead to a certain monotony of behavior?
After the question, the author gives an answer. You will rarely find a question without an answer. Look on page 15 to see how the **author answers** these questions.	Do you? **Probably not.** Why not? Why does that vicarious reinforcement fail to motivate you to engage in imitative behavior?

7C   Using Contractions in Academic Writing

You need to be careful about using **contractions** in academic writing. Some teachers will accept them in papers; others require the full form. Generally, very formal writing does not use contractions. Compare these two passages. The first is very formal and the second less formal. Differences in audience and purpose lead to different formality levels—and to different decisions about using contractions. Notice that the writer of the "pasta" passage did not use contractions in every sentence but mixed contractions with full forms.	formal academic writing from a textbook Inhabiting an area that is too dry to support either agriculture or the keeping of livestock, the !Kung are totally dependent upon hunting and gathering for their food. informal academic writing from an essay about eating habits of college students Pasta in all shapes and sizes is a popular meal. **It's** easy, cheap, filling, and versatile. When it is buried in different sauces, a student can almost fool herself into believing that she **hasn't eaten** it for five days straight.
However, writing that gives **advice** often uses contractions in commands.	**Don't** do anything silly to a computer. **Don't** spill things on it. **Don't** drop it. **Don't** hit it.
Its vs. *It's.* These two words are pronounced the same but they are **grammatically different.** *Its* is the possessive form. *It's* means "it is" or "it has."	**It's** really just not possible to pass on all math-related tasks to someone else. When a football team wins consistently, other teams copy **its** style of play.

7D   Using *You* in Academic Writing

You is used in academic writing to give some of the flavor of conversation to written material. Using **pronouns** correctly in academic writing can be a challenge. Writers need to look carefully at models for the kind of writing they will do. Examples are given here to show how writers have used *you* effectively.

When **giving advice,** writers often speak directly to the reader as *you.*	Put **yourself** in **your** instructor's head. What kind of questions would **you** ask?

Continued

Writers sometimes combine **question asking** with use of *you*.	Is it **your** first draft or **your** fourth rewrite?
In this passage, the writer first talks about consumers as *he* or *she* and then turns to the reader with an example about *you*. The writer is trying to **connect the material to the lives of the readers.** The whole example clarifies the concept "problem recognition" in terms of what *you,* the reader, could experience.	A consumer recognizes a need (or want) when something that **he or she** requires is found lacking. Some marketers call this "problem recognition." Events or conditions that stimulate need arousal vary. **You** may experience hunger pangs during your noon marketing class and realize that you need to purchase some lunch. Or **you** may visit with a fellow student and find out that his computer has graphics capabilities and hard drive capacity far superior to **your** old 1982 model.

7E   Using *We* in Academic Writing

Writers use the **pronoun** *we* to suggest a bond with their audience. *We* means that the writer and the reader share the same knowledge, ideas, experiences, or beliefs.

The writer of the psychology textbook material in Chapter 1 uses a mixture of personal pronouns, including *we*. The sentence can be changed by using the word *people*. While both sentences mean the same thing, the sentence with *we* suggests a closer **relationship** between the writer and the reader.	**We** achieve or fail to achieve a sense of self-efficacy in two ways. **People** achieve or fail to achieve a sense of self-efficacy in two ways.

7F   Using *I* in Academic Writing

Some writers think that they should never use the pronouns *I, me, my,* and *mine* in academic writing. This is not accurate. Some types of academic writing require the use of **personal opinions** and **personal evidence.** In other types of academic writing, the writer is supposed to use a more impersonal style. One of the tasks of a writer is to find out what style is expected for a particular type of writing. Persuasive writing is based on knowing about the expectations of the audience. Here are examples taken from the readings in this book to show how writers use *I* in academic writing.

The writer of the **survey questions** on pages 166–167 used *I* but not to refer to the writer. This *I* is actually the reader of the survey who fills out the form.	_____ 1. I do optional reading that my instructors suggest even though I know it won't affect my grade. _____ 2. I try to make time for outside reading despite the demands of my coursework.
In these examples, *I* shows the **voice of the author in an argumentative essay.** In this essay, the student clearly presents the opinions which are his. His teacher encouraged him to write in this manner. Other teachers would have different opinions about the use of *I* in an argumentative essay. Find out the opinions of your teachers and the customs in your academic major.	I think that a pass/fail grading system would be more just. Still, I think most students would work fairly well in order to learn the subject. At least, I don't think the grading system will affect it.
In the psychology textbook material in Chapter 1, the writer uses a highly interactive style mixed with features of informational writing such as complex noun phrases. This mixture of styles is frequently used in academic textbooks to present **technical information in a user-friendly manner.** Student writers in psychology courses will need help from their teachers to know whether or not to use this style in their own writing.	We achieve or fail to achieve a sense of self-efficacy in two ways. One way is by observing ourselves. If I have tried and failed to develop even simple athletic skills, I will have no sense of self-efficacy when I think of trying to duplicate the behavior of an Olympic medalist.

Section 8 Basic Grammar Terminology: How to Talk about Your Sentences

These are words that students and teachers often use when they talk with each other about the grammar of student writing. This section provides an overview of the uses of these **grammar structures in sentences.** The charts do not teach you how to use the grammar, but provide examples of the basic vocabulary used to talk about English grammar. The topics are presented in alphabetical order. Only the terms most likely to be used by teachers or textbooks are given here.

8A Adjectives

Adjectives are words like *good, useful, reliable, efficient, global, technological,* and many others that **describe nouns.** They are usually used with nouns in noun phrases.	a **good** student **useful** statistics a **reliable and efficient** system a **global technological** society
Adjectives can be used in the **complement** of a sentence.	<u>Math</u> skills <u>are</u> **necessary** for modern life.
Most adjectives have **comparative** and **superlative forms.** Depending on pronunciation, comparatives are made with *-er* or *more: happier* or *more effective.* Depending on pronunciation, superlatives are made with *-est* or *most: happiest* and *most effective. Good* has the irregular forms *better* and *best.*	Students can do **better** on tests by learning **more effective** study strategies. **The best students** do not all study the same ways. When you keep up with your class work, you feel **more confident** in class.
Another name for **relative clause** is **adjective clause** because it is like an adjective in its work.	adjective noun relative/adjective clause **interesting** materials **that I've learned in class**

8B   Adverbs and Adverbials

Adverbs are the kinds of words that give information about **time, place, manner, purpose,** and so forth. They answer questions such as *when, where, why,* and *how.*

This example has two single-word **adverbs.**	Breathe **deeply** and **slowly.**
Groups of words that have this grammar are called **adverbials.** There are **adverbial phrases** and **adverbial clauses.** The first example shows a prepositional phrase used as an adverbial phrase that tells when; the second, an adverbial clause that tells why.	They bought their daughter a car **in high school.** She got a job **because she had to make car payments.**

8C   Articles and Determiners

Articles are often used in noun phrases. The articles are the words *a, an,* and *the.*	**a** specific assignment **an** interesting class **the** first day of class
Sometimes the articles are described as **determiners.** The determiners are a larger group that also includes *this/that, these/those, each, much, no, another, some,* and several other words.	**another** argument **no** self-esteem and **no** interests
The **personal pronouns** can be called **determiners.**	**your** noon marketing class
The words *this/that* and *these/those* are sometimes called **determiners** and sometimes called **demonstrative pronouns.**	**these** classes **this** concept

8D Auxiliary Verbs

English verbs are either simple single words, or compounds of two or more words. For example, present and past progressive verb tenses combine a form of *be* with the *-ing* form of the verb. In this situation, *be* is called the **auxiliary verb.** Sometimes you will hear the term **helping verb,** which is just another name for **auxiliary verb.**	simple present tense **study, studies** simple past tense **studied** auxiliary verb + main verb (present progressive) **is studying** auxiliary verb + main verb (present perfect) **has studied** auxiliary verb + auxiliary verb + main verb (present perfect + progressive) **has been studying** auxiliary verb + main verb (a passive verb) **is required**
Questions and negatives can also require *do, does,* or *did* as an auxiliary verb.	How <u>do</u> I <u>pay</u> for my car? I <u>didn't get</u> home until 10:30 pm.
Modal auxiliary verb or **modal** is the name for the words *will, would, can, could, may, might, must, shall, should.* They combine with main verbs for verb phrases.	Children <u>can succeed</u> in mathematics. Students <u>will have</u> the rest of their lives to own an automobile and pay expenses.

8E Comma Splices

A **comma splice** is a compound sentence that has a comma but not a coordinating conjunction. A comma cannot be used alone to make a compound sentence. Both of these examples show comma splices.	A buyer often evaluates a purchase after it is made, the buyer may be happy or unhappy with the purchase. Time goes very quickly when I work on the computer, I am sometimes late to class.
To correct a comma splice, you can separate the clauses and make **independent sentences.**	A buyer often evaluates a purchase after it is made. The buyer may be happy or unhappy with the purchase. Time goes very quickly when I work on the computer. I am sometimes late to class. <div align="right">Continued</div>

You can add a **semicolon.**	A buyer often evaluates a purchase after it is made; the buyer may be happy or unhappy with the purchase.
	Time goes very quickly when I work on the computer; I am sometimes late to class.
You can add a **coordinating conjunction.**	A buyer often evaluates a purchase after it is made, and the buyer may be happy or unhappy with the purchase.
	Time goes very quickly when I work on the computer, so I am sometimes late to class.
You can use **subordination.** This method might require other changes in the sentences to get exactly the right meaning.	A buyer often evaluates a purchase after it is made with the result that the buyer may be happy or unhappy with the purchase.
	Because time goes very quickly when I work on the computer, I am sometimes late to class.

8F   Complements

Complements are often nouns, noun phrases, or adjectives. The complement describes or renames the subject. Notice that this structure is often used in definitions of terminology.	"Voluntary simplicity" <u>is</u> **a plainer, more basic lifestyle.**
	Consumers with this lifestyle <u>are</u> **cautious, conservative, and thrifty.**
A **linking verb** connects the complement to the subject. These are verbs like *be, become, seem,* and *taste.* (A list of linking verbs is on the WWW at http://www.gsu.edu/~wwwesl/egw/vanass-ch.htm.)	When you <u>become</u> **sleepy** in class, the problem <u>might be</u> **lack of oxygen.**
	Many students <u>feel</u> **fairly confident** when they take the first test in a class.

8G   Conjunctions

The two most frequently used kinds of conjunctions are **coordinating conjunctions** and **subordinating conjunctions.** (See http://www.gsu.edu/~wwwesl/egw/bryson.htm for more details.)

Coordinating conjunctions *for, and, nor, but, or, yet, so* are used to combine words and phrases. They are also used to make compound sentences and compound-complex sentences. The most common are *and, but, so*, and *or*.	<u>Family **and** friends help</u> with decisions. <u>These sources may</u> not <u>be</u> as relevant as others; <u>they may be</u> dated; **or** <u>they may be</u> inaccurate.
Subordinating conjunctions are used to make complex sentences and compound-complex sentences. Subordinating conjunctions create units that are called **subordinate clauses** or **dependent clauses.**	I don't spend much time reviewing the readings **because it would take too long.**

8H   Fragments

A **fragment** is a piece of a sentence, but not a complete sentence. However, a fragment may look like a complete sentence because it begins with a capital letter and ends with a period.

Using **fragments** is a feature of spoken English, but academic writing requires complete sentences. Many fragments would be correct in speaking, but they must be changed into complete sentences in writing. The use of adverbial clauses as sentences is a common error in student writing.	They were rewarded. **Because of their answers.** **When I get home from class.** I will start my research.
The simplest solution is to **join the fragment** to its related independent clause with correct punctuation.	They were **rewarded because** of their answers. When I get home from **class, I** will start my research.
Sometimes it is possible to **create two independent sentences** by removing the subordinating word and making other changes to create a complete sentence of the fragment.	**First, I** will get home from class. **Then, I** will start my research.

8I   Infinitives

An **infinitive** is the combination of *to* + verb. Infinitives are used in four major ways: as **direct objects, adverbials, with nouns,** and **with adjectives.** Example 1 shows the infinitive as the direct object. Example 2 shows the infinitive as an adverbial to tell why, and Example 3, a noun + infinitive. The last is an adjective + infinitive.	1. I want **to take only courses in my major.** 2. I came to the university **to study engineering.** 3. a cube-sized **refrigerator to store foods.** 4. It is **tough to reconcile 7:30 a.m. classes with late-night jobs.**
Notice that infinitives can have objects— and sometimes very long objects. The **objects** are in **bold** type.	to take **only courses in my major** to study **engineering** to reconcile **7:30 a.m. classes with late-night jobs** to store **foods**

8J   Nouns

A **noun** is a word like *student, computer, car, child, success, confidence,* or *mathematics* used in sentences as subjects, objects, complements, and a few other functions. The nouns in these sentences have been marked with **bold** type. See Sentences on page 260 and Phrases and Clauses on page 258 for more information.	A **student** needs a **computer.** **Students** need **computers.** A **child** should not have a **car.** **Children** should not have **cars.** **Success** can increase **confidence.** **Mathematics** contributes to **business, finance, health,** and **defense.**

8K   Noun Phrases

Noun phrase is the name for the combination of a noun with other words. The combination functions in a sentence just like the simple nouns do, as subject, object, and/or complement. The first two examples show the noun phrase as subject and direct object.	<u>**Your children**</u> are at risk. We now have **a world economy**.
A noun phrase can include several different kinds of structures.	article + adjective + noun the first **test** article + adjective + adjective + main noun an important first **step**
A **complex noun phrase** is a noun phrase that is long and complicated, with words attached before and/or after the main noun.	article + main noun + prepositional phrase (preposition + noun) a **system** for **students** article + adjective + main noun + relative clause the introverted **students** who have a hard time finding a place in the college scene

8L   Objects

The word **object** is used for two different types of grammar structures. Verbs can have objects. Prepositions have objects.

A transitive verb must have a **direct object.** Sometimes this direct object is just called the object of the verb. The direct objects are circled in these examples.	<u>Students</u> <u>choose</u> (their majors.) <u>Students</u> <u>have chosen</u> (their majors) and <u>should</u> consequently <u>prioritize</u> (the courses) to meet the requirements of their majors.
Some transitive verbs can have another object called the indirect object. **The indirect object** *(their children)* "receives" the direct object *(a car).* You cannot have an indirect object unless you also have a direct object.	<u>Many parents</u> <u>give</u> their children (a car.)
Prepositions *(in, for, before)* have objects. The combination of a preposition with its object is called a **preposition phrase** or a **prepositional phrase** (as in the three examples).	**in** a course **for** each class **before** the test

8M   Participles

The **present participle** is used to form present and past progressive verb tenses.	My parents <u>are **letting**</u> me get a car. Pascal <u>was **working**</u> for his father when he invented the calculator.
The **past participle** is used to form present perfect *(has changed)* and past perfect *(had worked, had gone)* verb tenses. It is also used to make passive *(is triggered)* verbs.	Society <u>has **changed**</u> over the years. He <u>had **worked**</u> until 10:30 pm and <u>had **gone**</u> to sleep after 11:30 pm. A need to make a purchase <u>is **triggered**</u> by finding out that a product is available.

8N   Phrases and Clauses

A **phrase** is a group of words that work together as a single unit. Phrases include **noun phrases, verbs phrases,** and **prepositional phrases.** The examples illustrate these three.	an important first step has learned from her friends

Unlike a phrase, a **clause** is built like a sentence with a subject and a verb phrase. The most important clause types are **adverbial clauses, noun clauses,** and **relative clauses.** The examples illustrate these three in order.
    Clauses can also be called **dependent, subordinate,** and **independent.**
    An **independent clause** is just another name for a simple sentence.
    The term **subordinate clause** is just another term for **dependent clause.**
	Many students feel fairly confident **when** <u>they</u> <u>take</u> **the first test in a new course.**
	The drawback with pass/fail classes is **that** <u>the students</u> <u>will</u> **simply not** <u>work</u> **hard enough.**
	The best students in a class have developed strategies **that work well for them.**

80   Prepositions

Prepositions are words like *on, by, at, from,* and many others. A related structure is the **prepositional phrase** or **preposition phrase.** This terminology refers to the combination of a preposition with its object. Prepositional phrases are often used as adverbials to tell *when, where, why,* and *how.*	Bowes had hardly a friend **on campus.** Research suggests that some people may harm themselves physically and mentally **by exercising too much.**
Prepositional phrases are also often attached to nouns in **complex noun phrases.** Research has shown that this combination is more common than the combination of a noun plus a relative clause.	• her pal Johan **from Sweden** • officials **at one school**—the University **of Maryland at College Park** • 35 minutes a week **per person of the total population**

Prepositions are also closely tied to some verbs and need to be learned as part of the structure of particular verbs. (See the following WWW site for a list of these prepositional verbs: http://www.gsu.edu/~wwwesl/egw/verbprep.htm.)	chat with	Every day she <u>chatted with</u> her pal Johan from Sweden.
	recover from	Bowes has since <u>recovered from</u> her on-line addition.

8P   Pronouns

Pronouns are words like *I/me/my, you/your, we/us/our, he/him/his, she/her/her, it/its*. These are also called **personal pronouns.**	I do optional reading that **my** instructors suggest.
Other words are also **pronouns.** These include the following types: 1. **demonstrative pronouns** (*this/that* and *these/those*) 2. **relative pronouns** *(who, whom, that, which, whose, where, when)* 3. **interrogative pronouns** *(who, whom, whose, why, how, what, when, where, which)* for making questions	demonstrative pronoun I haven't met anyone at **this** school. relative pronoun *who* at the beginning of a relative clause I get irritated by students **who** ask lots of irrelevant questions. interrogative pronoun **What** are the effects of this math avoidance?

8Q   Sentences

A **sentence** is a complete unit that contains a **subject** and a **verb.** In writing, a sentence begins with a capital letter and ends with a period, a question mark, or an exclamation mark.	<u>Students</u> <u>eat</u> junk food. How <u>do</u> <u>I</u> <u>pay</u> for my car?
Sometimes a verb requires a **direct object.** Direct objects are nouns, pronouns, and other words that complete the meaning of the verb. This kind of verb is called a **transitive verb.** *Junk food* and *cars* are the direct objects in the examples.	<u>Students</u> <u>eat</u> junk food. <u>Many students</u> <u>have</u> cars.
Sometimes the verb requires a **complement.** Complements can be nouns, pronouns, or adjectives (*difficult* and *Webaholic* in the examples). This kind of verb is called a **linking verb** because it links the subject to the information in the complement. (A list of linking verbs is on the WWW at http://www.gsu.edu/~wwwesl/egw/vanassch.htm.)	<u>The first test</u> <u>was</u> difficult. <u>She</u> <u>was</u> a Webaholic.
Sentences can also have **adverbials.** These answer questions like *when, where,* and *how.*	<u>You</u> <u>should breathe</u> deeply. Continued

| This example sentence does not have either a direct object or a complement. The verb is called an **intransitive verb.** An intransitive verb never has an object or a complement. It can be followed by an adverbial. | Speed kills.
 A need can arise naturally. |

8R   Subjects of a Sentence

| Subjects can be single nouns, longer noun phrases, complicated complex noun phrases, pronouns, and other combinations of words that can be used like nouns. In these examples, the subjects in these sentences are underlined. The last example includes a complex noun phrase as the subject. | Adults should make the decisions for their children.

 You do not automatically imitate the behavior of someone else.

 Optimistic thinking helps fuel success.

 Hard work and persistence are key ingredients to success.

 People's persistence or lack of persistence in coping with a difficult task is strongly influenced by their sense of self-efficacy. |

8S   Verbs in Sentences: Active or Passive

| Each English sentence must have a subject and a verb. The verb in a sentence is often called the **verb phrase.** | My parents are letting me get a car. |
| Verbs can be **active** or **passive.** In active sentences, the subject does the action. In passive sentences, the subject receives the actions that someone else does.

 In the active example, students do the choosing. In the passive example, the university does the requiring and the students just receive the requirement. Also, teachers grade the classes, and the registrar's office adds the grades to the GPA. | Most students choose their majors early in their university careers.

 Almost every student here at the University of Wyoming is required to take several courses which have little or no relevance to their field of study. Why is it that these classes are graded, and added to the GPA, as if they were ordinary major classes? |

8T   Verb Forms

Verbs are words like *want* or *write* used primarily in the verb phrase in sentences and also in infinitives.	<u>Students</u> <u>want</u> to make good grades. <u>Students</u> <u>write</u> several short papers and one long paper.
Want and most other verbs are **regular verbs;** they form their simple past tense and past participle by adding *ed* to the basic word. *Write* and many other verbs are **irregular verbs;** they form their past tense and past participle in ways different from the regular verb. (See the list of irregular verbs on the WWW at http://www.gsu.edu/~wwwesl/egw/jones.htm.)	Last quarter, <u>I</u> <u>wanted</u> to make a good grade in mathematics. Last semester, <u>the students</u> <u>wrote</u> several short papers and one long paper.

8U   Verb Tenses

simple present tense	A consumer <u>recognizes</u> a need and then <u>makes</u> a purchase. Consumers <u>pay</u> special attention to quality and price.
simple past tense	Most of the Norwegian students <u>gave</u> a very clear position on the issue of pass/fail grades. I <u>smiled</u> and <u>returned</u> to grading my students' essays.
present perfect tense	The students <u>have shown</u> themselves worthy of being treated as responsible young adults. Society <u>has changed</u> over the years.
past perfect tense	They <u>had bought</u> a car for their daughter.
present progressive tense or **present continuous tense**	My parents <u>are letting</u> me get a car. Working to pay for a car <u>is hurting</u> the academic work of many U.S. high school students.
past progressive tense or **past continuous tense**	French mathematician Blaise Pascal built the first calculator, probably to aid him in the accounting that he <u>was doing</u> at his father's office.

Credits

Chapter 1:
Page 7: *The Newbury House Dictionary of American English* (Boston: Heinle & Heinle Publishers, 1996).
Page 15: J. Kalat, *Introduction to Psychology* (Wadsworth Publishing Company, 1993).
Page 21: George Sheehan, "Anatomy of a Champion," *Runner's World* (Rodale Press, May 1993).

Chapter 2:
Page 34: Dave Ellis, *Becoming a Master Student*, 7th Ed. (Boston: Houghton Mifflin Company, 1994).
Page 35: J. N. Gardner and A. J. Jewler, *Your College Experience–Strategies for Success*, 2nd Ed. (Wadsworth Publishing Company, 1995).

Chapter 3:
Page72: T. L. Engle and Louis Snellgrove, *Psychology—Its Principles and Applications*, 7th Ed. (New York: Harcourt Brace Jovanovich, Inc., 1979).
Page 73: Susan Fernandez, Knight-Ridder/-Tribune Information Services, Lawrence (Kansas) *Journal World*, Nov. 28, 1995 3A.
Page 78: University of California at Berkeley Wellness Letter, Vol. 11, Issue 3, December 1994.
Page 81: Valerie DeBenedette, *The Physician And Sportsmedicine*, Vol. 18, No. 8 (August 1990).

Chapter 4:
Page 97: Gary Ferraro, *Cultural Anthropology* (Wadsworth Publishing Company, 1992).

Page 102: Susannah Baker, "College Cuisine Makes Mother Cringe," *American Demographics*, September 1991.
Page 107: Marion Burros, *The New York Times*, April 13, 1994.

Chapter 5:
Page 128: National Research Council, *Everybody Counts—A Report to the Nation on the Future of Mathematics Education* (National Academy Press, 1989).
Page 136: Carol Gloria Crawford, *Math Without Fear* (NewViewpoints/Vision Books, 1980).
Page 139: Theoni Pappas, *More Joy of Mathematics: Exploring Mathematical Insights and Concepts* (World Wide Publishing/Tetra, 1991).

Chapter 6:
Page 166: Ohmer Milton, Howard R. Pollio, and James A. Eison, *Making Sense of College Grades: Why the Grading System Does Not Work and What Can Be Done About It* (Jossey-Bass, Inc., Publishers, 1986).
Page 169: Lyla Fox, *Newsweek*, March 23, 1996.

Chapter 7:
Page 191: Marjorie J. Cooper and Charles Madden, *Introduction to Marketing* (New York: HarperCollins Publishers, Inc., 1993).
Page 200: Joel R.Evans and Barry Berman, *Marketing*, 7th Ed. (Prentice-Hall, Inc., 1997). Reprinted by permission of Prentice-Hall, Inc., Upper Saddle River, NJ.

Index